The Social Psychology of Power

This is a volume in
EUROPEAN MONOGRAPHS IN SOCIAL PSYCHOLOGY

Series Editor: Henri Tajfel

A complete list of titles in this series appears at the end of this volume.

EUROPEAN MONOGRAPHS IN SOCIAL PSYCHOLOGY 21
Series Editor: HENRI TAJFEL

The Social Psychology of Power

SIK HUNG NG

Department of Psychology, University of Otago, New Zealand

1980

Published in cooperation with
EUROPEAN ASSOCIATION OF EXPERIMENTAL SOCIAL PSYCHOLOGY
by
ACADEMIC PRESS
A Subsidiary of Harcourt Brace Jovanovich, Publishers
London New York Toronto Sydney San Francisco

ACADEMIC PRESS INC. (LONDON) LTD.
24/28 Oval Road
London NW1

United States Edition published by
ACADEMIC PRESS INC.
111 Fifth Avenue
New York, New York 10003

British Library Cataloguing in Publication Data

Ng, Sik Hung
The social psychology of power. - (European monographs in social psychology).
1. Power (Social sciences)
I. Title II. Series
301.15′52 HM141 80-40855

ISBN 0-12-518180-9

Phototypeset in Compugraphic Baskerville
by Dobbie Typesetting Service
Printed in Great Britain by
St Edmundsbury Press, Bury St Edmunds, Suffolk

Preface

This book is about power. It was written with the primary objective of providing a broad perspective for the development of a social psychology of power. Such a perspective, I believe, cannot be found in the social psychological literature; nor can it be generated from social psychology alone.

Conventional social psychology has addressed itself to only a restricted range of the problem of power, and has done so with insufficient regard to the important issues that the problem of power raises for man and society. This unsatisfactory state of the knowledge is one manifestation of the historical development of social psychology, which has tended towards an individualistic mode of approach and has shied away from social analysis. In seeking perspective on power, it has become necessary for me to look into the related disciplines of general psychology, politics, sociology and philosophy as well. The first three parts (Chapters 1 to 7) of the present volume contain a critical examination of the analyses of power which (as far as I can discern) are among the most important in social psychology and the above-mentioned disciplines.

It is difficult for an interdisciplinarian exercise of this kind to aspire to be exhaustive in every aspect. I have therefore chosen to assign emphasis to some aspects but not to others. The selective treatment was partly a direct consequence of my personal limitation, and partly guided by the following considerations. (1) Is there any instructive lesson that social psychology can learn from the success and/or failure of a particular mode of approach to power? In some cases, the lesson can be drawn fairly unambiguously by reviewing the cumulative debate over certain explicitly stated issues, as in the cases of political behaviourism (Chapter 5), and the relationships of power with social stratification and conflict (Chapter 4). In some other cases, the lesson can only be discerned by tracing the evolution of a particular discipline to uncover how the conceptualization of the problem of power has shifted in response to the changing nature of the problem. From the earlier works of N. Machiavelli and T. Hobbes to the more recent work of B. Russell, we can uncover a clear shift from an individualistic or interpersonal type of analysis to one which focuses on the corporate group or the organization (Chapter 1).

(2) What are the important issues of power which have been neglected or insufficiently dealt with by social psychology? This is a central theme which runs through the first three parts of the book and extends into the fourth, and final, part (Chapters 8 and 9). In summary terms, the issues are those raised by power in relation to (a) morality and psychological well-being (Chapters 1, 2 and 6); (b) two basic views of society (Chapters 3 and 4); (c) the identification of the locus of power (Chapter 5); (d) social influence and social exchange (Chapter 7); and (e) power change (Chapters 7, 8 and 9).

Since the present volume is intended to aid the development of the social psychology of power, the relatedness or complementarity between social psychology on the one hand, and the four related disciplines on the other, has to be pointed out. This must mean that there will be a lot of cross references in the pages that follow. In fact, I have done precisely that in numerous places apart from devoting one full section of the Introduction to the same purpose. If I appear to be verbose at times, it is with a purpose.

I wish to take advantage of a corner of the Preface to say a few personal things. This work would never have been started without the encouragement and interest shown by Henri Tajfel. His trusting attitude and helpful guidance have been directly (albeit nonconspicuously) instrumental in bringing the work to its completion. With this professional debt which I owe him goes a personal debt, which has started to accumulate soon after I became a graduate student at Bristol University. I wish to pay tribute to both debts I owe Henri Tajfel.

I wish to thank Margaret Gilkison, Jill Gillespie, and Carol Hunter in particular, for typing and retyping the manuscript; and also Raewyn Harray for her help with the references and preparation of the manuscript. I am most grateful to Peter McKellar for his careful reading of the manuscript and his constructive comments, and above all, for his interest in my work. I owe a special kind of debt to my wife, Grace, who in her own helpful way has borne with me and at the same time has borne our first child.

The present work bears the influence of my two sets of university teachers: those who are/were affiliated to the Psychology Department and those to the Sociology Department. I wish to thank them all.

August, 1980 SIK HUNG NG

Acknowledgements

I would like to thank authors and publishers for permission to reproduce passages from the following sources:

Bachrach, P. and Baratz, M. S. (1962). The two faces of power. *American Political Science Review* **57**, 641–651.

Brown, L. D. (1978). Toward a theory of power and intergroup relations. *In* "Advances in Experiential Social Processes, Vol. 1" (C. L. Cooper and C. P. Alderfer, Eds), pp. 161–180. John Wiley and Sons, Chichester.

Dahrendorf, R. (1968). On the origin of inequality among men. *In* "Essays in the Theory of Society" (R. Dahrendorf, Ed.), pp. 151–178. Routledge and Kegan Paul, London.

de Charms, R. (1968). "Personal Causation: The Internal Affective Determinants of Behaviour". Academic Press, New York.

Duverger, M. (1966). "The Idea of Politics: The Uses of Power in Society". (Translated by R. North and R. Murphy). Methuen, London. © Editions Gallimard, 1964, Paris.

Friedrich, C. J. (1963). "Man and his Government". © 1963, McGraw-Hill Book Company, New York.

Homans, G. C. (1961). "Social Behaviour: Its Elementary Forms". Routledge and Kegan Paul, London. © Harcourt, Brace and World, Inc. 1961.

Horowitz, I. C. (1963). An introduction to C. Wright Mills. *In* "Power, Politics and People, the Collected Essays of C. Wright Mills" (I. C. Horowitz, Ed.), pp. 1–20. Oxford University Press, New York.

Michiavelli, N. (1965). Discourses on the first decade of Titus Livius. *In* "Machiavelli: The Chief Works and Others, Vol. 1" (Translated by A. Gilbert), pp. 188–529. Duke University Press, Durham, North Carolina, 1965.

Mills, C. W. (1951). "White Collar: The American Middle Classes". Oxford University Press, London.

Mills, C. W. (1956). "The Power Elite". Oxford University Press, New York.

Nietzsche, F. (1883–1888). "The Will to Power" (Translated by W. Kaufmann and R. J. Hollingdale, and edited, with commentary, by W. Kaufmann). Vintage Books, Random House, New York, 1968.

Parsons, T. (1963). On the concept of political power. *Proceedings of the American Philosophical Society* **107** (3), 1963, June.

Contents

Introduction

The need for a broad perspective on power

There is as yet no definitive *social psychology* of power, nor is there a social psychology in general which alone can give birth to the social psychology of *power*. What I intend to do in this volume is to bring together several viewpoints from social psychology and other related disciplines to form a broader perspective on power than is currently available in the literature. Such a perspective, I believe, is both necessary and instrumental to the development of a social psychology of power. There are two reasons for holding this belief. In the first place, power occupies a significant place not only in social psychology, but also in the related disciplines of general psychology, sociology and politics. Secondly, the current social psychological thinking on power is fragmentary in nature and narrow in its outlook.

Two closely related facts indicate the significance of power in social psychology, even though its conceptualization of power is far from adequate. First, power is used as a central theoretical concept in the analysis of a number of basic social psychological problems. At the same time, power constitutes a substantive part of the content areas of social psychology. Both facts are also apparent in sociology and politics. General psychology, on the other hand, may seem to accord a relatively less prominent role to power. Nevertheless, it can be shown that a number of important concepts and basic areas in general psychology are in fact concerned with power, even though they are not always construed as such. Both as a concept and as a content area, power occupies a significant place in all the four disciplines. This observation will become more evident in the discussion contained in Parts II, III and IV of the present work.

To the extent that social psychology is intimately related to each of the other three disciplines, the least that a social psychology of power should be able to do is to point out where and how it stands in relation to the treatments given to power by the latter disciplines. This can only be achieved through the development of a broad perspective which recognizes fully the multi-disciplinary ramifications of power. To the best of my knowledge, a perspective of this kind is not available either in general or social psychology. It is not readily available in sociology or politics either. Much remains to be done. Towards this end, I will undertake a critical examination of the conceptualization of power in all the four disciplines. Since many of the issues relating to power have their antecedents in philosophy, and since these issues are more clearly and profoundly stated by the philosophers than by the social scientists, it is only appropriate that I should add a philosophical dimension to the framework which I am developing.

A broad, multi-disciplinary perspective of this nature does not automatically constitute a social psychology of power. Its true roles are, first, to give bearing to the social psychology of power, as we have already noted, and secondly, to facilitate the latter's development by providing an antidote to the fragmentary and narrow state of the conventional social psychological thinking on power. The following introductory review will bear out the inadequate state of social psychology with regard to its treatment of power.

The first major review of the literature was published in the late 1950s. The verdict then was that social psychologists in general had not given enough attention to the problem of power; those who did were "soft" about power (Cartwright, 1959a).* In the same year, two systematic theoretical frameworks of power were separately articulated. One of them was the field-theoretical framework elaborated by Cartwright (1959b) and others. The other one was the social exchange model worked out by Thibaut and Kelley (1959). Both were formulated at the dyadic level. Prior to that, Heider (1958) had made liberal use of the power concept in his analysis of the action of the individual, and had generated with insight several statements on the perception and attribution of power. Heider's contributions, like those made by Adler (1956), pertain mainly to the general psychological and dyadic levels. Power at the *group* level received much less attention. Such an omission was particularly conspicuous in contrast with the rapidly expanding field of small group research. Sherif (1962), for instance, remarked that the power dimension was the most neglected topic in small group research.

* The review was originally in the 1953 Presidential Address to the Society for the Psychological Study of Social Issues by Cartwright.

In the 1960s, empirical research on power was characterized by a strong tendency amongst the researchers to construe the problem from a single theoretical stance. The field-theoretical and social exchange systems dominated the field. New conceptual and theoretical developments of power (e.g. Berkowitz and Daniels, 1963; Schopler and Bateson, 1965) were limited in generality, and slow in pace in comparison with the advances in other areas. The stagnation was clearly reflected in two reviews (Schopler, 1965; Collins and Raven, 1969) in which the literature was comfortably accommodated within the familiar and conventional theoretical systems. The studies of coalition formation, a topic which is directly related to power, threw little new light on power in general (Wilke and Mulder, 1971). At the turn of the 1970s, the state of power research remained at what Kuhn (1962) has called the pre-paradigmatic stage, according to a review by Tedeschi and Bonoma (1972). No general paradigm existed then which could provide a theoretically coherent and broad approach to the subject and at the same time was attractive enough to gather around itself an enduring group of students.

With few exceptions, psychological conceptions of power are directed at the individual (intra-psychic) level, or the interpersonal level, or sometimes both the individual and interpersonal levels. Psychology seems to know no power apart from that which can be found in the psychological functioning of the individual and in interpersonal interaction. Power that is embedded in and works through the social structure and norms of a community seems to have no place in psychology, as if the analysis of power at the individual and interpersonal levels can be undertaken in a social vacuum. In a review of the power factor in attitude change, McGuire (1969) has also identified a similar situation: that psychologists have largely neglected the case of power as it operates in real communities, and through this, have left out a number of substantive issues of power.

The fact that even *social* psychology in its conception of power has stopped short at the community level, and that a good part of conventional social psychology is dominated by theories of the individuals and by the absence of social analysis in the design of the experiments and in the interpretation of data (Tajfel, 1972), seems very extraordinary in the light of the early history of social psychology.

As pointed out by G. W. Allport (1968), Auguste Comte (1798-1857) envisaged a "true final science", designated as *la morale*, which would answer the question: "How can the individual be at once cause and consequence of society?". *La morale*, which turned out to be psychology, can do this by an appropriate combination of the biological and sociological points of view. Comte, and Wundt and Tarde after him, insisted that all psychology is either physiological or social (Allport, op. cit.). The close link between social psychology and sociology was evident in the professional activity of their early practitioners. Thus, according to Allport again, the first book to bear the title of social psychology was written by a sociologist (E. A. Ross), and subsequently, sociologists have contributed almost as many social psychological textbooks as psychologists. It is unfortunate that later development has taken the form of two social psychologies, one written by psychologists and the other by sociologists, between which there has been too little contact (Armistead, 1974; Stryker, 1977). It is the more unfortunate since both of the two social psychologies have undergone various degrees of "psychologizing". Leon Festinger once remarked (retold by Claude Faucheux) that he ceased to be a *social* psychologist when he became a dissonance theorist. His cognitive dissonance theory (Festinger, 1957) has been so influential that it has swayed *both* of the two social psychologies to look into the cognitive elements within an individual's head. Conventional social psychology can hardly be called social by Comte's standard, and its contemporary development away from sociology must be, in the eyes of Comte, the great retreat. On the other side, attempts by sociologists to build a sociology on operant psychology (e.g. Homans, 1961, 1969; Emerson, 1972) create a largely premature impression that Comte's social psychology is finally in sight.

In conjunction with social psychology's movement away from sociology, and its preoccupation with the individual and interpersonal modes of analysis, is another feature which can be described as the softly, softly posture of social psychology. By this is meant the under-emphasis on the relatively more permanent, structural aspect of the power relation between people in favour of the more transient, and situation-specific aspect. The fact that the power inequality between people can become relatively long-lasting and generalizable across situations appears to be of little concern to social psychologists. Underlying this orientation is the implicit faith in the prospect of individual social mobility, and a belief in social Darwinism that individuals with the right ability will ultimately make it, and if they do not, it is because they have not got the ability. So that it is the individual, not the structure of the power relation, that is problematic.

Thus social psychologists seldom write about social stratification in general, and much less about the relation between structured inequality and power. The study of social conflict is mainly concerned with social competition, that is, the competition for status superiority (Turner, 1975b). No serious attention has been paid to the systematic discussion by sociologists and political theorists of the relationship between conflict and the power relation. Conflict resolution under the consultation of social psychologists has stopped short at the identification and fostering of superordinate goals without changing the basic power relation (Blake and Mouton, 1979). The human relations movement in organizational psychology failed to recognize that the "informal" norm was a product of the power relation between the subordinate workers and their superiors (Baritz, 1960). Milgram's (1974) study on obedience to authority tells us more about obedience than the nature of authority. It is only relatively recently that power change has received some persistent attention from social psychologists (e.g. Mulder, 1975; Brown, 1977).

As a result of the "softly" posture of social psychology and its preoccupation with the individual and interpersonal modes of analysis, many substantive issues of power are either left out completely, or are formulated in a partial manner which renders it difficult to relate the issues to one another. Several such examples have been cited above, others will be discussed later in the main text.

At the general psychological level, the concept of power is used more implicitly than explicitly. The power concept seems to have suffered a kind of terminological taboo. This in itself is the victim of a one-sided presumption that power can only corrupt. Instead of a systematic and coherent conception of power, a host of concepts have sprung up which nevertheless can be shown to be related to power in one form or another. These concepts include, among others, self-esteem and self-actualization (Maslow, 1943b), competence and effectance (White, 1959), personal causation (de Charms, 1968), perceived locus of control (e.g. Rotter, 1966), helplessness (Seligman, 1975), personal efficacy (Bandura, 1977) and stimulus (Skinner, 1938). Both individually and in conjunction with one another, they have exerted considerable impact on the development of contemporary psychology. The impact, however, will remain fragmentary unless the respective concepts can be related to one another through a more general, inclusive idea. Such an idea, I believe, can be found in the concept of power.

Against this background of the fragmentary nature and narrow outlook of the psychological conceptions of power, an increasing number of psychologists are expressing the need for a broader perspective of power. The study of the power motivation, which passed into oblivion in the achievement motivation studies (McClelland, 1961), has been resurrected and expanded in a series of studies, culminating in McClelland's recent book on power (McClelland, 1975). Another concrete expression of the need of a wider perspective and the relevance of power to psychological research can be seen in the objectives behind the first two Albany Symposia on Power and Influence (Tedeschi, 1974). The same is also apparent in psychoanalysis (Masserman, 1972).

As old problems are reexamined and new ones explored, authors in many areas have called attention to the relevance and necessity of a more adequate analysis of power. Noted examples are conflict and bargaining (Apfelbaum, 1974), authority relations (Zimbardo, 1975), equity (Homans, 1976), and intergroup relations (Billig, 1976; Apfelbaum, 1979). A similar need exists in the more specific area of intergroup discrimination (Ng, in press). Davis *et al.* (1976) concluded their review of the social psychology of small groups with the prediction that the experimental study of social interaction will increasingly address the basic questions of classical political economy. Zimbardo *et al.* (1977) appended the subtitle of their previous edition of "Influencing Attitudes and Changing Behaviour" to read, "An Introduction to Method, Theory and Applications of Social Control and Personal Power".

Two decades after Cartwright's (1959a) review of the literature on power, the study of power is still in search of a discipline. Whatever this discipline may be, it would be on shaky ground if it were to be erected only on the foundation of social and general psychology. What is also needed are two other layers of foundation, one to be derived from sociology and politics, and the other from philosophy. Few would quarrel with this multi-disciplinary stance, but not many have gone beyond paying it just lip-service. The present volume represents an attempt in this direction.

The plan of the book

The book is comprised of four main parts. The first three parts are devoted to an analytical examination of the conception of power in philosophy (Part I), sociology and political thought (Part II), general and social psychology (Part III). Part IV is concerned with power change, a topic which is of great relevance to the social psychology of power. Each of the four parts will be divided into two chapters, except Part II, which consists of three chapters.

Part I will discuss the analyses of power made by Niccolò Machiavelli, Thomas Hobbes and Bertrand Russell (Chapter 1), as well as Friedrich Nietzsche (Chapter 2). Machiavelli (1467-1527), of course, is widely known for his advice to the power wielder on matters like how to generate power, the pros and cons of different bases of power and their effective application in accordance with the situation. His advice is premised on a certain assumption of human motivation which reflects rather poorly on the moral state of mankind. A wise ruler must not rely on people's morality, but must conduct his rule as if people had lost their moral imperatives. He should, Machiavelli exhorted, also learn not to be good but to behave as the situation requires. There is nothing particularly striking about the contents of Machiavelli's advice, which is neither ingenious nor novel. What made his views so shocking to his contemporary Christian world was that he *publicly* advocated the autonomy of statecraft from the moral and religious realm. In this way, Machiavelli successfully brought to a head the controversy over the relation between power and morality. The controversy has remained a central theme not only in philosophy, but also in sociology, politics and psychology.

Hobbes (1588-1679) was a more systematic theoretician than Machiavelli. He attempted to erect a grand system of human behaviour and experience on the principles of motion and egoism (hedonism). His analysis of power was initially developed in conjunction with and as an adjunct to the principle of hedonism. How can egoistic human beings achieve their hedonistic pursuit? The answer, Hobbes said, is power. Hence the famous Hobbesian definition of power — power is the present means to secure some future good. The hedonistic motive gives rise to the desire for power. Hobbes' analysis of power, however, was not confined to hedonism. Power leads to competition, conflict, and finally a hypothetical state of nature wherein there is a general war of all against all. This gives rise to the Hobbesian problem of social order. How is society possible, given that its members are egoistic beings antagonistic to one another? The solution advocated by Hobbes is a covenant, a kind of social contract in which the citizens give up their individual power of hurting one another to a supreme body in return for the peaceful pursuit of individual ends and freedom from violent death. This supreme body (the Leviathan), Hobbes insisted, must be autonomous and *self-perpetuating*. In the latter respect, Hobbes went even further than Machiavelli's assertion that the political arena should be freed from the moral and religious realm.

Hobbes' solution to the problem of social order has not earned much orthodoxy amongst sociologists. As will be pointed out in Chapters 3 and 4, both the utopians and the rationalists have their own solutions. The Utopian's solution is normative consensus, or what Émile Durkheim would call the *conscience collective*. The rationalist's solution, on the other hand, is in terms of the domination by one group, or an interlocking network of elite groups, over the rest of society. Of the two solutions, the rationalist's comes closer to Hobbes' and assigns a greater theoretical role to power in the analyses of social order, social conflict and social stratification.

Both Machiavelli and Hobbes conducted their analysis of power primarily in terms of the desire and action of an individual or an aggregate of individuals. Russell (1872–1970), on the other hand, took the corporate group or the organization as the unit of analysis. In doing so, he was very much in keeping with the changing nature of power in industrial society. Compared to the power wielded in pre-industrial society, power in complex industrial society has become more impersonal, more anonymous, and is embedded more in organizational positions than in individuals. Because of these changes, a fuller understanding of power in modern society can only be gained by looking at the structure of society, its major institutions, the market system and the principal assumptions on which this system operates, as well as the ideologies. As will be discussed in Chapter 5, such an understanding can hardly come from either the one- or two-dimensional view of political behaviourism, which is premised on the dubious assumption that the locus of power in a community can be found in the acts of individual human beings. To a certain extent, Russell's major work on power (Russell, 1938) is true to its very title, which reads "Power: *A New Social Analysis*" (added italics). It is also noteworthy that Russell gave a more inclusive definition of power than the Hobbesian definition, namely, power is the production of intended effects. Contrary to Machiavelli, Russell discussed at great length the necessity of restraining power.

Too much of the current social psychological thinking on power proceeds from the same restrictive premise as political behaviourism. As will be pointed out in Chapter 7, the field-theoretical conception of power is a prime example of this mode of thinking. The conceptualization carried out within the social exchange framework, although less restrictive than that of field theory, can hardly provide a useful perspective on a problem as complex as power. This does not mean that the above two approaches are unproductive in generating ideas for research into power. The point is that they attend to only a narrow range of the phenomena of power and their underlying processes, and therefore cannot provide us with a broad perspective for formulating the problem in a socially and politically more relevant way. There is no convincing reason why the social psychology of power must remain at the pre-Russellian stage.

Nietzsche (1844-1900) wrote "The Will to Power" during 1883 -1888. The work has great relevance to the understanding of power at the general psychological level, even though he had not presented his work in a systematic and developed form. He used the term power both as an elastic concept as well as a specific concept. By means of the former, he was able to attribute a long list of apparently unrelated phenomena to the working of the will to power. On this and other grounds, he put put forth the claim that the will to power can provide a unifying psychological principle superior to either hedonism or Darwinism. What a man strives for first and most is power, pleasure and displeasure are accidentals. In opposition to the Darwinian emphasis on external, environmental forces, Nietzsche posited the will as having ascendancy over external influences. He deplored the diminution of the will as the sign of grave human weakness, and condemned as slander any teaching which leads to that deplorable state.

According to one interpretation, Nietzsche also used the concept of power specifically to mean self-overcoming through the process of sublimation. Strong and weak, or powerful and powerless, correspond respectively to a high and a low degree of self-overcoming. A person who does evil, who seeks to dominate and subjugate other people, does so not because he is strong or powerful, but rather because he is weak and powerless. Similarly, false morality and *ressentiment* are the signs of powerlessness and the diminution of the will, and not of powerfulness or the abundance of the will. In short, Nietzsche reached the point of asserting that the degrees of power would constitute a standard of moral evaluation.

It is noteworthy that Nietzsche did not treat power in isolation from the lack of it. Furthermore, his psychology of power and powerlessness is at the same time inextricably related to the problems of morality and ethics. From the outline that can be discerned in "The Will to Power", it is possible to derive a balanced and relatively broad view of power which can serve two interrelated functions. First, it offers an antidote to the exaggerated and oversimplified presumption that power must necessarily corrupt. Secondly, it provides a heuristic framework within which a number of concepts in contemporary psychology can be meaningfully related to power. These concepts range from self-actualization and competence to helplessness and efficacy. The relevance of these two functions will be amplifed when we discuss the psychological views of the power of the individual in Chapter 6. In addition to this, Nietzsche's thinking on power has some illuminating thing to say about social interaction involving freedom and justice (see Chapter 2).

The three chapters of Part II deal with the sociological and political conception of power. Chapter 3, the first of the three chapters, gives a digest of Max Weber's (1864-1920) work on power, and outlines two basic sociological views of society and their corresponding conceptions of power. Weber's work is more than a classic in the sociology of power. It is remarkably modern. Many authors in their discussion of social conflict and social stratification have found Weber's work highly relevant to the modern era. That is to say, Weber's work is not restricted to capitalist or post-capitalist democratic countries but is also relevant to socialist, communist and multi-ethnic countries. As will be pointed out in Chapter 4, the writings of Weber have been instrumental in the development of several important theories of social conflict and social stratification. To the extent that social psychology is interested in these two problems, the discussion in Chapter 4 would provide a useful background to the advancement of this interest.

Furthermore, Weber's work is also relevant to social psychology in at least two other areas. His delineation of the four types of legitimacy (traditional, rational-legal, charismatic and *Wertrationalität*) holds promise for a cognitive type of approach to social change, in which the emphases are on the belief structure of people and the cognitive conflict that an agent of social change may induce. In particular, Weber's treatment of charismatic legitimacy would be potentially useful for the further study of minority influence, as will be pointed out in a discussion of Moscovici's work (Chapter 7). Secondly, the so-called Weberian multi-dimensional model of social stratification is directly relevant to the rank equilibration theory (e.g. Galtung, 1966) and equity theory (Homans, 1976). The former, in turn, will be instrumental in the study of power change (see Chapter 9).

It has been mentioned above that Chapter 3 will also outline two basic sociological views of society. The two views (the Utopian's and the rationalist's views) have their roots in philosophy. Their manifestation in contemporary sociology and politics is closely related to two different approaches to power. There is considerable divergence between them with regard to the formulation of such basic problems as social order, social conflict and social stratification. Furthermore, they also differ in the selection of research questions and the determination of the relative importance of these questions. These points of divergence will be taken up in Chapter 4.

Chapter 5 is on political behaviourism. The initial, primary concern of political behaviourism was to launch an empirical approach to the question of the distribution of power in a community. This in itself was a significant milestone in the history of community power studies. The rigour of measurement has unfortunately squeezed out those elements of power which are not so easily quantifiable. It soon became very obvious that the initial approach, which consisted of finding out which members in the community have influenced the making of big decisions, barely scratched the surface of the question. This decision-making approach, otherwise known as the one-dimensional view of power, was later incorporated into a broader approach which covers the power of nondecision-making as well as decision making (the two-dimensional view of power). Nondecision-making power refers to the ability of limiting the scope of the political process to public consideration of only those issues which are comparatively innocuous to the power wielder. It is a power that is not so readily observable, but is no less real than the readily observable power of decision-making.

Despite the above difference, the two-dimensional view shares with the one-dimensional view the behaviouristic premise that the locus of power can only be found in the behaviour of individuals. It ignores yet another, more fundamental dimension. The life chances of people in a community are not so much the result of somebody somewhere making a series of decisions or nondecisions to that effect, but largely because certain social mechanisms, principles and assumptions are taken for granted. This dimension is quite beyond the reach of behaviourism.

From the beginning of the one-dimensional view to the end of the two-dimensional view, the relatively short history of political behaviourism should be taken seriously as a lesson to the social psychology of power. The lesson is not that the empirical method should be completely discarded. It is rather that we must keep in mind a broad perspective on power when we formulate the problem, design our research and analyse the data.

Part III will examine the general and social psychological works on power (Chapters 6 and 7 respectively). Chapter 6 deals with firstly a number of viewpoints which make use of power or a power-related concept as a latent, personality construct. The controversy over the relation between morality and power is as much evident here as in the political arena. More common than not, the psychological judgement is that power corrupts. This opinion is not invalid. It is, however, one-sided and over-simplified. We must recognize that inasmuch as power corrupts, power also enriches and uplifts life, and that powerlessness, no less, corrupts too. What is needed is again a broader perspective that would do justice to the complexity of power in relation to the psychological functioning of the individual. It will be suggested that Nietzsche's work can meet such a need. At the same time, his work provides a framework within which a large number of important concepts in psychology can be related to one another. The concepts, as noted earlier, include self-esteem, self-actualization, competence, effectance, personal causation, perceived locus of control, helplessness and personal efficacy.

Secondly, Chapter 6 will examine B. F. Skinner's experimental analysis of behaviour and F. Heider's analysis of the action of an individual. It is possible to argue that the essence of Skinner's experimental analysis of behaviour is an analysis of power. The concept of stimulus, which is central to Skinner's behavioural science, assumes a theoretical role that is more or less identical to the power concept. Once the similarity between stimulus and power is recognized, the strength and weakness of Skinner's views on society and the design of culture would become more apparent. In the light of the discussion presented in Chapters 1, 3, 4 and 5, Skinner's writing on society appears to be extraordinarily adventurous. It is a long leap from the general psychology of power (stimulus) to the sociology of power. The admirable quality of Skinner is his deep and persistent concern with the political and cultural relevance of his work, a quality which is all too lacking amongst *social* psychologists. As will be pointed out in Chapter 7, Skinner's idea of the reinforcing and discriminative stimuli can be readily translated into outcome and cue control at the interpersonal level.

The power concept is an essential part of Heider's "naive psychology" of the action of an individual. Like many of his other remarks, his statements on power are both suggestive and illuminating. Examples would include the attribution of and attitude toward power, and the functional relation between harm-doing and the assertion of power. The attribution of power is in turn related to attribution theory in general. Heider's statement on the attitude toward power has a bearing on the interesting thesis that dependence sometimes leads to a power relation such that the weaker (dependent) person can have power over the stronger person. Finally, Heider's suggestion that harm-doing can enhance the actor's power feeling is in agreement with the view of a number of other psychologists who see a similar relation between aggression and power.

Chapter 7 will discuss the field-theoretical and social exchange formulations of social power. The former is part and parcel of the conventional social psychological thinking on social influence. It bears the influence of K. Lewin on the one hand, and that of his students on the other. Its excessive and one-sided reliance on the notion of dependence has been strongly criticized by S. Moscovici, who in turn has proposed seriously to discard the concept of power from the study of social influence altogether. It can be shown that Moscovici's proposal is derived from a partial and selective image of power which does not seem to justify his assertion. Furthermore, his own study on minority influence would sooner or later lead to the problem of power which he so far has been trying to avoid. In view of this, Weber's work on charismatic legitimacy (Chapter 3) will be potentially useful.

The social exchange conception of power gives the most coherent view that is currently available in social psychology. P. Blau's approach, in particular, represents a serious effort of relating the sociological and social psychological modes of analysis to one another. Like the social exchange theory in general, Blau's analysis is unfortunately imbued with an excessive air of laissez-faire liberalism. This, as will be pointed out in the discussion, is most clearly reflected in the notion of "alternative".

Chapters 8 and 9, which make up the final part of this work (Part IV), are devoted to a study of power change. For reasons discussed in Chapters 1 and 4, a certain power relation can be regarded as an inevitable and permanent feature of society. In formal groupings and organizations, the presence of a power relation is obvious enough. As will be noted in Chapter 8, an increasing number of men and women are enmeshed in organizations wherein they stand in a relation of power towards one another. In the informal group setting, the power relation is less explicit but is nevertheless real. A large part of the social context within which people relate to one another is therefore characterized by the presence of a power relation. For this reason alone, a study of the changes occurring in the power relation would be highly relevant to the social psychology of power. In this regard, the pioneering work of a contemporary Dutch social psychologist, Mauk Mulder, provides a useful albeit preliminary paradigm. The rest of Chapter 8 is devoted to a critical review and further elaboration of this paradigm.

Chapter 9 is a direct continuation of Chapter 8. Mulder's general observation, which is further supported by our own work, is that the low-ranking group members are less inclined than their more highly placed counterparts to take over power from the top rank. Mulder regards this observation as an invariant finding. Subsequently, this finding has played a significant part in Mulder's proposal of gradual power change. However, there are historical and theoretical reasons to be skeptical of the generality of the finding in question. By combining the theories of social categorization and rank equilibration, it is possible to identify a new set of conditions which would raise the low-ranking members' tendency to take over power. Some tentative experimental results which support the expectation will be reported.

The reason why the subject of power change has been singled out for special attention is because of its important nature, and not because of the answers that have been proposed. The general aim is to raise research questions concerning the instigation of power change and to outline possible ways of approaching them.

I

Power in Western Philosophy

1

From Machiavelli to Hobbes and Russell

It is beyond the scope of this book to provide a representative coverage of the philosophical views on power. What follows is a selective account of the opinions of four thinkers in western philosophy. The selection can be easily shown to contain an assumption which ought to be made explicit at the outset. Conflict and co-operation, change and stability, are integral elements of social life. In times of co-operation and stability, social life smoothly flows on, like a gentle breeze over a calm ocean, and power in its more naked forms is largely concealed. When co-operation develops into conflict, or stability into change, the smoothness of social life turns into turbulence, and power in all its diverse, and particularly naked, forms suddenly confronts the consciousness of every woman and man. It would be enlightening, so I think, to listen to the philosophers who have witnessed turbulent times.

Partly guided by this assumption, and partly restricted by the limitation of space, I have chosen to examine the views of Bertrand Russell, Thomas Hobbes and Niccolò Machiavelli. Russell wrote his book on power (Russell, 1938) very much with the prospect of another world war in his mind. Hobbes' (1651) "Leviathan" was written when the English monarchy was under the mounting threat of the Parliament and the Civil War. Machiavelli was a political administrator and a military strategist of the Florentine government (Florence's diplomatist and the Secretary of the Ten of War) by profession, and an observant writer on statecraft by fame. He wrote "The Prince" in 1513 after being released from torture as a political suspect; and according to one translater (Gilbert, 1965), began his work on the "Discourses" around the same period, which was completed in 1517.

Power to these three thinkers, as far as I understand them, is not merely an intellectual subject. None of them indulged in the metaphysics of power. They, and Russell in particular, all treated power as the blood and water of life itself. Such a position was even more emphatically endorsed by Friedrich Nietzsche, whose opinions deserve more understanding. Nietzsche deplored what he perceived to be the advancing hegemony of the collective power of the weak and many over the strong and few, as manifested – according to Nietzsche – in Christianity, democracy and socialism. And even though it may sound unbelievable, Nietzsche abhorred the power of the unthinking, fanatic nationalism of *his* own country, the German *Reich*. In these regards, Nietzsche shared with the aforesaid philosophers the view that power is a basic social process. But he went much further than that and proposed that power is the unitary conception in psychology as well as a monistic standard of moral evaluation. To examine this proposal, a separate chapter will be devoted.

Niccolò Machiavelli

The doctrine that all power ultimately belongs to God is deeply ingrained in the Old and New Testaments, culminating in the Lord's prayer: ". . . For thine is the kingdom and the power and the glory, for ever". All governing authority is said to be instituted by God (e.g. Romans, Chapter 13). On the other hand, the doctrine of the two kingdoms and Jesus' admonition that his kingdom is not of this world strongly suggest that secular power is for worldly people. And being surrounded by a hostile pagan political order, the early Christians were understandably apprehensive of and distrusted secular power and government. How these political legacies of distrusting secular power and government have survived and become rooted in the Christian beliefs has been dealt with by Friedrich (1963, 1967).

When the Church established itself over and above the kings, politics and Christian morals were mixed up. The monarchs found it necessary to deduce the principles of statecraft from the Bible; or at least to pay lipservice to the Christian creed, even though many of them undoubtedly had followed the Ten Commandments in reverse and thus anticipated in practice the advice given by Machiavelli in "The Prince".

Against the Christian distrust of secular government, Machiavelli glorified the State. Against the religious tether placed on politics, he proclaimed the divorce of politics from morals and preached the gospel of realism and empiricism. In the spirit of the Italian Renaissance, Machiavelli approached the generation and use of power as an art, a skill that has to be perfected rather than as an evil which has to be chained. It was these qualities which furnished the shocking value of "The Prince" to the Christian world rather than the tactics articulated therein which were neither novel nor ingenious. "Han Fei Tzu", the book named after the last of the Chinese Legalist school (Han Fei, 280 B.C.-233 B.C.), would make the policies of Machiavelli's "The Prince" seem timid and vacillating (Creel, 1960). The historical significance of these qualities would not diminish even though Machiavelli might have written "The Prince", not as a serious objective treatise, but as a satire to embarrass the Medici family who had tortured him, as Mattingly (1958) has ventured to suggest. If "The Prince" were really intended as a satire, then Machiavelli would have been a "Machiavellian". In any case, the political ethos of the Middle Ages had been denounced in public; and whether that was done by means of a satire, or in the name of realism, or both, would not alter its historical significance. Since, too, the same themes reappear again and again in the "Discourses". The following discussion will mainly refer to the "Discourses", which is superior to "The Prince" both in scope and detail.

The ends sought by Machiavelli were national independence, liberty, security and workable laws. These cannot be achieved without a government. Machiavelli gave a brief explanation of the origin of government. As the inhabitants increase in number, they gather together, and "So that they could better defend themselves, defer to him among them the strongest and the bravest, and make him chief and obey him" ("Discourses", Book 1, Chapter 2).

Machiavelli distinguished between three varieties of government — kingdom (princedom), aristocracy and republic (popular government) — which succeed one another in the form of a "government cycle" (Book 1, Chapter 3). None of them is totally good or bad, so that the superiority of a government would lie in a mixed form which is in accord with necessity. A mixed government means division of power among the prince, the nobility and the people. Machiavelli spoke of the uniformity of humanity (all men in all ages are basically the same because their desires are identical). In "The Prince", he favoured greater power to be vested in the prince than the multitude. This preference was reversed in the "Discourses". The people, when they are rulers, are no better or no worse than the prince. And since government by a multitude, as compared to princedom, would be less susceptible to corruption by bribery, more able to shape their happiness and misery, more reliable, and whose fault can be cured by words rather than by steel, the people should have a greater share of power (Book 1, Chapters 58 and 59).

The change of one variety of government into another is mediated by conflict between the prince, the nobility and the people. Within a republic, such as the Roman Republic, discord between the people and the rich makes it free and powerful.

Having been divorced from morals, Machiavellian politics became autonomous. In "The Prince" as well as the "Discourses", Machiavelli spoke of the use of power in a manner that reflected the spirit of the Renaissance. The use of power is a skill, an art, the achievement of which is limited only by the creativity of the person who wields it. Creativity is part of the quality called *virtù*, which does not mean virtue, but vigour, emotional detachment, force of character, wisdom and action. Machiavelli's trust in the efficacy of *virtù* is best expressed in the manner he acknowledged and then minimized the role of Fortune in human affairs.

> I assert, indeed, once more that it is very true, according to what we see in all the histories, that men are able to assist Fortune but not to thwart her. They can weave her designs but cannot destroy them. They ought, then, never to give up as beaten, because, since they do not know her purpose and she goes through crooked and unknown roads, they can always hope, and hoping are not to give up, in whatever fortune and whatever affliction they may be. (Book 2, Chapter 29)

(Compare "The Prince", Chapter 25.) Christie and Geis' (1970a) "Studies in Machiavellianism" is a rigorous experimental investigation of *virtù* in action between individuals over non-political ends. To be fair to Machiavelli, it should perhaps be entitled "Studies of Machiavellian virtù in non-Machiavellian affairs".

Machiavelli did not define power. It is possible to infer, nevertheless, that Machiavelli used the term to denote the ultimate basis of the efficacy of means. For him, the end does not by itself justify the means. He would be as contemptuous of blundering tyranny as unworkable idealism. The means must also be justified by its efficacy. An extraordinary object or an exceptional situation would require drastic measures beyond the ordinary rules (the principle of *raison d'état*), but even then, these measures, such as cruelty, must be well used and not badly used ("The Prince", Chapter 8). With these qualifications, means is amoral, and so is power. The legitimacy or otherwise of power is relevant only in so far as it impinges on the efficacy of power. Thus a prudent ruler should use religion in order not to create resistance by default, but he must be able to be *not* good when the situation so requires. The ruler can use fear as much as love, so long as he does not incite hatred, lest he be forced to turn into a tyrant and become self-destructive. It is safer to be feared than loved because men can always — and easily — withdraw their love whereas fear is held by a dread of punishment that is hard to ignore. This follows from Machiavelli's belief that the goodness in men had been lost under the influence of the Roman Church (Book 1, Chapter 10), and by the presence of gentlemen (who without working live in luxury on the return from their landed possession — Book 1, Chapter 55). Thus a law-giver must, said Machiavelli, *assume* that all men are evil, and should not rely on morality. Force should be used in conjunction with fraud, without which force will never be enough.

Machiavelli saw the salvation of the then chaotic and corrupt Italy in the realistic and creative use of power, which was possible only when statecraft was liberated from religious and moral tethers. The power tactics he recommended are mostly expedient and rarely promise long-term solutions. He seemed to have ruled out the possibility of any long-term solution, and he may be right. His renaissance-styled faith in *virtù* and the almost limitless possibility of power stands in contrast with the fatalistic evolutionary view that laws cannot change folklores. The outbreak of the ideologically-inspired political movements in this century, both from the right as well as from the left, indicates the reality of Machiavelli's faith. Such a reality is terrifying to some people as it is heartening to others. The kingdom proclaimed in Machiavelli's amoral gospel of power is not yet decisively on earth, and probably never will. For the opposite view has never been silenced, and the controversy over the autonomy of power from morals remain a lively issue (e.g. Maritain, 1942; the American Watergate).

Thomas Hobbes

Like Machiavelli, Thomas Hobbes wrote with the explicit aim of persuading his country to adopt a certain rational political model which, in his case, was supposed to save the country from the imminent civil war and the subsequent disaster of anarchy. What was problematic to Machiavelli were the subordination of politics to ineffectual moral precepts and the inept wielding of power, not power itself or conflict. Hobbes, on the other hand, dreaded the conflict between the bourgeois Parliament and the Monarch; and he rationalized the inalienable need for a monolithic sovereign body (the Leviathan, or the Commonwealth) by a complex set of arguments which amounts to a grand theoretical system of human experience and behaviour containing, as one of its vital clauses, an intermediate conclusion that man's desire for power is socially harmful. His views are laid out in the "Leviathan", which was first published in 1651.

In his proposed system, Hobbes attempted to offer a theory not only of man, but also of nature. Expressed in terms of our present day learned disciplines, Hobbes aimed at building psychology on physiology, physiology on physics; and then partly on the basis of this materialist psychology, and more importantly on the basis of a consideration of social behaviour, Hobbes deduced political sociology. The starting point of this grand system had its source from Galileo's law of inertia — *motion* is the natural state of things. Hobbes' psychology is motion through and through. Light, colour, sound, odour, etc., are not in the external objects. They are sensations caused by the actions or motions of the external objects. The sensation itself is motion in the organs and interior parts of a person's body, being caused by the action of the external object. Moreover, all behaviours are motions, which can be *"vitall"* (involuntary) or *"animall"* (voluntary). An involuntary motion, such as breathing, begins in and continues throughout life, requiring no help of "imagination". All voluntary motions, such as walking and speaking, are "first fancied in our minds", since they always depend upon "a precedent thought of *whither*, *which way* and *what*". Thus a voluntary motion has an internal beginning; and the first internal beginning is imagination. Before a voluntary motion appears visible action, it is a motion within a person's body and is moved by passion(s). Passions that move towards something are called appetites or desires (love, hunger, thirst, good, etc.); while passions that move away from something are aversions (fear, hate, evil, etc.). The sum of passions continues till the thing is either done, or thought impossible. That state is called "deliberation", which is reached through foresight of the good and evil consequences. This chain of reasoning amounts to a hedonistic principle of human motivation. Furthermore, by assuming that passions are incessant, Hobbes drew a preliminary conclusion, "Life it selfe is but Motion, and can never be without Desire, nor without Feare, no more than without Sense". All that are in Chapter 6 of the "Leviathan". For a critical examination of the logical difficulties of Hobbes' psychology, the interested reader is referred to the article by Peters and Tajfel (1957). A general discussion of Hobbes' psychology can be found in Robinson (1976). Our focus here will be with Hobbes' conception of power.

Power enters Hobbes' system apparently through two doors. Hobbes' principle of hedonism naturally raises the question about the means for the pursuit of hedonism. Hobbes called the means power, defined as the present means to secure some future apparent good (Hobbes, 1651, Chapter 10). Power is thus ushered in as an adjunct to hedonism. I wish to call this the side door entry in order to highlight, by contrast, Hobbes' sophisticated analysis of power which finally transforms his principle of hedonism into one of power, and which also provides an independent theoretical base for the analysis of political behaviour.

The second entry is created through a social analysis of the active relation between individuals, in contradistinction to the aforesaid bio-physical analysis of human motivation which provides for the first entry. Hobbes asserted that men are by nature basically equal both in body and mind. Equality of physical strength consists in the fact that even "the weakest has strength enough to kill the strongest"; and of ability, in

> that howsoever they (men) may acknowledge many others to be more witty, or more eloquent, or more learned; Yet they will hardly believe there be many so wise as themselves . . . (And this proves that men are equal because) there is not ordinarily a greater signe of the equal distribution of any thing, than that every man is contented with his share. (Hobbes, 1651, Chapter 13)

The assertion of the equality of physical strength is a mere recognition of the tremendous equalizing power of lethal weaponry, and there is nothing striking about this except that it rectifies Machiavelli's erroneous dismissal of the importance of artillery. On the other hand, equality of ability, that is, that people esteem themselves as able as anyone else, shows great foresight of popular individualism that underlined the ascendency of the bourgeois. As well, it can be regarded as a forerunner of the concept of self-esteem in psychology.

Equality of body and mind then leads to some general statements of social interaction between individuals quite unanticipated by the principle of hedonism.

Hedonism alone has nothing definite to say about social competition and conflict. People may consent to a hierarchically ordered society, or to an ideology of natural inequality, and thereby eliminate any competition or conflict in their hedonistic pursuit. Equality of body makes competition at least entertainable. Then from the equality of ability, Hobbes reasoned, arises equality of hope. When two men desire the same thing, which they cannot both enjoy, they become enemies. (Retreat would amount to an acknowledgement of inferiority, and is hence unlikely.) Their subsequent interaction is characterized by competition and diffidence. In competition, *each* man uses his power to invade for gain, so that the power of one man necessarily resists the effects of the power of another, and hence real power consists only in the *excess* of the power of one above that of another. Competition turns out to be basically a power struggle. The effects and operation of power are no longer confined to the power wielder, for the main use of power now lies in subduing the power of another, or in transferring another's power to its own master. Power becomes socially harmful. Diffidence (the use of power for self-defence) results, and then "warre", which consists not only in actual battle, but also the will to and expectation of battle. The dynamics of equality would thus pull everyone into a constant struggle for power.

> So that in the first place, I put for a generall inclination of all mankind, a perpetuall and restless desire for Power after power, that ceaseth onely in Death. And the cause of this, is not alwayes that a man hopes for a more intensive delight, than he has already attained to; or that he cannot be content with a moderate power: but because he cannot assure the power and means to live well, which he hath present, without the acquisition of more. And from hence it is, that Kings, whose power is greatest, turn their endeavours to the assuring it at home by Lawes, or abroad by Wars: and when that is done, there succeedeth a new desire; in some, of Fame from new Conquest; in others, of ease and sensuall pleasure; in others, of admiration, or being flattered for excellence in some art, or other ability of the mind. (Hobbes, 1651, Chapter 11)

On the basis of the socially harmful nature of man's desire for power, Hobbes proposed what ought to be done. There should be consensus among all the people to enter into some kind of social contract (Covenant) wherein they agree to invest their individual power in a sovereign body in return for protection from violent death. The necessity of political protection is identical to Machiavelli's view on the origin of government. What makes Hobbes' civil sovereign body particularly provocative is the stipulation that the sovereign body should be self-perpetuating. It does not matter for Hobbes whether that body is a monarch, or even a parliament, so long as it is entrusted with the complete autonomy to appoint its successor(s). Such a stipulation follows from Hobbes' belief that unless the government can control its succession, it will be subject to the manipulation by *someone* on the other side of the covenant, and would thereby fail in its obligation of protecting *all* the members from violent death.

As pointed out by Macpherson (1968), Hobbes intended to persuade the bourgeois into accepting the need of a self-perpetuating supreme governing body which was designed not to deny men a life of competition and acquisition, but to ensure that they could have it securely without endangering civil peace. Hobbes failed to convince the bourgeois, who then succeeded in creating a state as prescribed by Hobbes. Hobbes' failure is understandable in the light of his own analysis. With their political power yet unassured, the bourgeois would not give up struggle as a means of securing their power, particularly when the conflict began to show them in favourable light. Hobbes' own analysis would have predicted that the bourgeois would be most unlikely to substitute "warre" by trust in his proposed system of government.

The way the bourgeois succeeded in creating a self-perpetuating government, according to Macpherson (1968), shows up a major error in Hobbes' analysis of power. Hobbes' method of analysis relies ultimately on some sort of extrapolation from the behaviour and passions of individuals. What he had failed to recognize was that the struggle for power was not only staged between "every man against every man", but more importantly, between groups. Power struggle might generate group differentiation which under certain conditions would lead to ingroup solidarity. The cohesive group could have a continuous life above and beyond the life-span of individual members through the recruitment and socialization of new members. In other words, whereas individuals are mortals, a cohesive group could be long-lasting. When such a cohesive and self-renewing group, in this case the bourgeois class, controlled the election of new government, the government would become a self-perpetuating sovereign body in fact, if not in name. Nevertheless, although Hobbes had erred for lack of a Marxian analysis of class, or for that matter, a social psychology of intergroup relations, his idea that power perpetuates itself has been a recurrent theme in political sociology, as manifested in the concept of power elite (e.g. Mills, 1958) and Michels' Iron Law of Oligarchy (Michels, 1962).

If one accepted the "Leviathan" as Hobbes' single most important philosophical work, then one must acknowledge that power occupies an important position in Hobbes' philosophy, even more important than hedonism. Power to Hobbes is no longer a servant to hedonism, but has a life of its own. Machiavelli, as we have noted, preached the autonomy of power. Hobbes, more a theoretician than a preacher, demonstrated theoretically that, given certain assumptions, power must be autonomous. Social life without the constant threat of violent death is possible only when the leviathan is entrusted with autonomous power, and without it, a relative power advantage is an end forced upon every person. Hobbes even went on to assert that the true value or worth of a man, is no more than it is esteemed by others, that is to say, "so much as would be given for the use of his power" (Hobbes, 1651, Chapter 10). This true value of a man, Hobbes insisted, should be distinguished from a man's self-esteem, which, as we have noted in connection with the equality of ability, is (according to Hobbes) always on a par with, if not superior to, any other man's self-esteem. In other words, Hobbes was arguing here that social status is a derivative of power.

Friedrich (1963) is critical of Hobbes' conception of power which puts too much emphasis on the substantive aspect of power, that is, on the superior resources (personal or acquired) possessed by a person. Such a conception, argues Friedrich, is both too broad and too narrow. It is too broad because when power is identified with the totality of resources, "wealth" becomes indistinguishable from "power", and hence economics is confused with politics. This is not so much a criticism as a difference of opinion regarding the generality of the concept. More noteworthy is Friedrich's charge that the Hobbesian conception of power is too narrow. The reason advanced is that power is primarily a relation among men which manifests itself in the behaviour of following. This relational aspect of power cannot be completely reduced to any calculus of resources because sometimes persuasion alone would be sufficient to bring about followership.

The most serious criticism advanced by Friedrich, in my opinion, is that both Machiavelli and Hobbes failed to distinguish the issues presented by authority as contrasted with the issues raised by power. Authority refers to the capacity of the power-wielder to elaborate what he prefers by reasoning which would make sense to those who follow him, if time and other circumstances permitted. Such a capacity for reasoned elaboration is distinguished from the sheer skill of the tongue by the qualification that reasoning becomes authoritative only when it is based on communal values, beliefs, interests and needs. Authority, argues Friedrich (1967), becomes important as soon as one is concerned with the operation of the state and the maintenance of a political order:

> As has been rightly said, you cannot sit for long upon bayonets, so you cannot long maintain an effective order with mere brute power; you must add to it this other element of authority. (p. 145)

I shall discuss the controversy over the relation between power and authority in Chapter 4.

It is unlikely that Machiavelli or Hobbes can defend themselves against the charge of an incomplete analysis of power. Power in social change may no longer be the same as in social stability. Yet a proper evaluation of the Machiavellian and Hobbesian emphases on the substantive aspect of power has to reckon with the particular issues which Machiavelli and Hobbes regarded as problematic, as well as the political and social context of their times. They were witnessing, each in his own time, an era of rapid and drastic social change; and they were both concerned with the problem of how to create a new social order. When in social change, the old structure of power relations was losing ground and value consensus (if any) gave way to dissension, would it still be effectual by appealing to morals or authority *à la* Friedrich? And would extraordinary resources, or raw power, not move to the foreground?

In a discussion of how to influence and create social change, even on a much more limited scale than that which occupied the attention of Machiavelli and Hobbes, Coleman (1971), for instance, has similarly placed considerable emphasis on resources. It is interesting to note, too, that out of the revolutionary career of Mao Tse-tung have come the following remarks: "Power comes out of the barrel of a gun", and "Revolution is unlike inviting guests to a meal". The analyses of power offered by Machiavelli and Hobbes, partial as they are, highlight the close relation between social change and substantive power.

Two further comments are pertinent before we leave Hobbes and Machiavelli. Power to them is wielded by individuals. Social mechanisms, such as the market mechanism and the implicit assumptions of how society should function, were not being considered as active agents in the power game. Secondly, the prevalence of bureaucratic organizations outside the church and the state since the Industrial Revolution has shifted the locus of power from individuals to corporate bodies. Institutional analysis of power becomes necessary. The best source of information on social mechanisms and institutions, to my knowledge, can be found in sociology. Modern sociology began long before Bertrand Russell wrote his book on power (Russell, 1938), and has produced statements on the topic of power far superior to Russell's, many of which actually predated Russell's views. Russell on power is like a philosopher taking on the language of a sociologist, and that makes his views worthy of note. For his work represents a serious effort on the part of a philosopher to come to grips with social processes and institutions in the analysis of power, and in doing so, picks up from where Machiavelli and Hobbes have left behind.

Bertrand Russell

Russell claimed to undertake a new social analysis of power the aim of which is "to prove that the fundamental concept in social science is Power, in the same sense in which Energy is the fundamental concept in physics . . . . The laws of social dynamics are laws which can only be stated in terms of power" (Russell, 1938, p. 10). Power, defined by Russell as the production of intended effects, is together with glory, the chief among the infinite desires of man. Power and glory are not identical. But since the easiest way to obtain glory is to obtain power, "The desire for glory, therefore, prompts, in the main, the same actions as are prompted by the desire for power, and the two motives may, for most practical purposes, be regarded as one" (p. 9). A distinction is made by Russell between "power desired as a means and power desired as an end in itself" (p. 275), and that the latter is "sure to arise in the course of an active career" (p. 276).

It is clear that Russell insisted on using power as a generic concept, both from his conceptualization of the concept as sketched above and further discussed below, as well as from his disagreement with the Marxian analysis of power. Marx's analysis, he said, focused on wealth and failed to see the totality of power, of which wealth is only one form. An elaborate typology of power forms the skeleton of Russell's book. Power over human beings is classified by means of three separate criteria, each criterion in turn produces its own forms of power. The first criterion is the manner of influencing individuals, which may be carried out through physical coercion, material inducements (including incentive and deterrent), or persuasion. The first and the last have been respectively identified as physical (coercive) power and propaganda; but the second one has not been given a special label.

Another criterion of classifying power is by the type of organizations involved. This includes, among others, military, economic and educational organizations. The types of power formulated by the previous criterion are used as bases of grouping the organization. The army and the police are being grouped together as organizations which exercise coercive power; economic organizations are lumped into one category which use inducement power; and schools, churches and political parties share another category on the basis that they aim at influencing opinion.

The third criterion is psychological. There are, according to Russell, three psychological sources of power. One is tradition, in the form of respect, such as respect for priests and kings. When people cease to respect the tradition, traditional power will gradually give way either to "revolutionary" power based on the belief in a new creed, or to "naked" power based on people's fear and the personal ambitions of those who seek it.

Apart from these three criteria and the various forms of power which they generate, several other terms have also been introduced, such as mechanical power, and the distinction between primary (military) and derivative (such as economic) powers. A vocabulary of power such as Russell's is useful for analytical purposes and may provide a frame of reference for a discussion of the transformation of various forms of power into one another, as Russell has done with regard to revolutionary, traditional and naked power.

Besides serving as a criterion for the classification of power, organizations constitute the focus of an extensive discussion in three of the eighteen chapters of Russell's book. An organization provides a mechanism through which power is exercised and propagated, as in the case of the church and the political party. Apart from this, every organization involves some redistribution of power in an unequal manner for the achievement of goals. Members of the same organization are hence brought into power relations with one another. Technical advancement in communication has faciliated the exertion of power at a distance from the centre. The degree of organizational control over the members, expressed as "density of power" (Russell, 1938, p. 165), depends on various factors among which the type of government has been singled out for special treatment, including monarchy, oligarchy and democracy. This is followed by a third chapter dealing with the pervasiveness of organizations (educational, economic, social, political, religious, voluntary and involuntary organizations) in the life-long experience of man.

Unlike both Machiavelli and Hobbes, who were mainly occupied with power in the political or governing arena, Russell found it necessary to bring into the orbit of analysis other major organizations and institutions. This, in a way, was necessary in view of the social changes occurring in western countries as they became more industrialized and complex. The basis of power is no longer confined to the control of political and religious events. Power has become much more diffuse and amorphous; and at the same time, the organizational structures within which power is generated and embodied have become more impersonal.

In these two respects (the necessity to investigate a wider range of the major institutions and the increasingly impersonal wielding of power), Russell's discussion is very much in touch with modern sociological thinking on the subject. As will be discussed in Chapters 3 and 4, these two themes run through the works of Max Weber, Ralf Dahrendorf, and in particular, C. Wright Mills. The basic premise of Mills' (1956) formulation of the power elite is that the elite are elite only by virtue of their positions in the great institutions.

> For such institutions are the necessary bases of power, or wealth, and of prestige . . . . No one, accordingly, can be truly powerful unless he has access to the command of major institutions, for it is over these institutional means of power that the truly powerful are, in the first instance, powerful. (*ibid.*, p. 9)

In contrast to pre-capitalist societies where power was known and personal, in modern societies, Mills (1951; cf. Mills, 1959, p. 39) asserts, power is wielded at a distance and is more impersonal and manipulative. As a result, the experience of powerlessness in modern times is not so much of direct coerciveness as of indifference and bewilderment. It is a kind of psychological coerciveness the source of which appears like Proteus. These must also imply that in order to identify fully the locus of power in modern complex societies, the method we use, as well as the conceptual framework within which this is carried out, should duly recognize the Proteus nature of power. This, in view of the cumulative debate presented in Chapter 5, happens to be a more defensible position than the alternative, behaviouristic position.

There is yet a third element which distinguishes Russell's discussion from that of Machiavelli and Hobbes. Russell was writing at a time when another world war seemed imminent. He was particularly impressed by the rising influence of communism and fascism, which demonstrated how rapidly collective power could be generated. He deplored propaganda and what he called the intoxication of power, and talked at length of the ethics and taming of power. The socially harmful aspect of individual power, as propounded by Hobbes, was more than confirmed by Russell – individual *and* collective powers were viewed by Russell as potentially dangerous to mankind and the natural environment, unless they are tamed. Note that Russell did not condemn power indiscriminately, as is made plain by his remark that power and the love of your neighbour go together. He was *ambivalent* toward power. It looks as though Machiavelli, who glorified power and treated it as a craft, was again held in suspicion, some four centuries later.

2

Friedrich Nietzsche's The Will to Power

My first encounter with Nietzsche's work on power was through reading his "The Will to Power", a collection of his notes written between 1883 and 1888. The notes were translated into English by W. Kaufmann and R. J. Hollingdale, and edited by Kaufmann. Nietzsche was a nihilist, yet he was not; he was anti-Christian, yet in some aspects he was most Christian; he was against morality, but only against some of its particular conceptions; he was a frank elitist, and held democracy and socialism in contempt, but then he had a vision of humanity, a humanity that is above society; he claimed the will to power to be the only unitary psychological principle, but unfortunately he had not put his claim into a coherent whole. At the end I was baffled. I even concluded that Nietzsche was a European racist, and decided not to wrestle with him. At that time, I was writing my doctorate dissertation. Afterwards, when I pulled myself together to work on the present book, I had a sudden seizure of intellectual impotence. Nietzsche would probably have scorned, "Here is another weak and decadent type, who even lacks the *will* to master!" It was bad enough to feel being *unable* to come to grip with Nietzsche's views on power; and worse, in lacking the very *will* to wrestle. My second encounter with Nietzsche's work, to be interpreted below, can be viewed as an anecdotal illustration of the will to power.

Toward a unitary conception of psychology

Power, and notions of strength and weakness appeared in Nietzsche's (1872) earliest published work, "The Birth of Tragedy". There, power mainly denoted worldly power and social success, and was characterized as evil. The same theme was further reinforced when Nietzsche convinced himself in the late 1870s that Wagner, whom he first met in 1868 and later learnt to admire, had become corrupted by belated success and power. To maintain and increase his success and power, Wagner conformed to the State, the Church and public opinion.

In about the same period, the phrase "will to power" made its first appearance (Kaufmann, 1950) and was meant to be a craving for worldly success which Nietzsche repudiated as harmful to man's interest in self-perfection. Two changes then occurred in the conception of the will to power. It became construed as a basic psychological drive as well as a monistic standard of moral evaluation.

Three considerations seemed to underline Nietzsche's conceptualization of the will to power as a basic psychological drive. The first consideration may be called observational. In various parts of his earlier writings, Nietzsche discussed a number of phenomena and attributed them, one after another, to the manifestation of the will to power. Kaufmann (1950) was able to cite the following phenomena from "The Dawn", which was first published in 1881. (1) Scapegoating: the quest by weak and impotent people to find somebody upon whom they can look down and to whom they may feel superior. (2) Power politics: prompted not only by the princes' lust for power but also by a desire among the lower strata of the nation for a feeling of might. (3) A lust for money which is wanted because it gives a feeling of power. (4) Self-sacrifice, which provides a feeling of power through identification with a greater power. (5) To determine one's manners, even one's shortcomings. Napoleon was said to be annoyed because he spoke badly. He decided to speak even worse, for he did not want to be the slave of his shortcomings, but wanted to have the power to determine his conduct. (6) Sexuality, as a foreground of the will to rule. (7) Pleasure, to which we shall return later.

Later, Nietzsche's (1883-1888) list of phenomena subsumed under the will to power becomes even longer. These include, among others, freedom, justice, love, invention of new values, submission to a larger whole, praise, gratitude, individualism, socialism and anarchism (see sections 774–776, 784). Of special interest is the way in which Nietzsche conceptualized justice, for it provides an instructive point of comparison with several ideas in contemporary psychology. A full discussion of this comparison will be given in the last section of the present chapter.

It would seem apparent that when Nietzsche attributed all the above phenomena to the will to power, the term power was no longer restricted to mean worldly power and success. Instead, power became an elastic concept. For obvious reasons, the elasticity of the concept in itself offered no persuasive rationale for turning the will to power into a basic psychological drive.

Two further, and more decisive, considerations turned the will to power into a basic psychological drive. One was related to Nietzsche's philosophy of nature and life, and the other to his refutation of Darwinism and hedonism. As told by Salter (1968), young Nietzsche was once caught in a thunderstorm and felt elated in witnessing the lightning, the tempest, the hail — free, non-ethical forces, pure will untroubled by the intellect. However, Nietzsche did not look up to nature as the model. He regarded nature as wasteful and criticized Darwinism in overestimating the influence of external circumstances. The essential thing in the life process, he said, "is precisely the tremendous shaping, form-creating force working from within which *utilizes* and *exploits* "external circumstances" (Nietzsche, 1883-1888, section 647). The will to life is not merely for self-preservation or even pleasure, but to incorporate, grow, overcome and self-transcend — that is, the will to power. Hence, "Life is not the adaptation of inner circumstances to outer ones, but will to power, which, working from within, incorporates and subdues more and more of that which is "outside" (Nietzsche, 1883–1888, section 681; cf. sections 728 and 704).

Nietzsche, as we have seen, criticized Darwinism for its excessive reliance on external influence. He then rejected Darwinism on the ground that natural selection and the struggle for existence, as formulated by Darwin, were not in accord with historical facts. The argument was spelt out in two lengthy sections (Nietzsche, 1883-1888, sections 684-685), and may be summarized briefly. The struggle for existence and natural selection would mean the death of the weaker creatures and the survival of the most robust and gifted in a slow but progressive manner. Every advantage would become inherited and hence grows stronger and stronger. Man as a species, Nietzsche observed, is however not progressing. Higher types had been attained, but they did not last; and the level of the species is not raised. Even worse for Darwinism, said Nietzsche, is that precisely the opposite of what Darwin and his school see or want to see has happened: the elimination of the strong by the dominion of the average, and the uselessness of the more highly developed types. Nietzsche obviously did not rejoice in Darwinism being proven wrong. Being a radical elitist, he was in fact sickened by the ascendancy of the mediocre. He rejected Darwinism because he thought it was untrue; and what Darwinism had failed to explain he proposed to explain in terms of the will to power. I shall return to Nietzsche's proposal in a later section.

Concerning hedonism, Nietzsche said

> Man does *not* seek pleasure and does not avoid displeasure: one will realize which famous prejudice I am contradicting. Pleasure and displeasure are mere consequences, mere epiphenomena – what man wants, what every smallest part of a living organism wants, is an increase of power.(Nietzsche, 1883-1888, section 702)

In other words, hedonism was rejected in favour of the will to power on the ground that pleasure and displeasure are epiphenomena, or accidentals, of a change in power. It is still conceivable, however, that the will to power may be an instrument for the pursuit of pleasure and avoidance of displeasure, even though they may be mere accidentals. Nietzsche himself admitted this (e.g. Nietzsche, 1883-1888, section 721). But then it is only the commoner sort of men who are after that. Hedonism cannot be a universal motivational mechanism because it will inevitably be superseded when men gather strength. Nietzsche then dealt a lethal blow to hedonism by denying the explanatory role of consciousness. Pleasure and displeasure are by definition conscious psychological states, whatever else they may be. Power, however, does not require self-consciousness. Everything of which a person becomes conscious, Nietzsche said, is arranged, simplified, schematized, and interpreted through and through. "We never encounter "facts": pleasure and displeasure are subsequent and derivative intellectual phenomena" and "cause(s) nothing" (Nietzsche, 1883-1888, sections 477-478).

Through these considerations, the will to power was turned into a holistic psychological principle. Nietzsche (1883-1888) designated such a holistic conception as the *unitary conception of psychology*, and proposed:

> That the will to power is the primitive form of affect, that all other affects are only developments of it; that it is notably enlightening to posit *power* in place of individual "happiness" (after which every living thing is supposed to be striving): "there is a striving for power, for an increase of power"; . . . that all driving force is will to power, that there is no other physical dynamic or psychic force except this (section 688)

Power and moral evaluation

The above account of Nietzsche's development of the will to power into a unitary conception of psychology gives the impression that Nietzsche used the term power as a general, elastic concept. It should be noted, however, that Nietzsche also used the same term as a specific concept. This brings us to an examination of the will to power as a monistic standard used by Nietzsche for moral evaluation.

When Nietzsche later put forward the will to power as a standard of moral evaluation, he spoke of power as a desirable end for man. He no longer meant worldly power or social success, but a power that required a will to power. He gave power an inner turn and the emphasis was now on will. Willing is a ruling thought, a command. He who wills believes that will and action are one, and ascribes the success, the carrying out of the willing, to the will itself, and thereby enjoys an increase of the sensation of power. *"L'effet c'est moi"* — *I* am the effect Nietzsche, 1886, section 19). Nietzsche saw the greatest danger for man not in the robber-animal inclinations, but in the inability to will. Do what you will, but first be such as *can will*, he would say.

That of course does not justify the setting up of a will to power as a monistic standard of moral evaluation. The common objection would be that *some* power, or a certain will to power, is nevertheless evil. Nietzsche got around this problem by postulating a *quantitative* ranking of power. Some power is bad not because some external standard says so — that would have destroyed the monistic stance — but because it is low down in the power scale. The difference here is subtle but significant, and it is important to note that the quantitative ranking of power evolved in Nietzsche's thinking prior to the monistic assertion. For instance, he observed (in Nietzsche, 1881) that whoever still wants to gain the consciousness of power will use any means, whereas those who have it have become very choosy and noble in their tastes (section 348). Further on, he noted that impotence, being oppressed, or having to repress one's desires may lead to cruelty and the desire to hurt in order to see the signs of suffering; whereas the powerful have no need to prove their might by hurting others, and if they do, they do so incidentally in the process of using their power creatively (sections 371 and 571). In this way, the "qualitative" differences between various modes of power were reduced to quantitative differences, and a scale of power was construed as a standard of values. This enabled Nietzsche to assert later,

> I assess a man by the quantum of power and abundance of his will: not by its enfeeblement and extinction; I regard a philosophy which teaches denial of the will as a teaching of defamation and slander . . . (Nietzsche, 1883–1888, section 382)

From this standpoint, good and bad became identical to strong and weak. It is important to note, on the other hand, that Nietzsche did not espouse the mechanical corollary that might should make right. At first sight, Nietzsche appeared to be contradicting himself. To examine this apparent paradox, we need to inquire into the specific (as opposed to the elastic) meaning of the will to power construed by Nietzsche. As interpreted by Kaufmann (1950), the specific concept is self-overcoming, and the process by means of which self-overcoming operates is sublimation.

According to Kaufmann's (1950) interpretation, it is the essence of the will to power to overcome itself. The will to power, which is the basic force, differentiates into the forces of impulse and reason. When reason overcomes impulse, the will to power will undergo self-overcoming. The two interplay in such a way that the will to power is both the agent and the object of overcoming. This is a dialectical *monism* which should be distinguished from dualism, such as that of Kant. Self-overcoming does not lead to atrophy, but to greater power through sublimation, a process which involves a simultaneous preserving, cancelling and lifting up. In self-overcoming through sublimation, the basic force (will to power) and the essential objective (power) are preserved; the immediate objective is cancelled; and the lifting up consists in the attainment of greater power. The immediate objective in which the will to power manifests itself can be diverse and ever-changing, and Nietzsche spoke of this feature as the "Proteus nature" of the will to power. Cancelling and lifting up can and should occur, but they do not necessarily occur. Nietzsche was vague about the means of ensuring sublimation, but he seemed to assign considerable importance to thinking.

In the specific sense of self-overcoming, Nietzsche's power scale can be seen as calibrated by degrees of self-mastery. At various times, Nietzsche placed the saint, the philosopher, and the artist on the pinnacle, as it were, of the power scale. *Near* the bottom of the scale would be those people who have strong impulses but have not yet learned to sublimate. For them the immediate objective may be to overpower others by coercive means. Yet they are still capable of self-mastery if only they would think. *Below* them are people whose very impulses have been extirpated. Kaufmann (1950) used the analogy of sinners and just men to characterize respectively people with strong impulse doing evil and people without impulse, and captured the essence of Nietzsche's power scale very well by saying, "In that sense, there is more joy in heaven over one repentant sinner than over ninety-nine just men — if the latter are just only because they are too feeble to have sinned" (p. 194).

In contrast to his earlier negative judgement of power, Nietzsche's will to power is doubly positive. Reason is desirable because it overcomes and lifts up impulse; on the other hand, impulse is indispensable, and because of the possibility of being sublimated, need not be abnegated. Thus Nietzsche lamented the Germans because they were "no thinkers any longer", and exclaimed, "But who knows? In two generations one will no longer require the sacrifice involved in any nationalistic squandering of power and in becoming stupid" (Nietzsche, 1883-1888, p. xxiii). And he attacked Christianity for the teaching that a good man is an emasculated man.

The will to power, construed as self-overcoming, through the process of sublimation (or its retardation, or impulse emasculation) establishes a power scale which serves for Nietzsche as a monistic standard of moral evaluation. The power scale also provides for Nietzsche a means of elaborating the will to power as a unitary conception of psychology. His starting point is that there will always be persons who are more lowly placed (i.e. weaker) than others on the power scale. The behavioural propensity characteristic of a weak person differs from that of a strong person. Mention has already been made of a weak person's violent and destructive outburst as a means of reducing the feeling of powerlessness. Such a tendency is part of a more general inclination which Nietzsche called *ressentiment*. Being unable to realize the will to power on one's own, the weak person may hate his own will to power, or devaluates the egoistic will to power of the strong person (Nietzsche, 1883-1888, section 373). The former is exemplified in Christianity as "guilt", and the latter, in "socialism". Both are herd moralities, the collective exercise of the will to power by "the weak against the strong and independent", "the suffering and unprivileged against the fortunate", and "the mediocre against the exceptional" (section 274). The ascendancy, as it were, of the herd majority over the strong, who is always in the minority, becomes a real possibility through equal rights, universal suffrage, parliamentary government and the press (sections 748 and 753), which legitimatize the rule by sheer numbers (section 53). Contrary to Darwin's expectation, the human race, according to Nietzsche, was on the decline. The decline became all the more rapid in the face of the political development of universal suffrage, equal rights, etc. Against this background, Nietzsche made a call that "one always has to defend the strong against the weak" (section 685).

The relevance of Nietzsche to modern psychology

In his scholarly work on the history and evolution of dynamic psychiatry, Ellenberger (1970) has this to say about Nietzsche.

> An entire generation was permeated with Nietzschean thinking — whatever interpretation was given to it — in the same way as the former generation had been under the spell of Darwinism. It is also impossible to overestimate Nietzsche's influence on dynamic psychiatry. More so even than Bachofen, Nietzsche may be considered the common source of Freud, Adler, and Jung. (p. 276)

Of a similar opinion is Ginsberg (1973). It can also be argued that in many respects, Nietzsche's "The Will to Power" may be considered a useful and rich source of the general psychology of power.

More than any one of the psychologists after him, Nietzsche had sketched the most balanced picture of power portraying not only the dark side of power, but also the bright side of power and the dark side of powerlessness. Through this, Nietzsche offered psychology a way of relating meaningfully several important but scattered ideas. These included, as will be pointed out in Chapter 6, the ideas of competence (White, 1959), personal causation (de Charms, 1968), internal/external locus of control (Phares, 1976), perceived control (Glass and Singer, 1972), self-efficacy (Bandura, 1977) and learned helplessness (Seligman, 1975). To the extent that these ideas share some commonality under a broader framework, Nietzsche's work is illuminating and potentially useful.

Self-actualization, as popularized by Maslow (e.g. 1968), seems to approximate Nietzsche's self-overcoming apart from the latter's asceticism and dialectical monism. Both self-actualization and self-overcoming are premised on an idealistic (as opposed to a materialistic) belief in the potential of the person's self-emanating force. This belief is part and parcel of the manifesto of humanistic psychology *à la* Maslow and his followers. It is perhaps summed up best by Nietzsche's aphorism that man is a kind of animal that promises. In holding this belief, Nietzsche was naturally opposed to Darwin's environmentalism. Over this Darwinian great divide, Nietzsche is clearly on the side of humanistic psychology rather than operant psychology, even though he would have detested the woolliness of Maslow's thinking.

Mention has been made earlier of the relation between power and justice, and how Nietzsche's formulation of the relation would provide an interesting comparison with several viewpoints in social psychology. Nietzsche dealt with justice in conjunction with freedom and love. They are manifestations of the will to power, and each represents an increase in the quantum of power in two ways. The first way is stated in terms of a person's strength. Among the oppressed, and slaves of all kinds, the will to power appears as the will to freedom – they are concerned foremost with liberating themselves. Among a stronger kind of man, the will to power appears as the will to overpower; and if it is unsuccessful, then it limits itself to the will to justice, i.e. to the same measure of rights. Among the strongest, it appears as love of mankind, of the people, of the gospel, etc.

The second way is explicitly expressed in terms of the relative power between people. A person desires freedom so long as he does not possess power. Once in possession of power, he desires to overpower; if he is still too weak to do so, he desires justice. (Here Nietzsche broke off and did not continue with love.) The process of reaching freedom and justice is mediated by struggle, and struggle ends temporarily with both sides agreeing to a new justice. The state of justice is however neither static nor terminal. Nietzsche offered a rather interesting reason why justice is inherently unstable. The instability lies in the tendency for a power relation to become unbalanced. Power imbalance or balance does not always correspond to actual inequality or equality. An objective inequality under a certain situation may be glossed over and therefore does not count. It remains always possible that such an inequality may be seized upon and becomes inflated enough to upset the status quo. The condition under which this will be more likely to occur is, paradoxically a state of justice. Nietzsche described the process as follows. When justice is achieved,

> The actual inequalities of force produce an enhanced effect (because peace rules on the whole and many small quanta of force now constitute differences that formerly did not count). Now individuals organize themselves in groups; the groups struggle for privileges and pre-dominance. Strife breaks out again in a milder form (Nietzsche, 1883-1888, section 784)

The first point to note is that Nietzsche's discussion of justice offers a striking contrast to the current social psychological formulation of the subject. It is the conspicuous characteristic of the latter that justice, or equity (as it is more popularly known), has been investigated in a power vacuum. A recent volume in the "Advances in Experimental Social Pyschology" is entirely devoted to equity theory, with the stated hope that equity theory will bring us toward a general theory of social interaction (Berkowitz and Walster, 1976). It is made up of six theoretical and review articles with a commentary by George Homans. Homans (1976) makes a general comment that he does not hear much in the volume about either status or power, even though, he argues, they have a close relation with equity. The relations between equity and power are "of the first importance" if "we are not just concerned with equity theory but with a general theory of social behaviour" (Homans, 1976, p. 242); and power is the more primitive phenomenon in the sense that "an equitable distribution of rewards may simply be a distribution by relative power . . . (And) an inequitable distribution may be no more than one that no longer reflects the actual distribution of power" (p. 244).

It stands to reason that a complete discussion of justice should include at least two interrelated but analytically separable questions. How are rewards *actually* distributed? What kind of distribution under what conditions will be *defined* as fair, and by whom? These two questions are already implied by Homans' statement quoted above, but should be more explicitly articulated because they bear on two respective problems. The question of how rewards are actually distributed is basically a problem of social stratification. This problem "disappears" in the experimental investigation of equity because of the transient nature of the laboratory situation, and more importantly, because the relevance of power and the wider social context have seldom been taken into account in the formulation of the research, design of the experiment, and interpretation of the data. In a typical experiment, the subjects would be placed in a position such that they *can* determine the distribution of rewards and are asked, either explicitly or implicitly, to do so in the light of the "input" factors manipulated by the experimenter. This procedure creates a situation which allows the participants freedom to distribute the rewards without regard to their power relations, and thereby removes power from the list of input factors. What has not been recognized is that by the same procedure, an equal power relation has been installed and it is within this particular power relation that the data are collected. In the world outside the laboratory, however, the allocation of rewards of any practical significance is determined more often by a few than by all, and this allocation is made with subtle but nevertheless real reference to the existing power relation. These facts must be considered if the experimental investigation of justice is to increase its mundane validity. We need to approach the problem in its proper context and relate it to social stratification. In Chapter 4, social stratification and the role of power will be examined in greater detail.

The second question (how justice is defined) has been the central concern of equity studies, and is usually cast in a modified version of Aristotle's classical formulation of justice. Of less concern is the active process whereby the participants reach a mutual equitable agreement. The experimental study of this process has been undertaken outside the conventional equity area. The studies by Thibaut and Faucheux (1965), and Chertkoff (1970), which were undertaken respectively in relation to the development of contractual norms in a bargaining situation and the division of rewards by coalition partners, are major examples. Both conceptualized the process in terms of the relative power of the participants, and the arguments they put forth are remarkably similar to Nietzsche's discussion of justice. In a bargaining situation, Thibaut and Faucheux (1965) reasoned that the lower-power member would appeal to the norm of fair-sharing in order to protect his interest against the high-power member's exploitative use of the power advantage. The latter, however, would appeal to the norm of loyalty in order to keep the low-power member from leaving the existing relation. When the power disparity was too great, the high-power member could safely ignore the low-power member's appeal to fair-sharing. It was only when the low-power member was provided (by the experimenter) with sufficient counter-power (through the presence of an attractive external alternative) that his appeal to fair-sharing, now being backed up by his convincing threat of disloyalty, succeeded in leading to the development of a contractual norm.

The division of rewards by the partners to a winning coalition, at and is conducted in terms of two norms (Chertkoff, 1970). The high-power partner would tend to emphasize the power differential to the effect that his share of the rewards should commensurate with his greater power (parity norm). The low-power partner, on the other hand, would emphasize the coalition itself and the indispensability of his partnership, such that the rewards should be shared equally (equality norm). The actual division, as shown by Chertkoff, was about half-way between these two contradictory claims.

Another point which we may note is that Nietzsche regarded justice as no more than a quasi-stationary state in the on-going will to power process between people who are socially related to one another in some way. The achievement of justice serves only to magnify psychologically whatever differentials there might still exist, and through this, the existent justice will be outmoded and strife breaks out in a milder form. At the door-step of justice there always lies a readiness of differentiating from and outranking one's equals. This readiness Nietzsche called overpowering, which should not be restricted to mean coercive control, but should be interpreted in its wider sense of reaching above from below. In this sense, Nietzsche's formulation of the problem bears an interesting parallel to the social categorization studies of intergroup discrimination (see Chapter 9).

Other points of interest can also be cited to highlight the relevance of Nietzsche's "The Will to Power" to psychology, such as his discussion of hedonism and the attribution of emotion. His remark that harm-doing and aggression are more likely to be committed by people lower down on the power scale than those who are higher up, bears a close resemblance to Heider's (1958) insightful discussion on the relation between agression and power (see Chapter 6).

"The Will to Power" deserves to be more widely known amongst psychologists. Had it been written by another author, it might have attracted more positive attention. It was more than a personal misfortune that Nietzsche had been misused by his sister, and later, the German Nazis; and that the Anglo-Saxon world, according to Bridgwater (1972), had prematurely misunderstood and rejected Nietzsche since the First World War. There are still clear signs that psychology has not yet emerged from the anti-Nietzschean legacy. It is disappointing to learn, for instance, that no mention is made of Nietzsche in the otherwise excellent volume by Robinson (1976). One can only hope that future development in pyschology will give no further chance for Nietzsche to say, again, that "My time is not yet, some are post-humously born".

II

Power in Modern Sociology and Political Thought

3

Introduction

An overview

For the purpose of introduction, modern sociological and political analyses of power can be seen as a continuation in the exploration of the problems posed by Machiavelli and Hobbes. What social and political means are available to bring about social change? How does human society cohere in the face of conflict and division? In all these problems — social change, social order, and social conflict as well as those related to them — the concept of power has been employed with varying degrees of enthusiasm by sociologists and political theorists. In this and the next two chapters, the views of a number of sociologists and political theorists will be exhibited, and (wherever possible) related to one another through the common issues to which they are addressed.

Dahrendorf (1959) has made a distinction between two views of society which highlights the differential use of the power concept amongst the academics. The "Utopians" view society as being based on a consensus of values among its members. The "Rationalists", on the other hand, see society as a product of constraint and domination. Of the two, the former accord much less theoretical importance to the power concept, and they tend to view power in a rather different way from the Rationalists.

Thus, since a Utopian's society coheres on the basis of a consensual normative order and its members are functionally integrated to the whole, there would appear to be no need to apply the concept of power to the Hobbesian problem of social order. Social conflict is then regarded as mere strains in the social system, and social change as the result of value and culture change. Where power is discussed, the tendency is to emphasize power as a facility for the accomplishment of the common good, not as a means which enables its holder to ensure his dominance over other people. On the other hand, social conflict and social change are on-going processes inherent in a Rationalist's society, which coheres as a result of constraint and through the domination of some people over others. Power, which is secondary to values and norms in the Utopian view, is primary in the Rationalist view. Whereas a Utopian can accommodate to an integrational view of power, a Rationalist sees power as always serving sectional interests before the common good. And whereas it is important to a Utopian to demonstrate the consensual nature of the normative order in society, a Rationalist has a vested intellectual interest in uncovering the unequal distribution of power as well as the pattern of dominance in society.

As pointed out by Dahrendorf (op. cit.), the divergent and sometimes contradictory images of society of the Rationalist and the Utopian reflect the legacy of two opposing social philosophies, and furnish a recurrent theme of debate in sociology and political thought. At the same time, the Rationalist-Utopian distinction is more than an academic distinction. It has a public counterpart and seems to reflect two basic images of society. In reviewing four national studies (United States, Germany, French Switzerland and Britain) of how people see society, Dahrendorf (op. cit.) draws the conclusion that the subjected class, for example, factory workers, are inclined towards a Rationalist view of society; whereas the middle class and above tend to have a Utopian view of society. A similar observation is made by Westergaard and Resler (1975). A parallel observation can also be noted. Social movements instigated by subordinate groups often make the avowed aim of achieving power, and label themselves accordingly. Thus there are more proclamations of "*Black* power" than "*White* power", more "*Sisterhood* is powerful" than "*Brotherhood* is powerful", and more "*Student* power" than "*Administration* power". It may well be probable that there exists a close relation between the Rationalist inclination among some academics and their sympathy for or identification with the underdogs.

Thus the Rationalist and Utopian images of society contain their respective conceptions of power which contradict or diverge from one another in several areas. Three such areas can readily be identified. The first, and most direct area is ideological: should one investigate *primarily* the power of men over men, or the ways in which power is and can be used for the promotion of communal goals? The controversy over whether the primary phenomenon of power lies in *power over* or *power to* is sharply articulated by C. Wright Mills and Talcott Parsons.

The second area is concerned with social conflict: which is the most basic form of conflict and what would its analysis entail? Marxism provides a pivotal case, not only because Marxism contains both Rationalist and Utopian elements in the analysis of conflict, but also because most of the subsequent analyses of conflict are responses to the Marxian challenge.

The entire range of Marxism simply cannot be categorized as Rationalist alone. The label fits the Marxian analysis of capitalism, but not the Marxian characterization of communism, which tends more towards a Utopian view. The Marxian analysis of power has thus been under double attack. On the one hand, the thesis that the economic infrastructure determines the ideological or normative superstructure, which is clearly a Rationalist formulation, has provoked reasoned criticisms such as Weber's Protestant Ethic and the Spirit of Capitalism (Weber, 1930). On the other hand, the Utopian thesis that the state will wither away in the higher phase of communism, and hence the disappearance of conflict between the state and the citizens, has been confronted several times. Weber (1947), for instance, has again argued that control over the governing bureaucracy provides a power base no less formidable than the control over the means of production. The two kinds of control do not necessarily correlate, and the former would tend to perpetuate itself instead of withering away in technologically advanced societies, even under communism. Elitist theorists (e.g. Pareto, 1935; Mosca, 1938; Michels, 1962) contend that the distribution of power in any society or large organization is and must be pyramidal, and that means power can never be completely under democratic control for long, let alone the eradication of power differences between classes. Somewhat related to the elitist's argument is what may here be called the power theory of conflict. Duverger (1966) advances the argument that the opposition between organized power (such as the state) and people who are subjected to it, can never be eliminated. Class conflict in the Marxian sense is being replaced by this form of power conflict as the fundamental conflict in modern industrial countries. Dahrendorf (1959), whose work has been quoted several times in this overview, formulates, after a documented critique of Marxism, a theory of group conflict in industrial society by coordinating group conflict to the authority structure of imperatively coordinated associations.

Analagous to the Marxian shift from the Rationalist to the Utopian view of power is the distinction made by Friedrich (1963 and 1967) between power and political authority. As has been noted in Chapter 1, Friedrich argues for a shift from power to authority as the state gains stability and becomes preoccupied with the routine of governing. This proposal from a well-known political theorist provides a welcome addition to the debate over the relation between conflict and power.

The third area in which the Rationalist and Utopian views diverge is social stratification. What is the origin of social inequality and by what mechanisms does inequality become structured and institutionalized? The Utopian approach to this problem finds its modern spokesman in American functionalism, which makes no admission of the role of power. Against this are the theses put forward by Dahrendorf (1968), Wesolowski (1962) and Lenski (1966), which tend towards a Rationalist explanation in terms of power.

In the ways outlined above, the Rationalist-Utopian distinction offers a central theme around which a number of major sociological and political analyses of power can be examined. These analyses will be grouped under three sections to be presented in Chapter 4. The first section, "Power Over and Power To", covers the views of C. Wright Mills and Talcott Parsons. The second section, "Power and Social Stratification", will discuss the role of power in social stratification. Following this is a section on "Power and Conflict". Here the views of Duverger, Friedrich, Dahrendorf, and the elitist theorists will be examined.

There are other major analyses of power that do not readily fall into any single one of the above-mentioned sections. Weber's (1947) discussion of power has great relevance to the development of subsequent analysis of conflict and social stratification. As well, his views form a system of its own which provide a way of looking at social change in terms of the changing nature of the legitimation of authority. A digest of the Weberian treatment of power will form the remaining section of the present chapter. A rather different approach to power, that of political behaviourism, will be discussed in Chapter 5. A major development in the political analysis of power has been associated with the advent of political scientism of a behaviouristic sort. One impetus to this development was the quest for a particular kind of empirical observation which would clarify the real distribution of power in a community, especially the issue of elitism versus pluralism raised by Mills "The Power Elite" (Mills, 1956). The immediate offspring of this development was the conception of power as observable decision-making (Dahl, 1957). Through demonstration of its own limitation, the conception of power in terms of decision-making gave rise to a nondecision-making conception of power (Bachrach and Baratz, 1962). In due course, the very behaviouristic orientation which underlies both the decision-making and nondecision-making conceptions has been questioned (Lukes, 1974; Westergaard and Resler, 1975). At the end, the protean nature of power reemerges.

Weber's conception of power

Weber's analysis of power and authority was most fully developed in "Wirtschaft und Gesellschaft". The English translation of "Wirtschaft und Gesellschaft" appears in the work of Henderson and Parsons (Weber, 1947). There, power is taken to be the equivalent of Weber's *Macht*. While this translation seems to be the most orthodox one, there are deviant views, notably those of D'Entrives (1967) and Banton (1972). With regard to authority, Henderson and Parsons take it to be the equivalent of Weber's *legitime Herrschaft*, which is far from appropriate in the light of other translations. In the following pages, Weber's conception of *Macht*, *Herrschaft*, and *legitime Herrschaft*, as translated by Henderson and Parsons, will be presented first. Then the terminological dispute over the identification of power and authority will be discussed.

The German political and intellectual atmosphere in which Weber breathed must be briefly mentioned before his conception of power is examined. Bendix (1965), amongst others (e.g. Parsons, 1942; Gerth and Mills, 1948), has described Weber's concern with the political development of the imperial Wilhelmian Germany. One of Weber's main concerns was the relation between power and culture. Germany after 1870, according to Bendix (1965), showed no unequivocal cultural gains that were commensurate with her increasing power. This ambivalent relation between power and culture has invited the unmasking critique of Nietzsche on German culture. In this the influence of Nietzsche on Weber was strong. Weber also shared with Nietzsche, along with the Freudian notion of libidinal impulses, the recognition that the quest for power in the form of imposing one's will on others despite resistance is a pervasive attribute of human actions. However, Weber's subsequent conception of power was not built on the organic or biological reductionism of Nietzsche or Freud. Instead, it is distinctly sociological. This is reflected, firstly, in his general definition of power which locates the imposition of one's own will in a social position rather than in man's biological make-up; and secondly, in his analysis of authority. To these we shall now turn.

By *Macht*, Weber refers to "The probability that one actor within a social relationship will be in a position to carry out his own will despite resistance, regardless of the basis on which this probability rests" (Weber, 1947, p. 152). *Macht* was translated by Henderson and Parsons into power. Subsequently, the Weberian definition of *Macht* has become the most frequently adopted sociological definition of power (Giddens, 1974). It covers completely the meanings attributed to power by Machiavelli, Hobbes and Russell, plus something more. In the first place, it explicitly recognizes the relational aspect of power and the context of social relationship within which an actor's will may be realized. This would save the definition from the criticism of Friedrich (1967) mentioned in the last chapter. Second, Weber's definition construes power as a probability. In so far as power designates the effecting of an actor's will regardless of the basis or the means, it is power to, and the substantive aspect of power is emphasized. Since this process takes place within a given social relationship, the relational aspect of power (power over) is given due consideration. When power is then expressed in probability terms, it becomes a variable, as opposed to a constant, and thereby opens up the possibility of quantification.

Obviously, the concept of power (*Macht*) "is highly comprehensive from the point of view of sociology", and so *Herrschaft*, translated as "imperative control" by Henderson and Parsons, is introduced with the explicit aim that it "must hence be more precise and can only mean the probability that a command will be obeyed" (Weber, 1947, p. 153). It is thus intended as a special sub-set of *Macht* (which is amorphous). A social organization wherein the positions stand in relation of command and obedience is called *Herrschaftverband*, such as the army, the state, or an industrial enterprise. *Herrschaft* therefore refers to a structural form of power relation which is embedded in a particular set of social organizations.

Weber then distinguishes *legitime Herrschaft*, translated as "authority" by Henderson and Parsons, from *Herrschaft* in general (Weber, 1947, p. 152). As will be pointed out later, this translation is far from satisfactory. Until then, "authority" will be taken to mean *legitime Herrschaft*. Weber has given elaborate treatment to the institutionalization of authority, beginning with his well-known typological construction of three ideal types of authority, namely, rational-legal, traditional, and charismatic authority, each of which corresponds to a particular claim to legitimacy (Weber, 1947, pp. 324-407). The legitimacy of rational-legal authority is based on rational grounds, resting on a belief in the legality of certain normative rules and the right of those elevated to authority under such rules to issue commands. Obedience is owed to the legally established impersonal order, not to particular individuals. It extends to individuals only in so far as, and by virtue of, their incumbency of the order, and even then obedience is owed to the formal legality of their commands within the scope of the authority of the office. The purest type of the exercise of rational-legal authority is that which employs a bureaucratic administrative staff.

Traditional authority, the second of Weber's ideal type of authority, rests on an established belief in the sanctity of traditions and the legitimacy of the status of those exercising authority under them. Whereas in rational-legal authority legitimacy is contained in the legality of enacted formal rules, in traditional authority legitimacy is bound by traditional precedents handed down from the past. Whereas the hierarchy of rational-legal authority is defined in terms of offices, traditional authority is defined by a system of statuses. The person who wields rational-legal authority is a "superior"; but he who exercises traditional authority is a personal "chief". A superior exerts authority over subordinate members by virtue of his office and does so completely within the legality of formal rules; the chief commands authority over his subjects or comrades by virtue of his status and does so partly within the limit set by traditions. When tradition leaves a certain sphere open, the chief will personally decide and can still call for obedience through the personal loyalty of his subjects.

Rational-legal and traditional authorities are, as pointed out by Parsons (Weber, 1947, pp. 56–77), to be found in organized "corporate groups" (*Verband*). In contrast to this, charismatic authority, the third type of *legitime Herrschaft*, is revolutionary because its claim to legitimacy lies in the conflict which it creates with the institutionalized order. It represents an emancipation from routine, and the charismatic leader "is always in some sense a revolutionary, setting himself in conscious opposition to some established aspects of the society in which he works" (p. 64). The revolutionary nature of charismatic authority and its distinction from the previous two types of authority may not be immediately obvious from Weber's initial characterization of the legitimation of charismatic authority, which is said to rest "on devotion to the specific and exceptional sanctity, heroism or exemplary character of an individual person, and of the normative patterns or order revealed or ordained by him . . ." (p. 328). It nevertheless becomes crystal clear later, as can be seen in the following characterization of charismatic authority, which is quoted below at length since I cannot improve upon it.

> The prophet has his disciples; the war lord his selected henchmen; the leader, generally, his followers. There is no such things as "appointment" or "dismissal", no career, no promotion. There is only a "call" at the instance of the leader on the basis of the charismatic qualification of those he summons. There is no hierarchy . . . no such thing as a definite sphere of authority and of competence, and no appropriation of official powers on the basis of social privileges . . . no such thing as a salary or a benefice . . . no system of formal rules, of abstract legal principles . . . no legal wisdom oriented to judicial precedent . . . . From a substantive point of view, every charismatic authority would have to subscribe to the proposition, "It is written . . . , but I say unto you . . ." The genuine prophet, like the genuine military leader and every true leader in this sense, preaches, creates or demands new obligation. In the pure type of charisma, these are imposed on the authority of revolution by oracles, or of the leader's own will, and are recognized by the members of the religious, military, or party group, because they come from such a source . . . . Charismatic authority is thus specifically outside the realm of everyday routine and the profane sphere. In this respect, it is sharply opposed both to rational . . . and to traditional authority . . . . Within the sphere of its claims, charismatic authority repudiates the past, and is in this sense a specifically revolutionary force (pp. 360-362)

The very revolutionary nature of charismatic authority means that it cannot become the basis of a stabilized order without undergoing radical change. "Indeed", Weber says, "in its pure form charismatic authority may be said to exist only in the process of originating. It cannot remain stable, but becomes either traditionalized or rationalized, or a combination of both" (p. 364). Weber calls this organizational transformation the "routinization of charisma". The need for some sort of organization is imposed by the task of the movement itself, and is thus a necessary concomitant of the movement becoming successful. As the followers become more full-time adherents to the movement and continue interacting among themselves as a group, there is a need for regularizing their relative statuses and functions. Finally, pressure towards routinization is generated by the problem of leadership succession. When the movement becomes a stabilized order, the successor can no longer base his claim to legitimacy on the same charismatic ground as his predecessor without declaring a revolution on the very organization which he intends to lead.

At this point, and before we move on to examine Weber's fourth type of legitimation, it would be pertinent to point out what seems to me to be a preemptive or reactive "antithesis" of charismatic authority. As Weber has pointed out, charismatic authority is derived from the alternative order which it reveals to the public. Through this revealed alternative, charismatic authority poses a revolutionary challenge to the institutionalized order. However, inasmuch as a certain alternative order revealed by the charismatic leader may pose a threat or a challenge to those who are in power, the latter may augment their own authority by revealing all kinds of foreseeable dangers that such an alternative, and indeed any other alternative, may incur to the people. By this, I mean not only inter-party politics at election time, but also at a deeper level something involving basic ideological opposites and national unity. The international news portrayed in the mass media keeps telling the citizens all sorts of terrible things happening elsewhere. News about unfriendly or ideologically opposing countries is worse than the already bad news. The citizens' own country may not be the best in the world, but so long as they do not opt for a radical alternative, it will not be as bad as what is happening in those places which follow *that* alternative. So said the message of the media. Just as race has come to be defined as a *problem* for the British people by the mass media (Hartmann and Husband, 1974), alternatives may be similarly defined as problems rather than solutions. Through this and other ways, alternatives will be largely foreclosed, and the people are left with the belief that there really is no viable alternative worthy of all the risks.

The above three types of legitimacy on which authority may be based are already well known in popular digests of Weber's discussion on power. Less well known is a fourth type of legitimation called *Wertrationalität*, which refers to the legitimacy of an authority based on a rational belief in its absolute value, thus lending it the validity of an absolute and final commitment. Bauman (1974) has expounded on this type of legitimation and its usefulness for the analysis of the authority characteristics of *socialist* societies. According to Bauman, the sole and indispensable legitimation of a socialist government is in the future, that is, the rulers justify their rule and demand obedience in the name of an ideal society they are set on building. The party, as the vanguard of the ideal society to come, needs no endorsement from the populace who should rather be educated to the correct line, because of the futuristic nature of its legitimation and its absolute value. Bauman has called this type of authority which is based on *Wertrationalität* the "partynomial" rule.

The translation by Henderson and Parsons raises some terminological dispute concerning the Weberian equivalents of power and authority. D'Entrives agrees to the close relationship between *legitime Herrschaft* and "authority", but contends that *Macht* should be rendered as "might" and *Herrschaft* as "power" (D'Entrives, 1967, pp. 10-11). To begin with, D'Entrives reckons that "might" is the direct equivalent of *Macht*. More substantively, he argues that the emphasis of *Macht* is on the effectiveness of effecting one's will, which is in line with the prime motive behind the exercise of "might". Secondly, the emphasis of *Herrschaft* is said to be on legality, which is hence equivalent to "power-conferring rules". D'Entrive's arguments are favoured by Banton (1972), who further buttresses the case on the grounds that "the sequence 'might', 'power' and 'authority' seems to me to express better Weber's intentions; it rids us of this monstrous expression 'imperative control', and it opens up new possibilities for analysis . . ." (p. 86). As an illustration of his last argument, Banton (1972) suggests that the state may be diagrammatically represented as possessing an inner circle of authority surrounded successively by its legal power and might (armed or unarmed force). Compliance on the part of the citizens will become less willing the more the state moves outward into the circle of might.

The contending trio of might-power-authority undoubtedly has superior aesthetic appeal, and it highlights the importance of psychological reactions (such as willingness) underneath overt compliance. Nevertheless, the difficulty here is that *Herrschaft* is being identified with legality and should, strictly speaking, be replaced by "legal power" or another more precise term. More objectionable is the rendering of *Macht* by "might", which overemphasizes the coercive aspects. The argument advanced by D'Entrives is, as we have noted, that "might" captures very well the spirit of *Macht*, which is said to be the effective realization of one's will, or in other words, overpowering other people. However, this is also precisely the spirit of "power" as used by Hobbes, Machiavelli and Russell on the one hand, and by a substantial number of social scientists on the other. In short, "power" would express what D'Entrives and Banton wish to convey by "might", but does not necessarily reduce *Macht* to force, so that on both counts "power" turns out to be a more satisfactory equivalent of *Macht* than "might".

After all, as I have noted earlier, *Macht* was intended by Weber as an inclusive concept. *Herrschaft* and *legitime Herrschaft* are subsets of *Macht* in the Weberian sense. Banton's (1972) typology of might-power-authority, however, would imply that *Macht* is on an equal ontological level with *Herrschaft* and *legitime Herrschaft*. Apart from this contradiction, Banton's classification can also be questioned on another point. What is the element common to all three concepts that brings them together in the first place? Presumably they all have to do with the means of eliciting compliance. Now the conspicuous thing is that Banton has not given any clue as to how such a common element may be named. Whatever that name may be, it is logically inevitable that a more inclusive concept must be used. For this purpose, the term power is undoubtedly the best candidate in the English language.

The translation of *Herrschaft* and *legitime Herrschaft* by Henderson and Parsons, on the other hand, is more in need of revision. Weber's discussion of *legitime Herrschaft* is centred on the types of legitimacy upon which *Herrschaft* may be based. The fact that he discusses legitimacy in such great depth seems to suggest, as pointed out by Rex (1961), that he regards legitimacy as problematic. That is, legitimacy does not spring spontaneously from the normative consensus of a society, but is a condition which requires explanation. From this interpretative point of view, Weber's construction of the ideal types of *legitime Herrschaft* is directed not so much at the delineation of the types of *Herrschaft* as the types of *legitimacy* upon which *Herrschaft* may rest. It would thus seem that *Herrschaft* and legitimacy are being conceptualized as analytically independent of one another. To identify *legitime Herrschaft* as authority must necessarily imply that authority can only be *legitimate* authority. This terminological issue can only be approached by a historical inquiry into the English usage of the term authority. Short of this, a suggestion can be made to regard authority and legitimacy as if they were independent of one another, on the grounds that such a distinction would be analytically more useful than otherwise.* In this way, not only authority, but also other forms of the manifestation of power, can be analysed with regard to their acquisition or loss of legitimacy. The problem of legitimacy would then apply to power in general, and should not be regarded as solved once authority is attained. Basically, this reasoning is merely an extension of Weber's distinction between *Herrschaft* and *legitime Herrschaft*. If the choice is between *Herrschaft* and *legitime Herrschaft*, then the former should be regarded as the equivalent of authority. As a matter of fact, this terminology is used in other translations (e.g. Weber, 1968, 1948) as well as discussion on power and authority (e.g. Dahrendorf, 1959).

The above cumbersome diversion into the terminological nuances would have been unnecessary were it not for the fact that Weber's treatment of power has great relevance to several discussions in the following pages. It will be useful to bear in mind the amorphous and inclusive nature of power as intended by Weber, from which (power) he then distinguishes authority (which is patterned and is structurally related to the organizational setting) and legitimacy. In Weber's treatment of power, authority and legitimacy acquire great significance. This, as pointed out by Parsons (1942), is a natural development from Weber's sociological orientation. Weber regards as a fundamental feature of all complex systems of human relationship the fact that a minority of men are put in a position of ability to control the action, to an appreciable degree and in a variety of respects, of the great majority. This fact is a power phenomenon in the general and amorphous sense: but at the same time, it is not structurally fortuitous. To uncover systematically the structural nature of this phenomenon, as well as the changes, constitutes a basic problem for sociology. The concepts of authority, legitimacy, and corporate groups provide Weber with the conceptual tools for examining this problem.

In a very instrumental way, these conceptual tools have paved the way for the development of an influential theory of conflict (Dahrendorf, 1959), which we will examine in the next chapter. Furthermore, Weber's insistence on the amorphous nature of power enables him to formulate a general framework within which the diverse relations between social stratification and power can be examined. The

* This point will be more fully discussed in Chapter 4, in relation to Friedrich's distinction between power and authority.

resulting multi-dimensional model of social stratification offers a heuristic guide not only to the problem of social stratification at the macro-level (as will be discussed in Chapter 4), but also to such problems of power change, social categorization and differentiation between groups at the micro-level (see Chapter 9). Finally, Weber's typology of legitimacy, and especially his characterization of charisma and the dynamic relation between charismatic legitimacy and other forms of legitimacy, are potentially useful for the further development of the study of minority influence and social change which has been ably begun by Moscovici and his associates (see Chapter 7). In all these respects, Weber's treatment of power should deserve much more the attention of social psychologists working in these areas [than, say, the attention given him by French and Raven (1959) in their well-known typology of the bases of power].

In at least one respect, however, Weber's treatment of power is primitive. His writing on force is minimal in comparison with his elaborate analysis of other forms of power. Of course, the use of physical force has been heavily regulated with the advent of the political leviathan, particularly in western stable democracies. Even then, as argued by Goode (1972) and Wrong (1976), the intricate and subtle influence of force and the threat of force, as well as the routine access to force by certain well-placed groups in society, require more recognition and fuller analysis. The inadequacy of Weber in this respect is related to the fact that Weber has not worked out a typology of power which would be comprehensive enough to illuminate the full range of power. A large number of articles by other authors can be found in the literature on the construction and delineation of power typologies. Some of them will be mentioned in the following pages when substantive issues are involved. Otherwise they will not concern us here, and the interested reader is referred to the detailed analyses by Goldhamer and Shils (1939), and Hamilton (1976, 1977).

4

Rationalist and Utopian Views of Power

Power over and power to

Integral to all the conceptions of power which we have examined so far is a certain hierarchical element. One person may have more or less money than another person, but power is always power *over* something or somebody. At the same time, power is also power *to* in the sense that some intended effect is being produced. Consensual or Utopian theorists emphasize power to and its integrational function. Conflict or Rationalist theorists highlight power over and its coercive nature. These contrasting positions are reflected respectively in the views of Talcott Parsons and C. Wright Mills.

The problem of power occupies a central place in the whole sociological thinking of C. Wright Mills. Power to Mills is ubiquitous in the social structure, and functions as an independent social variable. Although its form may vary, the fact of power remains constant. Horowitz (1963) sums up Mills' orientation in the following manner:

> In short, the settlement of the sociological question of how men interact, immediately and directly entails research into questions of superordination and subordination, elites and masses, rulers and ruled, ingroups and outgroups, and members and non-members. This is the fertile ground upon which Mills' sociology proceeds. (p. 9)

To ask whether any single base of power, such as money, is the exclusive foundation of power is a form of futile metaphysics to Mills. Instead, the study of the varieties of power and their continual transformation into one another should be a fundamental issue for the social scientist. With the exception of wartime experiences, men do not confront each other directly in power relations, but do so symbolically and politically. That is, power institutionalizes itself in human affairs. "Power translates itself into political activity, just as, at a more intimate level, power translates social interaction into group differentiation and rationalized authority" (*ibid.*, p. 11).

On the sociological level, Mills is extremely concerned with the pattern of dominance and what appears to him to be an increasing concentration of power in American society. As will be discussed below, much of the debate over Mills' work revolves around Mills' analysis of the distribution and exercise of power in American society. Before we examine this debate, it is worth noting that to Mills, there is always an intricate and theoretically profound relation between what is sociological and what is psychological.

The concentration of power in the hands of a few, which is a sociological phenomenon, to Mills means the increasing removal of power from the many. The loss of power by the many over their own actions and productive activities in turn has great psychological consequences, which the sociologists call "alienation". As will be discussed later in Chapter 6, the powerlessness which underlies alienation also underlies what psychologists call "external locus of control", "depression", and a host of other syndromes. These and other troubles of private individuals, Mills insists, must be related to the public issues of social structure. Ordinary man can seldom see beyond his personal troubles; and very often, much private uneasiness goes unformulated. On the other hand, much public malice and many decisions of enormous structural relevance never become public issues. The capacity to grasp biography and history, and the relation between the two within society, is the task and promise of the "sociological imagination". This imagination formulates the problem by translating undefined private uneasiness into articulated personal troubles, public indifference into public issues, and then by revealing the ways in which personal troubles are connected with public issues (Mills, 1959).

The problem of power, apart from being a central sociological question, is also central to the delineation of public issues. Mills devotes three books to the analysis of the distribution and exercise of power in American society, one book for about one social stratum. "The New Men of Power", the first of the three, is about labour leaders and their unions, covering the lower and lower middle class. The second book, "White Collar", is on the middle classes. They were published respectively in 1948 and 1951. The trilogy is completed with "The Power Elite" (Mills, 1956).

By the 1940s, the American labour unions had some fourteen

million members between them. The union is regarded by Mills as an institution established to accumulate power and to exert it. It is an army. The leader of the union is a member of the elite of power, not so much of money or of prestige. Because of the relatively recent history of the American labour movement, union leaders are *new* men of power. Their members are drawn from the "underdogs" of the economic hierarchy. Economically underprivileged, the underdogs are also socially and psychologically underprivileged, by which Mills means the habits of submission and acquiescence, the lack of information on the functioning of society, despondence, and lacking in the capacity for indignation (Mills, 1948, p. 267). For these people to be unionized, the union must go to them as a civilizing force, as it were, to remake them inside a union community. Mills is vague about the exact mechanism of unionization, but he makes the emphatic point that a new type of man must be built into the underdogs.

Mills (1948) does not define explicitly what he means by power. Nevertheless, it is clear that the power of the labour leaders would derive from the union as an organized institution, not automatically from the sheer size of union membership. Such a view naturally leads to an institutional analysis of the labour unions and their relationship with the employers' and business organizations as well as the political party system. Without going into the details, Mills' conclusion can be briefly stated. On the one hand, the balance of power between labour and business dips in favour of business, both in real terms and as perceived by the vast majority of the labour leaders. The perception of own weakness by the labour leaders is partly the result of their precarious basis of power. Unlike the corporation manager whose power does not depend on the loyalty of the men who work for him, a union officer is an elected official whose tenure of office depends on the members' loyalty and his vigilant responsiveness to their needs. On the other hand, the confrontation between the two sides makes for confusion and national inconvenience, which the public demands be remedied. "In turn, the public's demand that something be done is the most ostensible and important prod to the state" to move further to the side of business whose influence on the dominant political parties far exceeds that of labour (Mills, 1948, p. 238). The decision to do something about the situation is being made by the government and business behind the backs of the labour leaders. Thus, "within the present party system, labour organizations and union members do not have the power of decision: they are not even able to confront the live alternatives. Day after day they hear the clamour of the public that something must be done; but they don't know what to do, and they are afraid" (*ibid.*).

In his analysis of the American middle classes, Mills (1951) distinguishes between the "old" and the "new" middle classes. The former is made up of farmers, businessmen and free professionals; and the latter, managers, salaried professionals, salespeople and office workers. Between 1870 and 1940, the old middle class increased less than one and a half times, while the new middle class expanded sixteenfold. Several themes run through Mills' book; the one of immediate concern to us relates to the relative power position of the new middle class in the American society. Following Max Weber, Mills takes exception to the sociological assumption that political supremacy follows from functional and economic indispensability. This assumption underlies those theories which predict the new middle class to be the next ruling class on the basis of its indispensability in fulfilling the major functions of the social order. The same assumption is present in Marx's prediction of the inevitable ascent to power of the proletariat. Instead, Mills asserts that the accumulation of power by any stratum depends on three factors: will and know-how, objective opportunity and organization.

> The opportunity is limited by the group's structural position; the will is dependent upon the group's consciousness of its interests and ways of realizing them. And both structural position and consciousness interplay with organizations, which strengthen consciousness and are made politically relevant by structural position. (Mills, 1951, p. 300)

While conceding that the new middle class are better off than wage workers in terms of income and social prestige, and that some of their occupation lend them supervisory power over other white-collar and wage workers, Mills concludes that they are but the "assistants of authority; the power they exercise is a derived power" (Mills, 1951, p. 74).

The other themes of relevance to us include the increasing use of manipulation relative to coercion and authority; and the role of bureaucracy in the transformation and amplification of power. Putting aside these themes for the time being, the conclusions reached by Mills in these two books can be connected, for they pose a question in such an emphatic manner that would make Mills' third book appear like a belated sequel (it was published five years after the second book).

If the labour unions have no decision power, and the new middle class are mere assistants of authority, so that "history is made behind men's backs" (Mills, 1951, p. 350; cf. Mills, 1948, p. 238), where has the power gone then? Because of the then unprecedented power of America in the world, this question would have far-reaching implications.

The answer is almost implied by elimination. For if the American society were a class society, and since the other two classes were already disqualified, then the remaining, upper class would be the only contender. Yet Mills deliberately refrains from formulating his answer in this way. He does so on account of the diverse bases of power, of which the economic base is only one. The other bases are political and military. Each of these alone would be inadequate to locate the locus of power.

> The simple Marxian view makes the big economic man the *real* holder of power; the simple liberal view makes the big political man the chief of the political system; and there are some who would view the warlords as virtual dictators. Each of these is an oversimplified view. It is to avoid them that we use the term "power elite" rather than, for example, "ruling class". (Mills, 1956, p. 277)

Whereas Mills has not explicitly defined power in his two earlier works, he does so in the third by almost reiterating Weber's general definition (Mills, 1956, p. 9). From this general definition, Mills draws a more specific working definition. Power to Mills consists in making important decisions about the arrangements under which men live, and about the events which make up history. Ability to make up and carry through these decisions resides in the commanding positions of major institutions. All these are already implicit in the usage of the term power in the earlier works, and are consistent with that in latter ones (e.g. Mills, 1958). It should be noted that this definition is only loosely phrased, and Mills uses it only as a working definition. This is unlike the highly formalized and restrictive definition by Dahl (1957), which we will examine in Chapter 5. The emphatic point made by Mills, (1956, and then 1958) is that the economic, political and military institutions have acquired such dominance that the scattered institutions of religion, education and family are increasingly shaped by them. Mills' power elite thesis is simply this: power in the American society has become increasingly concentrated in the upper echelons of the three major institutions, which together would compose the power elite.

Referring to his contemporary America, Mills recognizes a noticeable degree of autonomy enjoyed by the elite in each domain. It is only in the intricate ways of coalition do they make up and carry through the most important decisions. In this sense, the power elite is not a completely meshed and totally united clique. One can well ask why is there one power elite and not three (Bottomore, 1964). To Mills, the crucial issue here is not the extent to which the three interlock with one another, but the context within which interlocking takes place. This context, Mills suggests, is made up of a weakened and formalized democratic system, the absence of any genuine civil service of skill and integrity and which is independent of vested interest, the coincidence of interest between those who control the major means of production and those who control the new technology of violence, and the pervasive feeling of powerlessness amongst the intellectuals and the masses.

From the point of view of power, Mills' image of the American society resembles the elitist more than the Marxian model. The concentration of power in the elite makes whatever power that the masses may possess irrelevant for most practical purposes. In terms of power, society has only one stratum – the power elite – others are *outside* it. Another way to describe this is that "history is made behind men's backs". This is the fundamental thesis of elitist theorists, from Pareto to Mosca to Michels (Olsen, 1970), and as such, is in sharp contrast to Marx's two-class model of society. The economically subordinate class is never outside the Marxian image of a society, in whose ultimate triumph Marx had unfailing faith. No one who studies Mills' trilogy in its chronological order can fail to be impressed by an increasing agitated pessimism.

Mills' "The Power Elite" comes under severe criticism in an extended review by Parsons (1957). Parsons' stated intention is to take issue with Mills' conception of power and the empirical base of the latter's thesis. The main attack, however, is waged on the conceptual level. Mills, he says, is too concerned with the distribution of power and the more ugly side of power. Using the analogy of wealth, Parsons asserts that before power can be distributed, it must first of all be produced. The distribution of power is thus a secondary and derived aspect. In elevating the distributive aspect into the central place, Mills puts the cart before the horse, so to speak. Then Mills is said to have interpreted power exclusively as a facility serving the sectional interests of the holders of power, and ignores its positive function in furthering communal goals. The result is a highly selective treatment of the whole complex problems of power, a treatment which Parsons designates as a "zero-sum" conception (Parsons, 1957, p. 139). Alongside this zero-sum conception, Parsons asserts, is Mills' tendency "to think of power as presumptively illegitimate; if people exercise considerable power, it must be because they have somehow usurped it where they had no right and they intend to use it to the detriment of others" (p. 140), a tendency which amounts to an indictment of power holders. Behind all this, Parsons asserts, lies a metaphysical position: a Utopian conception of an ideal society in which power plays no part, which Mills shares with a long line of indicters of modern industrial society.

Parson's review of Mills' conception of power is more than just a negative critique. For it sets the tone of some new developments in Parsons' later treatment of the problem of power. These subsequent developments are so different from Parsons' earlier thinking that the review in question must be regarded as something like an intellectual watershed.

In his first two major works (Parsons, 1937 and 1951) prior to the critique of the "The Power Elite", Parsons has assigned little prominence to the analysis of power. This is not so much a neglect through ignorance as part of a deliberate attempt to shape American sociological thinking. As pointed out by Rex (1961), Parsons in his first major work (Parsons, 1937) proposes a voluntaristic theory of action in place of positivistic and idealistic theories. Positivistic theories assume every actor to be an applied scientist whose conduct is seen as the rational pursuit of ends. The ends are random and taken as given, and normative elements are considered irrelevant to social action. In these two regards, positivistic theories are the polar opposite of idealistic theories. The latter view action as a process of emanation of self-expression of ideal or normative factors. These two types of theories concentrate respectively on instrumental and moral action-orientations, exclude one another, and make no room for expressive or cathartic action-orientation. Parsons' voluntaristic theory of action is an attempt to provide a theoretical framework wherein the normative and non-normative elements can be treated as positively interdependent with one another, as well as with the significant subjective elements. Parsons' later theoretical development in "The Social System" (Parsons, 1951), however, elevates the normative elements to such a central position as to make his theoretical system not unlike an idealist one (Rex, 1961). During this period, Parsons' conceptualization of power seems to be entirely subordinated to the normative elements.

Thus while accepting the Hobbesian problem of social order as a central problem in sociology, Parsons chooses to recommend Durkheim's solution. He seems to dislike Hobbes' leviathan because it stands "entirely outside the system, forcibly (keeps) order by the threat of sanctions" (Parsons, 1937, p. 314). Durkheim's solution is based on the regulatory and integrative functions of norms. A set of common norms – *conscience collective* – would not only regulate the means, but also shapes the ends. Thus social order would come about through normative regulation; and because the ends sought by individuals are shaped by common norms, they are no longer "individual" but contain a "social" element, so that the individuals no longer stand in antagonism to one another or to society, but are integrated into society. In short, Durkheim's approach "involves a complete rejection not only . . . of the utilitarian (Hobbesian) solution of the dilemma, but of the dilemma itself" (Parsons, 1937, p. 382). Furthermore, the condition of *conscience collective* is regarded to have positive psychological functions in the development of "integrated personality". When *conscience collective* is broken down, a condition which Durkheim calls *anomie*, the result is not merely the Hobbesian state of nature wherein there will be a general war of all against all. Apart from a break down in social order, a psycho-pathological state follows *anomie* in that individuals are no longer capable of acting rationally in their self-centred pursuits (as proposed by Hobbes) but may, in extreme cases, end up in suicide. Apparently, Parsons prefers Durkheim's solution to Hobbes' because the former holds promise for a much more far-reaching solution to social *and* psychological order. Having reached such a conclusion, Parsons assigns relatively little conceptual prominence to power in his sociology.

In so far as power is discussed in Parsons (1937), it reveals a conception which is no more than a selective reiteration of Hobbes' view: power is seen as the means to an end, consisting, in the final analysis, of force and fraud. Since the Hobbesian version of power acquires its importance from the problem of social order, now that the problem has been "solved", it would appear that power can be safely put aside in sociology. Nevertheless, Parsons clearly recognizes the important role of force. While agreeing with Pareto that the appearance of force and/or fraud on a considerable scale may be a symptom of social disintegration, Parsons asserts that there is a difference between force and fraud. Men of great faith, in order to gain conformity, readily turn to force the unpleasantness of which counts little in comparison with the absoluteness of the faith. Through the use of force, this faith may become the basis of a community of values. Thus, "Force frequently attends the 'creative' process by which a new value system becomes established in a society in part through the accession to power of a new elite" (p. 291). Fraud, on the other hand, is a symptom of a kind of individuation, the dissolution of community ties. In so far as Parsons admits that values and norms become consensual partly through force, power would retain a certain place even in his sociology. Since, too, fraud may also serve the same integrational function *à la* Machiavelli, if not *à la* Parsons.

Later in a discussion of the differentiation of the social system, Parsons (1951) presents a highly technical view of power. Structurally, a social system consists of differentiated roles which are functionally interrelated. Within this structure, "significant objects" – personnel, facilities and rewards – are distributed. Only facilities and rewards are related to power. Both are "possessions". A possession is a right or a bundle of rights. A facility is then defined as an instrumental possession for the achievement of goals. On the other hand, a possession which serves an expressive or symbolic function would be a reward. Then only "relational" facilities and rewards are related to power. Parsons' whole discussion is pitched at a highly general and abstract level. As far as I can understand it, the following concrete examples can be given, even though these may oversimplify Parsons' analysis. An example of relational facility would be the right of ego to ask alter to perform or not to perform a certain act. Ego's right to an attitude of loyalty on alter's part would be an instance of a relational reward. Parsons designates relational facility as power, and states that the "relational reward-possessions present an allocative problem just as do facilities, that is, through the power problem, and in the homologous way" (Parsons, 1951, p. 129). The technical details aside, what Parsons now calls power seems to mean simply a superordinate – subordinate relation of a legitimate kind. To him, power is power over; and because power is in scarce supply relative to its demand, it must be subjected to normative regulation, that is, legitimized. As pointed out by Lockwood (1956), Parsons attends to only a restricted and arbitrary range of the power phenomenon of the legitimate kind, and assigns the rest to the consideration of economists and political scientists.

Thus, Parsons' earlier conception of power, as far as it can be ascertained from the two books under consideration, actually contains a strong Rationalist component. Value consensus is at least in part the offspring of force, independently of the intention of the people who use force to translate their great faith into a community of values. Then, power as a relational facility, which is regarded as important in the differentiation of the social system, is still a hierarchical relation of dominance and subordination. Since power contains coercive and hierarchical elements, it is at least in part a zero-sum concept. Parsons' claim that the zero-sum aspects of power are only secondary to the nonzero-sum aspects would require for its justification a new theoretical rationale quite apart from those contained in his two books. However, this has not been done. Parsons later simply shifts the topic from power over to power to. Having made such a shift, he then develops a highly specialized conception of power to demonstrate its nonzero-sum quality, ignoring the counter-argument that even his new conception would still contain a zero-sum element. I shall return to this and other criticisms after presenting Parsons' later view on power.

In two articles, Parsons elaborates at length the concepts of influence (Parsons, 1963a) and political power (Parsons, 1963b). A third article is devoted to force, which was written for a conference on Internal War held in 1961 and was published three years later (Parsons, 1964). They are all reprinted in Parsons (1967), in which it is noted that the article on force has actually paved the way for the article on power.

Parsons' new conception of power relies heavily on what may be called a monetary model. The modern banking system, through the credit-creation mechanism, can expand the volume of money in circulation. When depositors entrust their monetary funds to a bank, they retain their property rights in those funds but at the same time make them available to the bank for lending. This would result in a net addition to the circulating medium, as measured by the quantity of new bank deposits created by the loans outstanding. The volume of money in circulation thus no longer remains a fixed-sum. Furthermore, when the system runs smoothly, both the depositors and the borrowers derive benefits from it, so that their respective interests are not mutually exclusive.

In the monetary system, the positive, nonzero-sum state of money is made possible and maintained not by gold but by mutual confidence or trust between the depositors and the bank, and by the binding contract which the bank stipulates on the borrowers. Furthermore, an increase in the quantity of money in circulation is economically functional only if it leads to a corresponding increase in productivity, and it is the productivity of the economy which forms the "ultimate basis of the value of money" (Parsons, 1964, p. 287).

Power is then conceptualized using the analogy of money. Analogously, for power, the counterparts of gold and productivity are respectively force and public interests. The effectiveness of power would depend on trust, not on force, although force may serve as its "symbolic basis of security" (Parsons, 1964, p. 296); and power becomes functional when it furthers communal interests and fulfils binding obligations. Now the hallmark of trust is its flexibility in the sense that the expectations on both sides must be stated without too definite advance specification of the rights and duties. Thus, power which is based on trust would enable the power holder to use power as a *generalized medium* in dealing with new and changing situations. The functional advantage of power as a generalized medium of the interaction process over power as a particularized medium is regarded as equivalent to that of money over barter. The analogy is brought to a climax with the proposed concept of a "power bank". Like the money bank, a "power bank" is insolvent in the sense that it cannot fulfil all its legitimate obligations if there is insistence on their fulfilment too rapidly. A mild pressure will force adoption of a rigid priority system, and extreme pressure will tend to bring about a serious breakdown, so that at the end of the road will lie the resort to force.

From these considerations, Parsons arrives at the following conception of power.

> Power then is generalized capacity to secure the performance of binding obligations by units in a system of collective organization when the obligations are legitimized with reference to their bearing on collective goals and where in case of recalcitrance there is a presumption of enforcement by negative situational sanctions — whatever the actual agency of that enforcement. (Parsons, 1963b, p. 308)

It would appear that Parsons is here focusing on power as a legitimate, generalized capacity whose wielder is morally committed to performing the binding obligations or otherwise would have to face negative sanctions. Who can apply these negative sanctions is not considered. The question of the distribution of power is acknowledged but not discussed; and similarly, the hierarchical nature of power (who has power over whom) is recognized but the emphasis is on the positive function that power may perform. Such an image of power is a highly selective and restricted one, to say the very least.

Parsons then distinguishes power from money and two other generalized media, namely, influence and generalization of commitments (Parsons, 1963a). The distinguishing feature of power as a generalized medium of mobilizing the performance of binding obligations is the application of tangible negative sanction in the form of deterrence, or of punishment in the case of non-compliance. Money, on the other hand, is a generalized medium of inducement which operates through the provision of tangible positive sanction for compliance. Influence is a generalized medium of persuasion which operates through offering reasons as to why compliance would be a good thing for the person who complies. Here the obligation is not binding and negative sanction is inapplicable. Finally, generalization of commitments, the capacity to motivate fulfilment of obligation through appeal to a subjective sense of commitment, does not involve the threat of tangible or situational negative sanction and is hence distinguished from power. Elsewhere (Parsons, 1963b), a distinction is made between power and authority. Authority is the institutional code within which the use of power is organized and legitimized.

Parsons' treatment of power as a generalized medium has subsequently been met with mixed reception. Mitchell (1967) deems highly of it as a "revolutionary" piece of analysis. Gouldner (1970) draws the different conclusion that "(Parsons') entire analysis of power, with its central and repeated analogy with money, yields consequences of absolutely no intellectual significance" (p. 292). In my opinion, both evaluations are overstated. In the light of Machiavelli's and Hobbes' contributions, Parsons' analysis hardly appears "revolutionary". The nonzero-sum functional view of power is but a modern, capitalist reformulation of Machiavellianism. Parsons' insistence on power being a *generalized* medium, together with the idea of a "power bank", revives, in effect, Hobbes' leviathan. All of these, of course, are with a difference, which is the moral or normative consensus imported by Parsons from Durkheim's *conscience collective*. Such a difference, however, can hardly wage a revolution; and in any case, Mitchell's applause is not primarily directed at the normative element. On the other hand, Parsons' analogy with money does yield one consequence of some significance in the history of the power concept. Unlike Machiavelli or Hobbes, Parsons addresses his analysis to advanced and relatively stable political systems. The very fact that he attends to the problem of power to, and does so in great length, signifies that the problem is not peculiar to periods of drastic social change, but it also abides in times of relative stability. By posing the question of power to, Parsons is in effect raising a problem as old as Machiavelli. And in posing such a problem in the context of advanced and relatively stable political systems, Parsons adds a conservative and expansionist facet to the problem. Machiavelli and Hobbes were dissatisfied with their contemporary political systems and they undertook their analyses of power with the explicit hope of helping to bring forth a better system. Parsons is apparently satisfied with the American system and his analysis is addressed not so much to social change but to the conservation and expansion of that system. Thus the practical relevance of power to is not limited to people who are committed to an anti-establishment stance but also to loyalists.

As a way of summarizing and analysing further the zero-sum controversy, the following classification may be considered. Assuming that both power over and power to possess zero-sum and nonzero-sum qualities, there would be four facets of power: (1) zero-sum power relation, (2) nonzero-sum power relation, (3) power as a zero-sum facility, and (4) power as a nonzero-sum facility. Mills' conception of power focuses on the first and the third facets. Parsons' later view is confined to the fourth facet. The status of the second facet is ambiguous. To Mills and others like Dahrendorf (1959), it is a contradiction in term. Parsons' attack on the zero-sum conception of power does not hinge on a refutation of facets (1) and (3), but on the assertion that they are secondary to (4). There are, however, strong reasons against this assertion. Giddens (1968), among others, has criticized Parsons for assuming the existence of consensual collective goals to the neglect of the fact that these goals may actually or predominantly represent the interests of the power wielders. So that the payoffs accruing to the nonpower-wielders represent only crumbs. Hence, both (4) and (3) would be equally present. Related to this is another criticism. Suppose that consensus does exist, and the payoffs procured by the use of power are commonly desired by all parties. But if the payoffs are differentially allocated in a non-random fashion, then (4) and (1) are inextricable. Let us suppose further that both the conditions of consensus and equal allocation are met. In so far as individuals or groups are not completely interchangeable so that some people are more likely than others to exercise that power, there would still be room for doubting Parsons' assertion that (4) is the primary facet of power. It is thus hard to accept the recent statement made by Parsons, that "the issue has been resolved, at least in principle, in favour of the economic nonzero-sum model, as generalizable to the power case" (Parsons, 1976, p. 100).

Finally, it is important to bear in mind that "zero-sum" and "nonzero-sum" are economic and game-theoretical terms. It would be relevant to raise the question of how would these terms further the discussion of the relation between power on the one hand, and social conflict and social order on the other hand. As already noted, Parsons abandons the Hobbesian solution in favour of Durkheim's in his analysis of social order, and thereby reduces the role of power in his discussion of social integration. When later he introduces the terms zero-sum and nonzero-sum, and asserts that the primary aspect of power is its nonzero-sum quality, he assigns a new role to power in social integration. This role seems to me to be analogous to the role of economic growth in the theory of embourgeoisement. According to the latter, the rising standard of living brought about by economic growth relaxes class antagonism and contributes to social integration. Analogously, the achievement of collective goals by power (as a generalized medium) would soften the opposition between power wielders and those subjected to them, and thereby enhances social integration.

To the extent that the benefit of power is seen to be fairly distributed, trust in the power wielders will be enhanced. However, as our later discussion on the relation between power and conflict will show, there remains a basic contradiction between the power wielders and people who are subjected to them. For this reason, the most that the power wielders can hope for is the regulation of conflict, not its elimination.

Power and social stratification

Social stratification generally means the arrangement of groups into a hierarchy of strata or positions that are unequal with regard to the value being distributed to them (Tumin, 1967). Alternatively put, social stratification is institutionalized or structured inequality. The pervasive existence of some form of social stratification is well documented in the ethnographic literature (e.g. Murdock, 1949) and requires only brief mentioning here. Means of livelihood, population size, and permanence of residence are themselves interrelated and they in turn have a decisive bearing on social stratification. A hunting or food gathering economy, small community size (of less than a hundred or a thousand), and a nomadic type of settlement are associated with less social stratification than an agricultural economy, large population size and permanent settlement. The former set of conditions is a limiting case of an approximate "egalitarian" society, and nowadays a rare one anyway (Fried, 1960).

The intellectual history of the inquiry into the origins and mechanisms of social inequality, as reviewed by Dahrendorf (1968), dated back to the philosophical speculation of Aristotle in which *social* inequalities were assumed to reflect and were in congruence with the *natural* inequalities existing between free men and slaves, male and female, the Greeks and the barbarians. When it was thus assumed that humans are by nature unequal, and that the natural inequalities are responsible for social inequalities, there would be no place for any inquiry into the origin of social inequalities that seeks the answer in sociological or social psychological factors. Only when this Aristotelian presupposition was challenged, notably by Rousseau, and later gave way to the antithetical axiom that humans are born equal, did the inquiry into social inequalities take a new form. The subsequent sociological explanations, according to Dahrendorf (1968), fall into three broad epochs. The eighteenth century advanced an account based on private property; the nineteenth century on division of labour; and the twentieth century so far, on American functionalism. All three major accounts, however, are found by Dahrendorf to be inadequate. These accounts, as well as Dahrendorf's and others' views, can be better understood if we insert here a brief summary of Weber's descriptive model of social stratification.

There are, according to Weber (1948), three types of grouping within a community, namely, classes, status groups and parties. Classes are generated by the market-situation and differ among themselves on the basis of their respective relations to the production and acquisition of goods. Status groups are stratified according to the prestige, esteem, or honour which they can command on the basis of the consumption of goods as represented by a particular style of life. How status honour is distributed in society is not systematically propounded by Weber, although the following point has been lucidly articulated. Status honour is deemed to be exclusive to a status group. Concern for status honour is manifested in the prejudice against the *nouveaux arrivés*, particularly against the *nouveaux riches*.

> If mere economic acquisition and naked economic power still bearing the stigma of extra-status origin could bestow upon anyone who has won it the same honour as those who are interested in status by virtue of style of life claim for themselves, the status order would be threatened at its very root . . . Therefore all groups having interest in the status order react with special sharpness precisely against the pretensions of purely economic acquisition. (Weber, 1948, p. 192)

This raises the general question of whether and to what extent status and class are interrelated. While insisting on the general point that status honour has diverse sources, Weber saw a tremendous effect of class on status. During and immediately following technological and economic changes, class is pushed into the foreground and threatens the existent stable status relation among the groups, as can be seen in the *déclassement* of the nobility. When the bases of economic stratification become relatively stable, stratification by status is revived, incorporating perhaps elements of the new class order but always consists of other criteria which differentiate the distribution of honour.

Parties, finally, are specifically oriented toward the acquisition of power, that is to say, toward influencing a communal action. Examples are political parties, trade unions and pressure groups. They are structures struggling for domination through various means ranging from violence of any sort to canvassing for votes with coarse or subtle means.

Social inequality or stratification in a community can hence be seen in terms of the disparity within each of the three groupings. On a more abstract level, social stratification can be portrayed as having three dimensions, namely, the economic, social (social-evaluative) and political dimensions; which correspond to the three groupings. As well, social stratification can be seen in terms of the distribution of power in the general sense; or as Weber puts it, classes, status groups and parties are all phenomena of the distribution of power in the community. Here as in the discussion of power (*Macht*), Weber uses the power concept as a general, inclusive concept. The stratification within each grouping then reflects the unequal distribution of power.

Considerable confusion, if not misunderstanding, can arise from undue recognition of the fact that Weber has used the power concept in a general sense. The popular trilogy of class, status and *power* (e.g. Bendix and Lipset, 1967; Runciman, 1966) should not be regarded as a literal equivalent of Weber's class, status and party, unless power in the former is explicitly intended to mean political power. That this point should be mentioned is not so much for the sake of terminological accuracy as for the autonomy which Weber has assigned analytically to the three groupings or dimensions in his model. Within this model, all the three dimensions are assumed to be autonomous. Whether or not the dimensions will converge or diverge in a particular community is beyond the scope of this model, awaiting further theoretical elaboration and empirical investigation. Weber's position is possible from the point of view that all the three dimensions represent the distribution of power. This position would no longer hold if one of the dimensions is power and the others are not, for the reason that the power dimension, so distinguished, must by implication of its definition be the focal dimension towards which the other, non-power, dimensions will converge. Weber's model has since been called the multi-dimensional model of social stratification.

Two comments about the multi-dimensional model should be made at this point. Should social inequality or stratification be conceived in such a broad perspective as to include three major dimensions, or should it be more specifically formulated to cover only the unequal distribution of rewards such as wealth and prestige? There are views on social stratification which opt for the more specific conception, as for instance the views of American functionalism and Dahrendorf, to which we shall turn soon.

Another comment is that there is a certain bias inherent in the multi-dimensional model. In assuming that the three dimensions are more or less autonomous from one another, the model makes it relatively easier to enlarge on the divergence or incongruence between the dimensions than otherwise. Some instances of dimensional incongruence can always be cited in support of the model as well as to the embarrassment of those students who undertake to demonstrate the primary importance of one dimension over the others in a particular type of society. When the model lends itself to the foreclosure of significant congruence between the dimensions by emphasizing the incongruence, it would lose its heuristic value. It would become as deterministic as other models which insist on the centrality of one dimension over the others. Because of this, Weber's model should be used cautiously, as a searching spotlight rather than as a dogma. Used in this cautious manner, the multi-dimensional model can be of high heuristic value. More than any other model or theory of social stratification, it highlights the political party as an autonomous grouping, which is more than confirmed by the emergence of modern socialist and communist states. Because of this, it possesses unique relevance to the analysis of social stratification in these countries (e.g. Parkin, 1971; Bauman, 1974). Furthermore, as pointed out by Parkin (1971). Weber's model is relevant to multi-racial society in which glaring dimensional incongruence has persisted. The model is also useful in highlighting some of the consequences of social stratification. This point is worth pursuing in some detail and I will do so before proceeding to an examination of the explanations of the origin of social stratification.

Since Weber's model assigns a large degree of autonomy to each of the stratificational dimensions, it enables us to envisage a wide range of situations in which the dimensions can interact with one another in various ways. At one extreme is the situation where there is complete dimensional congruence. Here a group (or an individual) which is high on, say, the political dimension is also high on the economic and social-evaluative dimensions; whereas another group which is low on one dimension is also low on the others. A situation like this is rigidly and nonambiguously stratified. At the other extreme is the situation where there is complete dimensional incongruence. That is to say, a group's rankings on the dimensions are negatively correlated. The configuration of social stratification of a particular society or group can lie anywhere along this continuum.

There has been considerable research into the social and psychological consequences of dimensional congruence and incongruence. The research appears in both the sociological and social psychological literature and is known by various names, including "rank equilibration" (e.g. Benoit-Smullyan, 1944), "status equilibration" (e.g. Kimberly, 1966, 1972), "status crystallization" or "status inconsistency" (e.g. Lenski, 1954, 1967; Geschwender, 1967), "status congruence" (e.g. Sampson,

1969), and "rank equivalence" (e.g. Galtung, 1966). A representative review and integration of the consequences of dimensional congruence/incongruence can be found in the works of Galtung (1966) and Geschwender (1967). A list of the consequences would include social integration, equality, "peace of mind", social mobility and social change attempts, prejudice, social isolation, symptoms of psychological stress, and emotional reactions such as anger and guilt.

The relation between dimensional congruence/incongruence on the one hand, and the occurrence of a particular consequence on the other is a complex one. The earlier focus on the *degree* of incongruence has oversimplified the relation by not taking into full consideration the *type* of incongruence. An ethnic group which has a low ascribed ethnic status but a high economic ranking would react to the situation differently from another group which has a high ascribed ethnic status but a low economic ranking, even though the degree of incongruence may be identical in both groups. Furthermore, the earlier assumption that incongruence is always psychologically aversive is no longer tenable. A group which used to be consistently low on all dimensions does not necessarily feel more deprived or dissatisfied when it achieves a higher ranking on one of the dimensions. The sum of a group's ranks may be more superior in predicting the consequence than the discrepancy of the ranks. Despite these and other complications, the central thesis still holds: the configuration of social stratification contains the structural root of a large number of social and psychological phenomena. Social psychology has been instrumental in clarifying some of the intermediary, intervening variables (Geschwender, 1967). As will be reported fully in Chapter 9, it is useful for the study of power change to combine the idea of social categorization (Tajfel, 1970) with the multi-dimensional model of social stratification, and particularly, the idea of rank equilibration.

After the above diversion, and bearing in mind Weber's multi-dimensional model of social stratification, we can now proceed to an examination of the three major explanations of the origins of social stratification. The eighteenth century explanation in terms of the ownership of private property, as articulated by Rousseau and later by Marx, regards as central the economic or class dimension towards which the social-evaluative and political dimensions would converge in the long run. In a large part, the validity of this explanation can be granted in so far as classical capitalism is concerned. The generality of this explanation is however very much in doubt, particularly since the converse of the explanation can no longer hold in the face of modern societal development. The absence or near absence of private property in some countries has not been accompanied by the withering away of the social-evaluative and political dimensions. Dahrendorf (1968) quotes the Soviet Union, Yugoslavia, and the Israeli kibbutzim to show that even though private property has been reduced to virtual non-significance, and stratification being prevented temporarily from manifesting itself in differences of posession and income, the "undefinable yet effective force of prestige continues to create a noticeable rank order" (p. 159).

The nineteenth century explanation, which was based on the division of labour in society, was separately advanced by Schemoller as well as by Engels and Marx. As pointed out by Dahrendorf (1968), in order to explain why division of labour, which results in lateral or horizontal social differentiation, can lead to stratification, some intermediate agency has to be inserted. Otherwise, there is the error of misidentifying stratification with lateral social differentiation.

Whereas the theory of division of labour does not contain an intermediate clause between horizontal social differentiation and stratification, the theory of functionalism, as represented by the Davis-Moore theory of social stratification (Davis and Moore, 1945), attempts to explain precisely the ubiquity and inevitability of the unequal distribution of economic advantage and prestige which associate with a high level of social differentiation. Briefly, the functional argument is as follows. Every society needs a mechanism of inducing people to acquire the necessary skills to fill certain positions which are more complicated and functionally more important than others. It also needs a mechanism for motivating people to perform conscientiously these functions once they occupy the position. The necessary inducements are provided in the form of rewards which are differentially distributed according to the positions. The rewards consist of economic payoffs and prestige. Since the rewards of different positions must be unequal, division of labour, and hence social differentiation, must necessarily lead to social stratification on the social-evaluative dimension (prestige) and a specific aspect of the economic dimension (economic rewards).

A similar functional approach to stratification of status and other rewards in small groups is evident in the work of Bales (1950). He views stratification as a result of the group's response to the increasing demands of the environment. As functional problems increase, functional/role differentiation will occur. The importance attached to different functions or positions forms the basis of a status hierarchy and leads to the emergence of differential rewards.

Subsequently, the functional explanation has become the subject of an extended debate, so much so that in the second edition of Bendix and Lipset's (1967) reader on social stratification, a half of the first section is solely devoted to it. Tumin (1953a, 1953b) and Wrong (1959), among others, have called into question several of the major assumptions of the functionl explanation. In the first place, it is difficult to be specific on the exact meaning of functional importance, and the question of "important to whom" has to be raised. Alternative motivational mechanisms other than those leading to stratification may be equally successful. The functions served by stratification (i.e. in getting people to acquire the necessary skills and in motivating them to do a good job) may turn out to be dysfunctions. A stratified system may in fact be more stratified than it is necessary to effect the assumed functions. Noting these and other criticisms, Dahrendorf (1968) draws the conclusion that there can be no functional explanation of the origin of social stratification. It merely asserts the ubiquity of social inequality.

Afterwards, Dahrendorf (1968) formulates his own theory of social stratification. To him as well as to the proponents of the functional explanation, social stratification means specifically inequality of wealth and prestige. His starting point is that every society is a moral community in the sense that any society must have certain behavioural expectations or norms to regulate people's behaviours so that behaviours do not occur randomly or by chance. The compulsory character of these norms is based on the operation of positive and negative sanctions to be discriminantly applied to conformity or deviant behaviours. When norms are thus enforced through the application of sanctions, a rank order of "distributive status" inevitably arises regardless of whether the status is measured in terms of prestige or wealth, or both. Social stratification in this narrow sense is therefore an immediate result of social control through the application of positive and negative sanctions.

Up to this point, Dahrendorf's theory is solely concerned with the social-evaluative dimension and the wealth aspect of the economic dimension of stratification. With regard to the former, the proposed stratification mechanism is remarkably similar to the social psychological hypothesis that a person will gain status and prestige by conforming to the normative expectations of the group, such as that formulated by Hollander (1958), and Homans (1961).

Further development of the theory takes Dahrendorf into the area of power. At one stage, a distinction is made by Dahrendorf between distributive and nondistributive values, defined in a footnote respectively as intransitive and transitive (in the grammatical sense) values. Wealth and prestige are distributive or intransitive values, while power is nondistributive or transitive. His theory of social stratification discussed so far is therefore a theory of distributive inequalities. What then is the relationship between distributive and nondistributive inequalities? Or to put it in another form, what is the relationship between inequalities of wealth and prestige on the one hand, and inequalities of power on the other?

Dahrendorf asserts that a system of norms and sanctions can only function in a society sustained by a power (*Macht*) and an authority (*Herrschaft*) structure. Society is possible because there are norms to regulate human conduct; this regulation is guaranteed by the incentive or threat of sanctions; the possibility of imposing sanctions is the "abstract core of all power". Thus the explanation of distributive inequalities in terms of the necessity of sanctions cannot at the same time explain the power structure of society because the possibility of applying the very sanction is a function of power. The conclusion is that the system of distributive inequalities is only a secondary consequence of the social structure of power.

In a telling footnote, Dahrendorf relates his intellectual conversion to a view of society that regards power as the primary, transitive or nondistributive force. For a long time, he says, he was convinced that there was a logical equivalence between the analysis of social classes and constraint (conflict or coercion) theory, and between the analysis of social stratification and integration (consensus or functional) theory. Then,

> the considerations developed in the present essay changed my mind. I have now come to believe that stratification is merely a consequence of the structure of power, integration a special case of constraint, and thus the structural-functional approach a subset of a broader approach. The assumption that constraint theory and integration theory are two approaches

> of equal rank, i.e., two different perspectives on the same material, is not so much false as superfluous; we get the same result by assuming that stratification follows from power, integration from constraint, stability from change. Since the latter assumption is the simpler one, it is to be preferred. (Dahrendorf, 1968, footnote 20)

It is apparent that Dahrendorf is dealing here with the economic and social-evaluative dimensions of social stratification only. The political dimension has been left out of the discussion. In so far as he is concerned with economic dimension, the focus is on the differentiation of wealth rather than of class. For him, the problem posed by social stratification means specifically inequalities of wealth and prestige. The origin of social stratification, so defined, is sought in the differential application of sanctions, that is, the power structure of society. It should be noted that Dahrendorf does not use the concept of power in the general Weberian sense, but in the more specific sense of the ability to apply sanctions.

Lenski's (1966) theory of social stratification resembles Dahrendorf's in many respects. Both are concerned with the distribution of material rewards (which Lenski calls privilege) and prestige. Like Dahrendorf, Lenski regards power as the primary factor in the differentiation of privilege and prestige. Unlike Dahrendorf, however, Lenski takes into account the developmental stages of society and uses the power concept both in the general Weberian sense as well as the more specific sense of force.

When the economic product of a society remains at the subsistence level, men will divide it amongst themselves not according to the power which they can wield, but according to their respective needs in order to insure the survival and continuing productivity of those others whose labour is necessary or beneficial to themselves. When there is surplus of material rewards (i.e. privilege), its distribution will be determined primarily by power and secondarily by altruism, power being defined in the Weberian sense. Therefore there is a positive correlation between technological advancement, which increases productivity and hence surplus, and the importance of power in the distribution of privilege. In other words, goods and services available to technologically primitive societies will be distributed on the basis of need; whereas in technologically advanced societies, an increasing proportion of the goods and services will be distributed on the basis of power. Power, and also privilege, would largely determine the distribution of prestige, which in turn would have some direct influence on the distribution of power (but not on privilege).

The difficulty with this part of Lenski's theory outlined above is his use of the power concept in the general Weberian sense. The important role of power, as suggested by Lenski, would simply follow from its definition. As such, Lenski's proposal is tautological, although he makes the point that the survival needs of a society will limit the use of power. In the other part of Lenski's theory, which will be examined below, power acquires a more specific meaning which renders the argument very similar to that of Dahrendorf.

Lenski assumes that survival is the basic concern of the great majority of the people, and hence "force", or the ability to take life, is the most effective form of power in the sense that more men will respond more readily to the threat of the use of "force" than to any other. Hence force is the foundation of the distributive system in every society where there is a surplus to be divided. It is also the foundation of political sovereignty because no government can expect to survive once its monopoly of force is challenged. However, because the use of force is costly and does not confer honour on its user, force is not the "most effective instrument for retaining and exploiting a position of power and deriving the maximum benefits from it", and thus, "those who seize power by force find it advantageous to legitimize their rule once effective organized opposition is eliminated" (Lenski, 1966, p. 52). In other words, the rule of might has to be transformed into the rule of right. Various means of transformation are available, which can be grouped into two categories. One is the use of coercive force to create a new consensus which lends ideological and normative support to the regime. Another is the generation of institutional power to facilitate or ensure that the benefits flow automatically to the power holders without having to invoke force. Power, based on force and through its transformation into institutional power and consensus, would then significantly determine the distribution of privilege and prestige.

Like any other discussion of the *origin* of a social phenomenon, Dahrendorf and Lenski's discussion of the origin of social stratification must remain speculative. The inquiry into the origin of social stratification would have no theoretical or practical relevance unless it can also further our understanding of social stratification as an on-going process. In the latter regard, the views of Dahrendorf and

Lenski would have the following implication. The inequality of wealth and (to a lesser extent) prestige is eradicable; here the opposite conclusion given by American functionalism seems less tenable. The inequality of power, on the other hand, is a permanent ingredient of human society. This does not mean that power equalization is impossible. There is however a limit to power equalization because social control (which is essential to society) must always presuppose a power structure for the differential application of sanction and force.

It is interesting to note that Wesolowski (1962) has painted a similar picture of the inevitability of power differentiation in groups and society. In an article originally published in the "Polish Sociological Bulletin", Wesolowski (1962) gives a critique of the importance attached to material rewards and prestige by the functional theory of stratification. The necessity of stratification, he argues, does not derive from the need of inducing people to prepare for and perform different roles, but from the very fact that human beings live together in groups. Any large scale group life involves the inner structuralization of the group resulting in the emergence of "positions of command and subordination". The occurrence of power relations of this kind is thus "inevitable" in every complex social structure, and consequently, differentiation of power would be inevitable.

On the other hand, stratification along the dimension of material rewards cannot be regarded as inevitable or universally necessary because the motivational force of material rewards depends largely on the cultural values of a society and socialization. Even if one assumes that people have to be motivated, it is conceivable that the relatively high positions in the power relation created by group life may be sufficiently attractive in themselves to make material differentials unnecessary.

With regard to stratification along the prestige dimension, Wesolowski concedes that it is more ubiquitous than the stratification of material rewards. If differences of prestige were to be eliminated completely, there must be a system of values in which "equality" *per se* holds supreme command, plus some mechanism to ensure objective equality among the people. In reality, Wesolowski asserts, "It is hard to imagine that a world without differences of prestige is imminent". The reason for this is that the very fact of power differentiation may lead to different prestige being accorded to the high and low positions of power. The correspondence between power differentiation and prestige differentiation is of course subject to cross-cultural variation. The general point is, however, that since power differentiation is inevitable, there will always be some objective ground for people to lay claim to a high or low prestige.

The foregoing argument that power differentiation is socially inevitable has at least three implications. As will be examined in the next section, an important type of conflict has its root in the power relation. If power differentiation is inevitable, then there will always be some form of power relation and consequently there will always be conflict. Secondly, the inevitability of power differentiation would pose a great problem for the "design" of Utopia and culture, as for example, the proposal by B. F. Skinner which will be examined in Chapter 6. Thirdly, to the extent that power differentiation and the subsequent formalization of power inequality are basic social facts, it would be pertinent to raise questions concerning the instigation and process of power change. These questions will be examined more fully in Chapters 8 and 9.

Power and conflict

M. Duverger introduces his political essay by discussing the definition of politics and concludes that the real nature and true significance of politics is to be found in the fact that it is always ambivalent. The ambivalence of politics is due to the very nature of power that constitutes the subject matter of politics. Power in its organized form, such as the political state, is inherently ambivalent because it always contains an element of antagonism or conflict, as well as an element of integration or harmony. Power breeds privilege, and enables its wielder to dominate over others. As a result, it leads to political conflict on two planes. On the horizontal plane, man opposes man, and group opposes group, in the struggle to attain, share, or influence power. On the vertical plane, there is opposition between those who hold power and others who are subjected to it. Power is therefore divisive and leads to antagonism and conflict. At the same time, power is also a means of ensuring a particular social order and integrating people into a collectivity. The divisive and integrational elements of power always co-exist, though their importance varies with time and the circumstances. The true image of power, according to Duverger, is the statue of the two-faced god, Janus. In the same way as the two faces of Janus are inseparable from one another, so are the divisive and integrational elements of power. Like Janus, power looks different depending on whether it is the divisive or the integrational element that is in the foreground.

From this springs the ambivalence of power, and hence the ambivalence of politics. Thus when in opposition, every political party conceives politics as conflict: once in power it sees politics as integration. On a more general level are two opposite interpretations of politics.

> The oppressed, the unsatisfied, the poor, the wretched, whether as individuals or as a class, cannot see power as assuring a real order, but only a caricature of it behind which is hidden the domination of privilege; for them politics means conflict. Those who are rich, well provided for, satisfied, find society harmonious and see power as maintaining an authentic order; for them politics means integration. It often happens that the latter succeed to some extent in persuading the former that political strife is dishonest, unhealthy, sordid, and that those who engage in it seek their own selfish interest by dubious means. To disarm opponents in such a way is to secure a considerable personal advantage. "Depoliticization" always favours the established order, immobility and conservation. (Duverger, 1966, pp. xii–xiii)

"Depoliticization", we may add, also works through the foreclosure of alternatives in the manner which I have tried to point out in Chapter 3 where I discussed the counteraction of charismatic legitimacy.

The two faces of power set the dominant tone of Duverger's essay, which contains a lucid analysis of conflict and integration, as well as the dialectical relationship between them. For Duverger, the analysis of organized power in general, and the political state in particular, is first and foremost an analysis of conflict and integration, and the interplay between them, which co-exist, in varying proportion, in all societies and at all times.

C. J. Friedrich (1963) sees power mainly as a *relation* among men, which manifests in the behaviour of following or conformity. The bases of a power relationship are infinitely broad, since virtually anything that human beings value can become the basis of a power relationship in its broadest sense. Two categories of power relation are distinguished. One is based on consent, another on coercion. Coercion has three sources: physical, economic and psychic. All three sources may also generate power which is based on consent, particularly in the case of psychic coercion (e.g. propaganda) which renders the distinction between coercive and consensual power extremely elusive. Such a distinction, however, serves to articulate a cumulative law of power. Both the growth and decline of power are said to be cumulative.

> The growth is cumulative up to the point of full employment of the resources of the power-seeker (coercive power) and of full realization of the common values and purposes of the power-followers (consensual power); beyond that point it starts to disintegrate. The decline of power is cumulative up to the point of complete exhaustion of the resources of the power-holders (coercive power) and of the disappearance of common values and purposes of the power-followers (consensual power). (Friedrich, 1963, p. 176)

As noted in Chapter 1, Friedrich in a later work (Friedrich, 1967) criticizes Machiavelli and Hobbes for their failure to understand the issues presented by authority as contrasted with the issues raised by power. The lack of interest in authority was due in part to their preoccupation with the problem of how to organize power to bring forth a new form of the political state. It is only when one is concerned with the operation of the state and the maintenance of a political order does the problem of authority move into the foreground. The same distinction between authority and power is also maintained by Friedrich in his later work (Friedrich, 1972). By authority, Friedrich refers to those power situations which are differentiated from others by the power wielder's capacity of reasoned elaboration. This capacity presupposes certain value consensus which enables the power wielder to explain to his followers the reasons he acted in a certain way and why he preferred them to act likewise. Apart from this consensus is the ability of persuasion, but persuasiveness *per se* is of secondary importance because it alone can never constitute authority. Friedrich (1963) characterizes such a consensus as a community of opinions, values and beliefs, as well as of interests and needs. Without such a community, there can be no authority. Given such a community, authority is the manifest sign of it. In this sense, authority "*results from* what is in the minds of the community" (Friedrich, 1963, p. 227).

There is obviously a strong element of Utopianism in Friedrich's conception of authority. In its extreme form, authority can only work for the common good and is devoid of coerciveness. It would also become like air that is freely and equally available to all. Any intelligent member of the community would then be capable of issuing an authoritative command, so that every member can be an authority to everybody else. This conception of authority makes it impossible to delineate any line of domination or subjection, and in this respect, it is fundamentally different from Weber's *Herrschaft*. That of course is not exactly as Friedrich would have intended it. There remains a certain element of manipulation in authority. In the maintenance of a political order, power wielders strive to transform their coercive power into consensual power, or to keep consensual power consensual as it acquires coercive potentiality. At the same time, they strive to acquire authority either by providing the reasoned elaboration themselves or through the priests and propagandists "who surround the throne" (Friedrich, 1963, p. 224). Thus to a certain extent at least, authority is the product of manipulation. In this way, the causal relation between authority and community may be two-way. Inasmuch as authority may result from what is in the minds of the community, community may result from the very process by which power wielders acquire authority. There is also an element of inequality in authority, for unless the individual members of a society are completely interchangeable in their social position, it is inevitable that some people are more likely than others to issue authoritative commands.

The moral overtone of authority, particularly when authority is contrasted with power, often conceals the elements of manipulation and inequality. Given the presence of these elements, however, one may question in what significant ways would Friedrich's authority be different from Hobbes' leviathan. One may as well question the rational purity of authority in complex, industrial societies. Authority, that is, the capacity for communal reasoned elaboration, is not a straightforward reasoning on the basis of certain consensual values. These common values, if they exist at all, have to be interpreted and articulated in such a way as to convince the potential followers that orthodoxy is on one's side. This would require an ideology, not reason *per se*.

The analyses made by Friedrich and Duverger provide two different conceptual approaches to the twin problems of conflict and integration. These problems, according to Friedrich, are problems raised respectively by power and authority. They overlap in a manner which we have noted above. Nevertheless, Friedrich insists that authority designates a vital political phenomenon which is distinct from other power situations (Friedrich, 1963, p. 223; cf. Friedrich, 1972, p. 55). Such an approach is quite different from the approach of Duverger (1966), who takes a more conceptual identification of a shift between the (coercive) power- (consensual) authority dichotomy is superficial because the shift only reflects a change in the mechanism whereby organized power operates. Thus it is not fruitful to conceive separately the problem presented by social order or integration as one of authority, and the problem presented by social conflict as one of coercive power in the manner distinguished by Friedrich.

Furthermore, Duverger's analysis of conflict and integration indicates that the achievement by the state of pure authority in Friedrich's sense is impossible in any significant way. The main reason is that integration and conflict always co-exist. Conflict contains the seed of integration in that every attack on the existing social order implies the image and anticipation of a more authentic order. Integration, however, remains incomplete because of "irreducible conflicts". Economic penury is not the root of all social conflicts and hence economic affluence can never be the panacea of conflict. A situation of economic plenty, under certain conditions, would alleviate economic conflict and push it to the background, so to speak. At the same time, it allows penury in other areas which can also create social conflict come into the lime-light. To the extent that some scarcities cannot be eliminated, conflict over them will remain. Furthermore, the divisions between the sexes, as well as between the generations, always remain a potential source of conflict. More importantly, even if economic affluence and technical progress reduce all conflicts on the horizontal plane, the conflict on the vertical plane between organized power and people who are subjected to it has no foreseeable end. In the more developed countries, the opposition of citizens to organized, bureaucratic power becomes the fundamental conflict. The most acute division, according to Duverger, is between the citizens and the state. From this point of view, pure authority in Friedrich's sense would be either a sociological or political myth, or a psychological illusion in highly complex, industrial countries.

Duverger's argument that the opposition of citizens to the state is the most fundamental conflict in developed countries is generated by two considerations. Technical advance has not led towards the withering away of the state but rather towards its growth and its bureaucratization. Through its bureaucratization, the state becomes a machine the very nature of which is oppressive, independently of the intentions of the officials or representatives who constitute it. Its growth results in a greater dependence of every citizen on the state. The citizens' relationships with the state become multiplied and so are the occasions when its rule is felt. On the other hand, the tendency for leaders to abuse their power has not been reduced by technical progress but has been increased. In short, the divisive element in organized power is resistant to technical treatment and hence will remain as the fundamental conflict in modern industrial countries, regardless of their ideological differences. Duverger anticipates a socialist convergence from both communist and capitalist countries. Communism moves towards socialism through increasing liberalization. On the other side, capitalism is on the way to socialism through increased effort of centralized planning. Class conflict in the Marxian sense *was* the most fundamental conflict, it has now given way to the opposition between organized power and people who are subjected to it. No technologically developed countries, whether communist, capitalist, or socialist, can sail clear of this type of conflict on the vertical plane which arises from the divisive element in organized power.

Duverger's analysis of conflict is opposed to Marxism in at least two significant aspects. Economic class division in advanced capitalist countries is secondary in comparison to the division between organized power and people who are subjected to it, particularly when the division is between the state and the citizens. Secondly, the opposition of citizens to the state continues even under communism. These divergent views seem to follow from the different perspectives of power adopted by Duverger and the Marxists. Unlike Duverger, who adopts a more inclusive perspective of power and assigns a greater autonomy to the state, the Marxists hold the view that the state is the executive arm of the ruling class whose real power base lies in their control of the economic infrastructure. The division between the citizens and the state is thus secondary in comparison to that between the proletariat and the capitalist classes. In the higher phase of communism following the socialization of the means of production, distribution and exchange, dictatorship of the proletariat, and so on, a classless society will be formed wherein the state will wither away.

The extent to which a communist transformation of the economic infrastructure would resolve the contradiction between organized power and people who are subjected to it remains to be proved. At the theoretical level, there are arguments which lead to the conclusion that the contradiction can never be completely eliminated. The arguments to be examined now are much more strongly and deterministically phrased than the argument developed by Duverger. These are the arguments presented by Pareto (1935), Mosca (1938) and Michels (1962). Since these arguments have been thoroughly examined by Bottomore (1964) and are summarized by Olsen (1970), the following discussion will be brief.

Pareto and Mosca make a general observation that in every society there is a minority elite who actually rules. This governing elite is composed of those who occupy the posts of political command and those who can directly influence political decisions. Over time, the elite undergoes changes in its membership by recruitment of new members from the lower strata of society, or less frequently, by incorporation of new social groups or complete replacement by a "counter-elite". These changes, called the circulation of elites, are confined to changes in the composition of the elite but do not alter the basic distinction between the elite and the masses in society. Michels in his study of political parties and labour organizations draws a parallel observation that a ruling oligarchy would inevitably emerge.

As to the reasons for the inevitability of a governing elite in organizations and society, they range from psychological to sociological. Pareto proposes that individuals who gain positions of power are those with superior sentiments who are necessarily few in number. Mosca adds to this the idea that elite families tend to be self-perpetuating because their children are in a more advantageous position than children from non-elite families in the competition for positions of power. Michels' argument leans heavily on the structural requirement of organizations. Every organization undergoes some division of labour which in turn requires coordination and leadership. Under this condition, the oligarchical and bureaucratic tendency becomes a technical and practical necessity, particularly during the more advanced stage of the development of the organization. In carrying out their roles, the executives acquire skills and knowledge in running the organization which the rank and file lack. The technical expertise so acquired further reinforces the legitimacy of commands coming from the top of the hierarchy. Ordinary members have to content themselves with the idea that those on top know better, and to leave unquestioned the content and rationale of the commands. Over time, the minority on top become organized around common vested interests through a web of personal relations solid enough to influence the succession of leaders. Democratic control thus undergoes a progressive diminution, and is ultimately reduced to an infinitesimal minimum. This "Iron law of oligarchy", which is implied by the very principle of organization, knows no ideological boundaries and operates in all organizations.

The power to govern, whether it is in the form of the state over the citizens, or an organization over its members, cannot be completely democratized or communalized according to the above three theorists. Government *by* the people would be psychologically, socially, and technically difficult to realize; and so is a classless society because there is always a class distinction in terms of power, if not in terms of wealth as well.

The responses to the Marxian analysis of class conflict made by Duverger and the elitist theorists can now be summarized. An unequal distribution of power in the state as well as other forms of organized power is seen as inevitable. This is their common starting point. The elitist theorists then proceed to argue for the existence of a concentration of power in the hands of an organized minority in all forms of organizations. Duverger presents an argument linking conflict to the asymmetrical relation of power. He is however vague on exactly who would constitute the parties to the conflict. What are the roles or positions that constitute the "organized power" on the one hand, and the "people who are subjected to it" on the other? This leads us to the theory proposed by Dahrendorf (1959).

Dahrendorf's (1959) theory of conflict is based firstly on a documented critique of Marx's analysis of class and class conflict and its inadequacy for modern industrial society. Secondly, it is formulated through an elaboration of Weber's analysis of *Herrschaft*, *Herrschaftsverband* and bureaucracy. In the preceding chapter, we have noted the Weberian concept of *Herrschaft* and how this is translated by Dahrendorf, among others, into "authority". Instead of power, authority is taken as the starting point in Dahrendorf's theory. This is clearly a legitimate starting point and requires no justification other than a demonstration of its fruitfulness. However, Dahrendorf does provide a justification which unfortunately appears to be unnecessary as well as misleading. The stated reason is that "power is essentially tied to the personality of individuals" and therefore power relations are "structurally fortuitous", whereas authority is always associated with social positions and roles (p. 166). The characterization of power as essentially tied to personality must be regarded as unwarranted in view of the fact that power in Weber's sense is a general construct of which authority is a more specific one. Power need not, and should not, be conceptualized as a personal attribute alone. Dahrendorf's use of authority as his starting point does not need to be justified by underplaying the power concept at all. Indeed, it is one of the merits of his analysis in demonstrating the significance of the authority relation as a determining factor of systematic social conflicts of a type that is germane to class conflicts. In any case, the choice of authority as the starting point necessarily follows from the very nature of *Herrschaftsverband*, which constitutes the unit of social organization in his theory of conflict. After this diversion, we can now turn to his main thesis.

A *Herrschaftsverband*, an imperatively coordinated association, is any social organization in so far as its members are, by virtue of a prevailing order, subject to authority relations. The most important examples of imperatively coordinated associations are the industrial enterprise and the state. An authority relation is one of domination-subjection, or super- and sub-ordination. Domination is the right to issue authoritative commands, and subjection is the duty to obey them. These are necessarily implied in Weber's conception of authority and are fully elaborated by Dahrendorf. The distribution of authority in an imperatively coordinated association is not only unequal, but more importantly it is dichotomous. Amongst the positions of dominance there is often considerable differentiation with the result that some positions are vested with more authority than others. Such differentiation, important as it is, leaves unaffected the existence of a borderline somewhere between those who have whatever little authority and the "outs". The latter can always be analytically and empirically identified in any imperatively coordinated association in so far as there are always people who cannot participate in the exercise of authority. Workers in an industrial enterprise are the subjected aggregates, and employers are the dominant category. In the state, "mere voters" stand in subjection to the high officials in the judiciary, legislative, and executive branches. However, in the industrial enterprise and particularly in the state, the existence of an administrative bureaucracy complicates the identification of the borderline between domination and subjection. Without going into Dahrendorf's elaborate analysis, his conclusion can be briefly stated. A bureaucracy is characterized by its double dependence: it merely administers, by virtue of its delegated authority, general orientations which are conceived and formulated *elsewhere and by others.* Despite such dependence, a series of arguments lead to the statement that bureaucratic roles are roles of domination. As a medium and instrument of domination, bureaucracy is at the disposal of whoever controls it. It is a mercenary reserve army of authority, so to speak.

Having established the dichotomous distribution of authority in imperatively coordinated associations, Dahrendorf then proposes that inherent in the positions of domination and subjection are antagonistic interests which are contradictory in substance and direction. These are respectively the interests in maintaining or changing the status quo. In so far as the interests are inherent in the authority relation, they are latent interests. They may become manifest interests when they are internalized and articulated by the individuals. In that event, the resulting antagonistic relation between the organized collectivities of individuals on both sides of the authority relation would give rise to group conflict of the class type (in the traditional sense of the concept of class — see Dahrendorf, 1959, pp. 201-205). Factors which would facilitate the transformation of latent interests into manifest interests include the blocking of social mobility within the imperatively coordinated association, presence of leaders and ideology, opportunity for communication, and freedom of coalition making.

Dahrendorf's theory then proceeds to the course of class conflict and articulates a number of factors which underlie the intensity and violence of conflict. The crucial element in this part of the theory are the twin concepts of superimposition and pluralism or dissociation. Within an imperatively coordinated association, the distribution of authority on the one hand, and that of rewards and prestige on the other, may be correlated to various degrees. When the distribution of authority is negatively or only marginally correlated with the distribution of rewards and prestige, a condition of dissociation or pluralism obtains, which would decrease the intensity of conflict. If however the authority relation and scales of socioeconomic status become congruent, a condition of superimposition results, which would increase the intensity of conflict. In the superimposition condition, so much is at stake that both of the opposing groups are likely to invest as much energy as they could in the conflict. A particular version of superimposition of this kind is furthermore related to the *violence* of conflict. This refers to the situation wherein subjection is bound up not only with a lower socioeconomic status but with a socioeconomic status so low that it is below a physiological subsistence minimum or poverty line. Such a condition of absolute deprivation coupled with exclusion from authority makes for greater violence, although the militant conflict motivation may give way to apathy and lethargy instead.

A second kind of superimposition — pluralism is obtained when the connection of the authority relations in different imperatively coordinated associations is considered. At one extreme is the condition of complete dissociation, wherein those who have authority in one imperatively coordinated association are excluded from authority in other associations. At the opposite end is complete superimposition. Here the authority relations of different associations are superimposed. The result would be a two-class society wherein authority is generalized across associations. In such a society, class conflicts of different associations become superimposed — the opponents in one association meet again in identical relations in another association — and hence more intense.

A third and final kind of superimposition — pluralism refers to the separation or combination of class conflict and other types of social conflict, such as the conflict between town and country, Protestants and Catholics. A condition of superimposition obtains when the conflict groups generated by the authority relation correspond to the conflict groups in other types of social conflict. This would then intensify the conflict.

In society where all the three kinds of superimposition are present, there is the likelihood that an intense and inclusive conflict will emerge which would split society into two. "Political class conflict, industrial class conflict, regional conflicts, conflicts between town and country, possibly racial and religious conflicts — all are superimposed so as to form a single and all-embracing antagonism" (Dahrendorf, 1959, p. 316). Approaching such an "ideal type" of situation was the capitalist society of the Marxian type. Among the modern post-capitalist countries, the totalitarian countries have a monistic social structure closest to being completely superimposed. There is, however, an important difference between the modern totalitarian and the Marxian capitalist countries. In the latter, Dahrendorf points out, superimposition was centred on the authority relation in the industrial enterprise. In the modern totalitarian country, the centre of power lies in the political party. The ruling and subjected groups of industry and the state are identical, with the orthodox political party exercising its power in both associations. Where the party ends, the subjected class begins.

On the other hand, the "free" countries in the post-capitalist era have moved away from complete superimposition. The institutional isolation of industry and industrial conflict, Dahrendorf suggests, has severed the superimposition of industrial and political authority, and thereby reduces the likelihood of social cleavage along the division of domination and subjection in industry. As a result of this and other factors, class conflicts are pluralistic.

Thus in the post-capitalist countries, whether totalitarian or free, the fronts of class conflict in imperatively coordinated associations can no longer be extrapolated from class conflict in the industrial enterprise, let alone the fronts of social conflict in general. This would necessitate a more general theory of class conflict than the Marxian theory in order to cover not only the industrial enterprise, but also other types of imperatively coordinated associations. Dahrendorf's theory of class conflict in terms of the authority relation in imperatively coordinated associations and the notion of superimposition is precisely such an attempt. It clarifies what Duverger has loosely termed "organized power" and "people who are subjected to organized power".

The importance of the issues relating to power and authority may not be immediately apparent in conflict situations. Many conflicts do not start off in the form of a struggle for power or authority, but rather in the form of a quarrel over some specific issues which are for the time-being remote from any question of authority. This may happen in class conflict as well as social conflict in general. In the course of conflict escalation, there is almost inevitably an expansion of the specific issues into questions of legitimacy and authority. The controversy over policy content becomes a battle over the decision right. The "outs" want to be in, while the "ins" resist the prospect of losing their power either in absolute or relative terms. The rhetoric may sound Utopian (e.g. "democratic participation", or "freedom to information", versus "autonomy", "understanding", or "moderation"), but the bone of contention is power. A vivid account of the escalation of conflict into issues of legitimacy and authority is given by Baldridge (1971) in relation to the campus conflict at New York University.

The relation between power and conflict can now be summarized.

Individuals and groups which do not stand in a relation of superordination and subordination come into conflict with one another as they struggle to attain or share power. This gives rise to conflict on the horizontal plane referred to by Duverger. Here the struggle for power arises for the reason that power is a scarce resource for the achievement of goals, including the goal of domination. This type of conflict resembles the Hobbesian state of nature.

Secondly, individuals and groups which stand in a relation of superordination and subordination have antagonistic interests which furnish the potential for conflict. Dahrendorf's theory of conflict provides us with a theoretical elaboration of how the latent conflict will be actualized and the course it may take. This type of conflict is what Duverger has called the conflict on the vertical plane. Conflict of this nature is irreducible so long as the relationships of superordination and subordination cannot be eliminated from the social context. The arguments put forth by the political elitist theorists in this section, as well as by Dahrendorf, Lenski, and Weslowski in the preceding section, suggest that the relationships of superordination and subordination are indeed inherent in the social context. The inescapable conclusion is that conflict on the vertical plane is irreducible; and is, in this sense, the fundamental conflict. An understanding of this type of conflict must be sought in the nature of superordination and subordination. The discussion so far has concentrated on the structural aspects and the inevitability of the relationships of superordination and subordination. We now turn to the more dynamic aspects of those relationships.

Simmel, whose analysis of social conflict is often quoted by sociologists and social psychologists alike, has discussed at great length the relationships of superordination and subordination (Simmel, 1950, pp. 181-303). Man, Simmel says, has an intimate dual relation to the principle of subordination. On the one hand, man wants to be dominated; on the other hand, he wants to oppose the leading power. Then, he wants to be liberated from subordination. Simmel has given a vivid account of the dynamics of liberation which is not dealt with by Dahrendorf's conflict theory. His central thesis is that the liberation from subordination is rarely an end in itself. One not only wants to have *freedom*, but also wants to use it for some purpose. After freedom is achieved, one wants to be equal to the superior; and *equality* is only the point of transition through which *superordination* can be gained.

Subordination, freedom, equality and superordination are therefore dynamically interrelated. The resemblance between Simmel's view and Nietzsche's discussion of freedom and justice (equality) is striking (see Chapter 2). From both points of view, conflict arising from a relationship of superordination and subordination would proceed through a series of phases. The first phase involves conflict over freedom; and then, conflict over equality or justice; and finally, conflict over supremacy. Thus, the type of conflict in question is not only fundamental in the sense that it is irreducible, but also because it is intimately related to the struggle for freedom and equality, which are central moral values. This brings us to Simmel's discussion of the intensification of conflict (Coser, 1956).

Simmel distinguishes between two types of conflict: that in which the goal is personal and subjective and that in which the object of contention has an impersonal, objective quality. Objectified conflicts are more radical and merciless than conflicts over immediately personal issues. There are two situations wherein objectification may occur. Firstly, it occurs when individuals enter as representatives of superindividual groups or ideas in which they have invested part of their personalities. Conflict assumes a more intransigent character as the participants act out their role of representing some collectivity. It is fought with more vigour since the participants are imbued with feelings of power derived from the power they ascribe to the collectivity. The situation in which the participants no longer engage as private individuals but as representatives of collectivities resembles the "intergroup" end of the interpersonal - intergroup continuum proposed by Tajfel and Turner (1979) and Tajfel (1978a).

Secondly, objectification occurs when the participants are imbued with a sense of respectability and self-righteousness. Thus when a group instigates conflict in the name of freedom, equality or truth, the members are filled with a good conscience and will fight all the more radically and mercilessly. It makes little difference here whether the morality of freedom, equality, or some other ideal cause is a disguise of self-interest, so long as the morality is believed by the participants as embodying some superindividual ideal. Austin (1979) has elaborated on this form of objectification in relation to triadic conflict.*

* Austin's treatment of justice and freedom departs from that given by Nietzsche and Simmel. A discussion of Austin's treatment would introduce a lengthy diversion and is unnecessary for the present purpose. The central point here is that moral righteousness intensifies conflict, regardless of whether it is more (as claimed by Austin) or less (as argued by Nietzsche and Simmel) authentic.

There is a further point about Simmel's discussion of equality which is worth noting. This concerns the question of equality to whom. The answer provided by Simmel is consistent with the prediction of social comparison theory (Festinger, 1954). The first objective is equality with the immediate superior. Hence, for instance, the resentment of the proletarian usually turns against the bourgeois instead of the highest classes. "For it is the bourgeois whom the proletarian sees immediately above himself, and who represents to him that rung of the ladder of fortune which he must climb first and on which, therefore, his consciousness and his desires for elevation momentarily concentrate" (Simmel, 1950, p. 275). This view has an important implication for the study of power change. It implies that the subordinate member of a power hierarchy would, in the nature of things, seek to improve his relative position in a gradual, step-by-step manner. This is precisely the proposal of power change advocated by Mulder (e.g. 1972 and 1975). I will examine this proposal in greater detail and suggest an alternative view in Chapter 9.

Power can therefore be related to conflicts on the horizontal and vertical planes in the manner which we have outlined above. Furthermore, power is also related to conflict in a more general way. The relationship is a reciprocal one and can be stated in two parts. Individuals and groups compare their relative power positions. Some of the reasons which call for power *comparison* are the same as those which call for social comparison: in the absence of clear physical standards, it is only through comparison with similar others that one can assess and evaluate one's strength. Quite apart from the needs for cognitive appraisal and social identity (for a detailed discussion of these needs, see Tajfel, 1974), there are at least two other considerations which render *power* comparison a matter of necessity. Individuals and groups need to find out their relative power positions in order to define whether their share of the privilege and prestige is fair or unfair. This is only an assumption but seems reasonable in the light of our earlier discussion of the relation between distributive inequality and the power structure (notably the views of Dahrendorf and Lenski). Secondly, people need to be convinced of their relative strength or weakness before they will accept, or continue to accept, their position in the superordination-subordination relationship. The question is how do people go about assessing their relative power. This brings us to the second part of the argument.

Power comparison is difficult to attain. The amorphous nature of power makes it hard to define, and impossible to quantify. It is always problematic, therefore, for individuals and groups to assess exactly their relative power; and consensus is rare, particularly in situations characterized by a high degree of social change. When an individual or a group suspects that it actually has got more power now than before, how would it verify the suspicion and convince others of the same? By fighting it out.

Unlike social comparison, power comparison is often made with turbulence through conflict. In this way, power generates conflict. Conflict, in turn, establishes a new order of power relation which prevents momentarily further conflict.

Simmel arrived at a similar conclusion concerning the reciprocal relation between power and conflict from a different starting point. How can conflict be prevented, he asked. The answer, as well as the conclusion in question, are elegantly stated as follows.

> The most effective prerequisite for preventing struggle, the exact knowledge of the comparative strength of the two parties, is very often attainable only by the actual fighting out of the conflict. (Coser, 1956, p. 133)

In conclusion, it should be clearly noted that the discussion in the present section is concerned with the relation between power and conflict, and not with conflict in general. Conflicts on the horizontal and vertical planes, as well as conflict arising from power comparison, are important in themselves but they do not exhaust the whole range of the problem. The work of Simmel (Coser, 1956), and the summary of studies given by Williams (1947) and Brickman (1974) are indicative of the diversity and complexity of the problem of social conflict. A recent collection of articles by social psychologists illustrates again the wide range of factors which are relevant to the problem (Austin and Worchel, 1979; see specially the contributions by Tajfel and Turner, 1979, and Triandis, 1979). By focusing on the roles of power in conflict we hope to demonstrate the importance of power in the analysis of conflict. The latter, as pointed out by Plon (1974) and Apfelbaum (1979), had not been accorded the right kind of attention by social psychologists.

5

Political Behaviourism and the Protean Nature of Power

Commenting on the history of political studies of power, Dahl (1968) notes that it has been dominated by speculative and impressionistic analyses until the 1950s. Of the few systematic empirical studies of power now available, most are said to be investigations of power relations in American communities. The distinctive feature of the approach adopted in the study of community power is its insistence on the empirical measurement of the distribution of power in a community. This is necessitated partly by a determination amongst the practitioners to develop a *science* of power, and partly by the need of providing an empirical answer to the controversy over the extent of power centralization. The result is a behaviouristic conception of power which identifies power with observable decision-making in public issues deemed by the researchers as important to the community. Within such a conceptual framework, it is possible to measure the relative power positions of individual group members by analysing their respective influence on the outcome of group decisions. The works of Dahl (1961) and Polsby (1963) are exemplifiers of empirical research guided by such a conception, the analytical and theoretical arguments of which are laid out in Dahl (1957).

The notion that power consists in the capacity of making important political decisions is of course not entirely new to political theorists. It forms, for instance, an integral part of the overall conception of power formulated by Lasswell (1948). When the decision-making conception of power developed by Dahl is compared to that by Lasswell, a clear shift towards *observable* decision-making power becomes obvious. This shift represents also an important development from Dahl's own initial working definition of power.

Lasswell's (1948) task is to understand the interaction of personality and power in order to provide an informed answer to the question of whether or not there are early experiences which, impinging upon a basic biological type, culminate in personalities oriented towards power. He draws heavily on the psychoanalytic literature in the analysis of personality; but unlike the later studies on authoritarianism, the positive and functional relation between personality and power is emphasized. Here we shall concern ourselves only with Lasswell's conception of power. Lasswell uses the term power to designate relations in which severe deprivations are expected to follow the breach of a pattern of conduct. The concept of influence is reserved for the relation which does not contain the expectation that severe deprivations will be inflicted on the deviant. However, "*any human situation can be converted into a power relation*" as soon as a participant invokes, or convincingly threatens to invoke, deprivation (Lasswell, 1948, p. 16). Thus power relations are not confined to the government, but are ubiquitous.

Lasswell then proceeds to relate power specifically to decision. A decision is a policy which is expected to be enforced against an obstructor by the imposing of extreme sanctions. From this it follows that the degree to which an actor influences a decision will be a measure of the *weight* of his power. Later, a formal definition of power is completed by introducing the concept of value, which means a desired or goal event. "*Power* is participation in the making of decisions: G has power over H with respect to the values k if G participates in the making of decisions affecting the k policies of H" (Lasswell and Kaplan, 1948, p. 223). The value concept also delineates the *range* and *scope* of power: the range is the list of values affected by the decision, whereas the scope is the degree to which the individual range values are influenced. Finally, the *domain* of power is defined in terms of the number of people affected by the decision.

Lasswell's conception of power in terms of decision and values, together with the corollaries of the weight, range, scope and domain of power, provides a series of consistently interrelated statements for the analysis of power in political science. Only some mathematical transformation would be necessary to operationalize the conception into a quantifiable paradigm such as the one proposed by Dahl (1957). On the conceptual level, the distinction between the speculative and the empirical is not unbridgeable. It should also be noted that although Lasswell has narrowed the power concept to the area of decision-making, he does not lose sight of the more general aspects of power. His insistence that any human situation is a potential power relation in the more general meaning of the term has already been pointed out. The idea of the transformation of one value into another one, which has been further elaborated in Lasswell and Kaplan (1948), generates a rich vocabulary for the description of the complex and dynamic nature of power. The decision-making approach developed later in community power studies has paid insignificant attention to this dynamic aspect. It seems appropriate that an overview of the decision-making approach to power in political science should present this earlier dynamic aspect in a summary form.

Eight values are listed by Lasswell and Kaplan (1948): power, respect, rectitude, affection, well-being, wealth, skill and enlightenment. They affect one another. Power can affect the other values as well as being affected by them. The influence of power over respect is called *homage*. Power may influence rectitude or the moral process by the *inculcation* of a moral code. The influence of power on affection is called *fealty*, while that on well-being is *compulsion*. Power can acquire wealth, such as by taxation or the granting of franchises, and the result is known as *polinomic power*. The influence of power over skill is *directorship*, as for example when a union leader directs the exercise of skills of his members. Finally, *indoctrination* is said to occur when enlightenment is influenced through power. Conversely, the power process may be influenced by the other values. The influence of respect is *councillorship*; rectitude, *mentorship*; affection, *personal influence*; well-being, *violence*; wealth, *ecopolitical power*; skill, *expertness*; and enlightenment, *advisory influence*. Lastly, the influence of power on power is *political power* in the narrow sense, such as the veto power of the president. This results in a complex picture of the manifestation and exercise of power, as well as the ways in which the power process may be influenced.

The one- and two-dimensional views of power

Dahl (1957) initially sets out with an "intuitive" definition of power which at first sight is similar to Weber's: "A has power over B to the extent that he can get B to do something that B would not otherwise do" (pp. 202-203). The similarity lies in the overcoming of resistance. The difference between the two definitions is more striking, however. As already noted, Weber defines power positively in the sense of enacting one's will. This is in line with Russell's definition of power as the production of intended effect, Hobbes' present means of procuring some future good, as well as the achievement of some positive goal implicit in Machiavelli's conception of power. In Dahl's intuitive definition, power is primarily negative in so far as it is identified foremost with daunting another person's will — which may not necessarily be the same as carrying out one's own will. The overcoming of resistance if necessary, which is a secondary feature in Weber's definition, becomes in effect the primary and exclusive element of Dahl's definition.

Dahl (1957) then defines the *amount* of power of an actor in terms of the magnitude of a change in the probability of compliance which the actor can instigate. Note that it is the probability change, not the probability *per se*, that is the criterion of power. Mathematically, the amount of power is expressed as follows.

> Let the amount of power of A over a regarding a's compliance x be M (from *Macht*), then $M = P_1 - P_2$, where $P_1 = P(a,x/A,w)$, which reads "the probability that a will do x if A does w", and $P_2 = p(a,x/A,\bar{W})$, which reads "the probability that a will do x if A does not do w".

In this way, the amount of power is coordinated to the change of probability of eliciting compliance by the performance of certain acts. From this point of view, the locus of power can and must be traced back to certain acts emitted by person A. At first sight, this approach seems reasonable enough: for unless person A has acted, it would be hard to gauge the amount of power he has. Indeed, as we will examine fully in Chapter 7, this is also precisely the starting point adopted by K. Lewin in the analysis of interpersonal power.

In its general form, Dahl's formulation can draw our attention to some very interesting behavioural aspects of power. One important class of behaviour is communication: threats, promises, distractive and issue-confusing statements, bluffs, etc. Power is not a static or fixed entity, it depends on the creative behaviour of the person. This is one of the reasons why Machiavelli was so optimistic about *virtù*. Much of real politics, for instance, is talk, and talk. There is a definite advantage in locating the source of power in behaviour. Nevertheless this approach is inherently restrictive, particularly in the form elaborated by Dahl.

The acts which interest Dahl and his associates most are those of individual actors which affect the *decision-making* of the group or the community. Using the above formula, and by introducing a few restrictive assumptions, the respective powers of individual actors over a series of group decisions can be quantified. When the conditions in a group allow, or are assumed to allow, power comparability, the quantified findings can then be used to rank the power positions of the group members. Thus in a study of the American Senate reported in Dahl (1957), Dahl *et al.* (1956) were able to rank the power positions of 34 Senators who held office continuously from 1946 to 1954 by analysing their roll-call votes in relation to the final outcomes of the Senate's decisions.

The same behavioural conception and methodology have been applied to a more complex set of phenomena, namely, the distribution of power in the community. In "Who Governs?", Dahl (1961) measured the distribution of power in New Haven by several methods, the most crucial of which was the determination of the extent to which particular individuals had influenced events in three issue areas. Decisions made in each issue area were examined. For each individual who had participated directly in the making of these decisions, a tally was kept of the number of successful vetoes or initiatives and the number of failures. Participants were then ranked according to the relative frequencies of their successes. The main empirical finding was that decision-making power was pluralistically distributed among the individuals in the community, rather than concentrated in the hands of a few. Dahl found that each issue area had its own set of "influentials". It was assumed that the results from the chosen issue areas could be generalized to the community at large. Dahl claimed to have uncovered who *really* influenced decisions.

Two criticisms, one minor and one major, from among political scientists have been voiced against the behaviouristic decision-making approach to power. If power were to be observed through the exercise of a certain act and its effects, the exercise itself would incur cost to the user. In order to effect a probability change of compliance of a certain magnitude, one actor may have to incur great cost to himself whereas another actor can achieve the same change with relatively little cost. Since the cost may vary among various actors, the cost factor has to be considered before the power positions of the actors can be compared or ranked. This argument has been articulated by Harsanyi (1962), who also extends the notion of cost in an attempt to conceptualize the *strength* of an actor's power over another. The greater the opportunity cost which A can inflict upon B for noncompliance, the greater will be

A's strength of power over B. In a series of mathematical transformations, Harsanyi concludes that the *amount* of power in Dahl's sense varies directly with the *strength* of power but the relationship is not a linear one.

The substantive contribution made by Harsanyi lies in the explanatory potential of his cost analysis. Although the concept of the strength of power is descriptive, Harsanyi argues that because the cost factor as perceived by B could constitute a determinant of B's incentive to comply, an analysis of the cost pertaining to B would acquire some explanatory value. Furthermore, since the strength of A's power is itself a function of the cost *he* is prepared to bear, the cost factor (pertaining to A) would be relevant to the explanation of the strength of power which A can or will exercise.

The "economism" of cost analysis seems persuasive enough. The strength or amount of power surely cannot be equated with the probability change alone. It is also necessary to look behind the observable behaviour of both the agent and the target of power to uncover how much cost is involved in the power relationship. The classical definitions of power offered by Hobbes, Russell and Weber must also be modified accordingly.

As will be discussed in Chapter 7, cost is a central element in a number of social psychological analyses of power. Cost is intimately related to the principle of reinforcement. It is thus not surprising to find that the analysis of power carried out in relation to the reinforcement principle would assign a conspicuous role to the cost factor. A notable example of such an analysis is the one by Thibaut and Kelley (1959). A more refined conception of cost is the idea of "subjective utility" which plays an important part in the analysis of social influence by Tedeschi *et al.* (1973).

Another, major, criticism of Dahl's decision-making conception of power comes from Bachrach and Baratz (1962). In their aptly titled paper, "Two faces of power", they put forth their argument succinctly in the following manner.

> Of course power is exercised when A participates in the making of decisions that affect B. But power is also exercised when A devotes his energies to creating or reinforcing social and political values and institutional practices that limit the scope of the political process to public consideration of only those issues which are comparatively innocuous to A. To the extent that A succeeds in doing this, B is

> prevented, for all practical purposes, from bringing to the fore any issues that might in their resolution be seriously detrimental to A's set of preferences. (p. 948)

When a person or group — consciously or unconsciously — creates or reinforces barriers to the public airing of policy conflicts, that person or group, according to the authors, has power. It is not even necessary for the person or group to participate in decision-making, since the occasion of decision-making never arises in the first place. To distinguish this face of power from the power of winning a decision, the authors coined the term "nondecision-making" power.

Quoting Schattschneider (1960), Bachrach and Baratz (op. cit.) point out that nondecision-making power is inherent in all forms of political organization. Organization is the mobilization of bias: some issues are organized into politics while others are organized out. What has been organized out is not so easily observable; and if we look only at the decisions made by individuals, we can never find it. As the reader may recall from our earlier discussion of the work of C. Wright Mills (Chapter 4), the ability of relating personal troubles to the public issues of the social structure, and of translating public indifference into public issues, would require an exercise of the "sociological imagination".

The two faces of power are therefore decision-making and nondecision-making. A parallel and more general distinction is made by Hamilton (1977) between "interactive power" and "environmental power". The former involves in most cases some direct communication and interaction between the two parties; the latter is exercised by the manipulation of the environment or by altering the other's perception of his environment. Cartwright's (1965) concept of "ecological control" bears a close resemblance to environmental and nondecision-making power.

The argument of and the substance behind the two faces of power pose a formidable challenge to the one-sided *decisionism* of the decision-making approach to power. To the extent that it calls attention to the hidden face of power which may not be overtly or directly observable, Bachrach and Baratz's conception of power also undermines the validity of Dahl's political behaviourism. However, their subsequent thinking and empirical work both contain strong elements of behaviourism and even decisionism.

In Bachrach and Baratz (1963), they delimit the existence of power by stipulating the following as its necessary conditions. There must be conflict of interests between A and B; that B actually complies with A's demands; and finally, that A can threaten to invoke sanctions. From this perspective, power is equated with compliance produced by the exercise of sanction in a conflict situation. This conception actually resembles closely the picture painted by Dahl. The new dimension is, of course, nondecision-making power. Yet nondecision is later defined as "a decision that results in suppression or thwarting of a latent or manifest challenge to the values of interests of the decision-maker" (Bachrach and Baratz, 1970, p. 44). The process of nondecision-making therefore consists of observable (which may not be overt) manoeuvres resulting in the scope of actual decision-making being limited to "safe" issues, e.g. the use of sanctions against the initiator of a potentially threatening demand; cooptation to stifle opposition without having to alter policy; the mobilization of existing bias in the political system (a norm, precedent, rule or procedure) to squash the opposition such as by branding the demand for change as "red" or by establishing additional rules and procedures for processing the demand. In other words, nondecision-making, the hidden face of power, constitutes but another set of *strategies* for deploying power (see, for example, the classification scheme on p. 54 of their book).

Both Dahl's and Bachrach and Baratz's views represent rigorous attempts to conceptualize power in a manner which would render it amenable to empirical investigation. In trying to identify power through the analysis of the actual outcomes of decision- or nondecision-making, these authors have provided a viable alternative to the earlier, reputational approach (e.g. Hunter, 1953) in the study of community power structure. This alternative enables them to examine more closely the powers that be, and not just the power that people think there is. However, despite this relative advance over the earlier approach, there is a pluralistic bias which is inherent in the behaviouristic approach. As pointed out by Walton (1966) in a review of over 33 empirical community power studies, the sort of community power structure being portrayed is a function of the methodological approach. Inasmuch as the reputational approach tends to discover pyramidal power structures, the decision-making approach tends to find factional and coalitional power structures.

More importantly, on the conceptual level, certain aspects of power which cannot be encompassed within political behaviourism have been left out. This brings us to the "Three-dimensional view" of power.

The three-dimensional view of power

A recent attempt to relax the behavioural constraints comes from S. Lukes. In "Power: A Radical View", Lukes (1974) criticizes Dahl's and Bachrach and Baratz's views as one- and two-dimensional respectively. Among his substantive criticisms, two are particularly impressive. The first is what he calls the bias of methodological individualism which misplaces the focus of power processes on a series of individually chosen acts instead of locating it in the "socially structured and culturally patterned behaviour of groups, and practices of institutions" (p. 22). He argues that a more adequate view of power should consider the many ways in which manifest and potential issues are being influenced, through individuals' decisions and nondecisions, as well as through the operation of social forces and institutional practices. He subsequently labels this type of view the "three-dimensional" view of power.

Interestingly, the same criticism of methodological individualism is levelled at Weber's definition of power, presumably because the latter is phrased in the singular tense conveying the impression that Weber was talking about individuals. That may be a valid criticism so far as the phraseology of the *definition* is concerned; but unfortunately Lukes does not substantiate his criticism with respect to Weber's *analysis* of power. Lukes set out an exposition of methodological individualism and its application to Weber's method, amongst others, in a former work (Lukes, 1973). Indeed, Weber has advocated that sociology can only proceed from the actions of one or more individuals (the hypothetical actor) and must therefore adopt strictly individualistic methods. His analysis of action is explicitly premised on the individual's intention and ability to take into account the behaviour of others, all of which, according to Weber, must be taken into any sociological account. Such a stance would deserve, rightly or wrongly, the criticism of methodological individualism, and puts Weber in sharp contrast to Marx, and particularly Durkheim.

It seems to me, however, that once the analysis is under way, it does not take long for Weber to open up and attend to those unique properties that emerge from the macro or collective level. The final picture that he produces, of power as well as of bureaucracy, is contained in a historical and sociological perspective wherein the "socially structured and culturally patterned behaviour of groups, and practices of institutions" occupy a central place. The point is, therefore, that the criticism of methodological individualism cannot apply with full rigour to the entire span of Weber's analysis. The debate between methodological individualism and methodological collectivism is too involved for us to go into any length beyond remarking that inasmuch as a naive methodological individualism cannot serve sociology and *social* psychology, neither can a fixated methodological collectivism. And certainly Weber is not a naive methodological individualist in his analysis of power.

Lukes' (1974) next criticism which we shall consider is that both the one- and two-dimensional views have associated power with and only with the presence of observable conflict of interests. Consequently, this has left out the most effective and insidious use of power: for "A may exercise power over B by getting him to do what he does not want to do, but he also exercises power over him by influencing, shaping or determining his very wants. Indeed, is it not the supreme exercise of power to get another or others to have the desires you want them to have . . .?" (p. 23). By shaping or determining the desires and wants of the community, no issue would ever arise in the first place and consequently there is no need to resort to nondecision-making or decision-making. But power is still there, only that it now works through the consensual values which it has created. Indeed, as Berger and Luckmann (1967) have stressed, power in society includes the power to produce reality. This power, Mills (1951) and Marcuse (1964) observe, has become more manipulative in the sense that it is wielded in an indirect, anonymous and more pleasant manner unbeknown to the people who do not participate in it. In this third-dimensional realm of power, no resistance needs to be overcome because resistance has been removed. Thus the identification of power should not capitulate on the overcoming of resistance.

By way of parentheses, Lukes lays the same charge on Weber as well, this time because Weber has included the overcoming of resistance in his definition of power. It is true that as D'Entrives (1967) has pointed out, Weber's conception of power, as opposed to authority, emphasizes the effectiveness of realizing one's will even to the extent of over-powering others despite resistance (see Chapter 3 in this volume). Such a definition therefore explicitly relates power to the potentiality of conflict; and is in this regard sharply opposed by Parsons' definition of power as a generalized capacity for the attainment of collective goals (see Chapter 4). However, power to Weber does not stipulate on the presence of resistance. As we have noted on a few occasions, Weber used the power concept in a general way which is not restricted to the overt or direct overcoming of resistance. Legitimacy, a subset of power, would cover those power relationships in which resistance is absent.

Lukes seems to have misidentified "conflict of interests" with "resistance". This is unfortunate because the concept of interests is central to his three-dimensional, radical view of power. Before examining the concept of interests, the misidentification in question can be briefly stated. Conflict of interests, of course, is accompanied by resistance when both parties are conscious of the antagonistic nature of their interests. When there is no such consciousness, conflict of interests in the "objective" or from an external observer's point of view may not be accompanied by resistance at all. Thus the notion of "false consciousness" comes in play, referring to, for instance, the antagonism of one working class group against another working class group instead of against the capitalist class. Resistance, on the other hand, may arise even though the power wielder is actually acting in the best interest of the other person. This can easily occur when the power process is perceived to be threatening to the person's sense of freedom or autonomy, as most parents would know from their experience of the contrary behaviour of their children.

The absolutely basic common core to, or primitive notion lying behind, all talk of power is the notion that (person) A in some way affects (person) B" (Lukes, op. cit., p. 26). Not every instance of affecting, according to Lukes, should be regarded as an exercise of power — but only those which are significant in some way. The criterion of significance is interests: when person A affects person B in a manner contrary to B's interests, A is said to exercise power over B. Unlike the two-dimensional view of Bachrach and Baratz, which admits only observable (overt and covert) conflict of interests, Lukes' view also admits latent conflict of interests. The distinguishing feature of the "third" dimension is therefore made up of *latent* conflict of interests. So the crucial question is this: how do we know there is a conflict of interests if it is latent? If an observer insists that there is a conflict of interests between A and B which neither A nor B would admit, who are we to believe?

Lukes does not seem to have an answer, but his position is quite clear. By way of parentheses, he states that he "would maintain that any view of power rests on some *normatively* specific conception of interests" (p. 35, added emphasis). This is because the notion of interests is an irreducibly evaluative notion. Accordingly, there are three normative conceptions of interests: the liberal, reformist and radical conceptions.

The liberal takes men as they are and relates their interests to what they actually want or prefer. The reformist also relates men's interests to what they want or prefer, but allows that this may be revealed in more indirect and sub-political ways. "The radical, however, maintains that men's wants may themselves be a product of a system which works against their interests, and, in such cases, relates, the latter to what they would want and prefer, were they able to make the choice" (p. 34). Lukes suggests that there is a one-to-one correspondence between these conceptions of interests and the three views of power. The one-dimensional view of power presupposes a liberal conception of interests, the two-dimensional view a reformist conception, and the three-dimensional view a radical conception.

According to the radical conception, a conflict of interests can exist where none is observable. This presumption can be a licence for all kinds of arbitrary attributions which in their extreme form are totally removed from verifiability as well as beyond the experiential and cognitive imagination of the individuals concerned. One can always invoke some bit of Freudian psychology where the Marxian analysis of interests begins to sound bizarre to the ordinary man. *However*, the radical conception is no more a licence for arbitrariness than the liberal conception. Take for instance a "happy" serf's perception of his interests. A naturalistic or unobtrusive assessment would probably indicate that the serf is contented with his lot. On the other hand, an obtrusive assessment made after the serf's consciousness has been raised would yield a different picture. Which one is more scientific? Is the arbitrariness involved in the latter assessment necessarily more than that involved in the former assessment? It would be hard to answer in the affirmative.

As pointed out in Chapter 4, it is one of C. W. Mills' arguments that the deprivation of power is often associated with a psychological deprivation. Subordinates can perceive their situation experientially. Most of them, however, are unable to relate their personal troubles to public issues. Because of this, they are not being able to define their "real" interests in terms of the social structure. If we take objective poverty as an index of power deprivation, Mills' argument receives some support from sociolinguistic studies of the poor.

Within the same culture, the poor and the powerless speak a different language from the rich and the powerful (Lind and O'Barr, 1979). The political implication of this is spelt out by Mueller (1973) as follows. The language of the hard-core poor is a restricted speech code. The categories of his language allow for a grasp of the here and now; but they cannot be used in a reflective way and they do not permit an analysis, hence a transcendence, of his social context. In narrowing his ability to discriminate, to conceptualize, and to analyse, the language of the poor renders his condition more acceptable to him. At the same time, it inhibits the development of his political consciousness.

In view of the above discussion, the radical conception of interests is less naive than the liberal and reformist conceptions. They all contain a certain amount of arbitrariness, which is inevitable because the very notion of interests, as Lukes points out, is evaluatively irreducible. Every view of power must also by implication necessarily embody a certain form of moral appraisal.

The three-dimensional view of power, I believe, is superior to either the one- or two-dimensional view. There are several reasons for holding this belief. The three-dimensional view presupposes a conception of interests which is, as just noted, less naive than those presupposed by the other two views. Another reason has already been cited from Lukes' work: a person's wants are socially conditioned, hence it is pertinent to go beyond decision-making and nondecision-making to examine how the social conditioning works and reinforces the existent pattern of dominance.

Related to the second reason is what Lukes calls the methodological individualism of the one- and two-dimensional views, which misplaces the locus of the power process in the acts of individuals. It is not so much that individuals and their actions are irrelevant to the identification of the locus of power. The point is that there is a "super-individual" locus of power which is beyond the scope of the one- and two-dimensional views, and which is of fundamental importance. This point is well articulated by Westergaard and Resler (1975). Non-decisions involve more or less direct and deliberate manipulation by a well-placed group to mobilize bias or pre-empt decisions. However, in any society, the life chances of people are not so much the result of somebody somewhere making a series of decisions or nondecisions to that effect, but largely because certain social mechanisms, principles, and assumptions are taken for granted. No strings need to be pulled, but the outcome is still that *some* people passively enjoy advantage and privilege because of "the way things work", and because those ways are not challenged. Power derives more from the routine application of effectively unchallenged assumptions than from the manifest dominance of one group over others in open conflict. A major source of power for dominant groups is simply the routine operation of social institutions. This is part and parcel of the institutionalization of power referred to earlier when we discussed the works of Russell (Chapter 1), Mills and Lenski (Chapter 4).

To a large extent, th Proteus-like nature of power must already imply that a behaviouristic analysis, rigorous as it is, cannot be adequate for the task. The inadequacy is revealed most clearly at the community or societal level where the transformation and operation of power are taking place in a historical context. A slice of what is observable can only yield a trace of the mist but hardly the underlying current. So long as the slice is made up of the acts of *individuals*, the personalized locus of power is overemphasized out of proportion and to the neglect of the anonymous and superindividual locus of power. It is as if we were asked to take a flight back to the Hobbesian state of nature, which by virtue of its ahistorical nature can only be examined through an individualistic mode of analysis.

The individualistic mode of analysis has also been found to be inadequate at a seemingly more simple level of analysis, namely, the analysis of power in families. Earlier studies have relied on the self-report (mostly the self-reports of the wives) method to decide which member in the family has more or less power. It turned out that when the self-reports of different members in the family were compared, little consensus was found. Investigators then went into the families to see things for themselves by observing how family members would interact and reach decisions. Several observational indices were used: the number of decisions won by a given member, the proportion of directive or interruptive acts emitted by the members, who talked the most and initiated the most discussion, etc. Methodologically, the investigators were as rigorous as Dahl, if not more so. The number of studies is too numerous for us to examine here. A representative review of the methodological issues by Olson and Cromwell (1975) reaches the following conclusion: "Except for the latter measure [the number of statements in which a spouse accepts the instructions from the other], these all appear to tap interactional behaviour that might better be labelled as individual assertiveness than power" (p. 149). An earlier comment by Ryder (1970) is even more pertinent, namely, that "In dyadic (or higher order) interaction, power does not necessarily reside with anyone: the interactional system may just operate as a system" (p. 52).

Too much of the current social psychological thinking on power proceeds from the same individualistic premise as political behaviourism. To a certain extent, the individualistic mode of analysis is appropriate to the kind of situations contrived by social psychologists, which usually have no past, no future, and only a transient present. Furthermore, the preoccupation with the dyad would make it only natural that the analysis starts from the individual. As will be discussed more fully in Chapter 7, the field-theoretical analysis of power is the most notable example of this mode of thinking. In line with the Gestaltist perspective, the field-theoretical analysis of power is remarkably comprehensive. Not only does it attend to the effect or outcome of power (which is conceptualized as "influence" in general), it also covers the bases and processes of power. For the analysis of the power between a dyad in an ahistorical situation, the field-theory has done a fine job. Nevertheless, it rarely reaches beyond the two-dimensional view of power.

The cumulative debate outlined in the present chapter indicates again the necessity of a broad perspective on power when we formulate the problem, design our research, and analyse the data. Whatever the unique and distinctive quality of the social psychology of power may be, it is important to situate it in relation to a wider framework such as the one provided by the three-dimensional view.

III

Power in Psychology

6

Psychological Views of the Power of the Individual Person

Introduction

Fortunately or unfortunately, contemporary psychology has largely surrendered the scientific study of society to other academic disciplines. In so far as psychology has ventured into the analysis of society, the enthusiasm stems largely from psychoanalysis and Marxism, with B. F. Skinner representing some sort of a third force. It is somewhat of a paradox that in this regard, social psychology has been less keen than other branches of psychology. The advent of psychological social psychology, as mentioned in the Introduction of this book, has kept social psychologists sufficiently preoccupied with the individual, the dyad and the small group. The general retreat from the analysis of society and societal processes by psychology (environmental/ecological and community psychology are minor exceptions) has one immediate implication for the present and the next chapter. The Rationalist-Utopian distinction which has been discussed and employed in Chapters 3 and 4 is no longer fully applicable to the following exhibition of the psychological views of power. Instead, a broad distinction will be made between those views which pertain to the power of the individual person and those which address to the power relation between people. They are to be dealt with in Chapters 6 and 7 respectively. Such a distinction corresponds broadly to that made by Minton (1967) between latent and manifest power.

At the most general level, the power of the individual person is conceived as a latent, dispositional construct. Power predisposes an individual to feel, perceive, and act in a certain manner. At a more specific level, three varieties of power constructs can be discerned in the literature. Not all the authors whose works will be discussed below use the power concept explicitly. Their inclusion is thus a matter of interpretation on my part.

(1) Power as a *motivational* construct. Typical of this are the notions of power striving (Adler, 1956), power motive and the experience of power (Winter, 1973; McClelland, 1975), and effectance (White, 1959). (2) Power as a *cognitive* construct. This includes personal causation (de Charms, 1968), locus of control (Phares, 1977), and self-efficacy (Bandura, 1977). (3) Power as a *behavioural* construct. Heider (1958) uses the power concept as part of the "can" factor in his naive psychological analysis of the actions of an individual. In Skinner's experimental analysis of behaviour, the concept of stimulus (Skinner, 1938), has acquired an explanatory role which seems to be equivalent to that of power.

The above classification is not supposed to be exhaustive. There are realms of human experience which are beyond the conventional motivation/cognitive/behavioural taxonomy, such as spiritual experience and consciousness. Psychological constructions of the power of the individual cover the latter's heart, mind, and body – but not the soul. Power as a spiritual construct remains to be developed, or to be uncovered from the works of the old masters. As such, it is beyond the scope of this book.

Instead of organizing the present chapter entirely according to the above classification, I shall centre the discussion on three major themes. Firstly, I shall discuss the presumption that power corrupts, a presumption which seems to me to be unduly widespread in psychological thinking. I shall try to argue that as much as power corrupts, power also uplifts and enriches life; and that powerlessness, no less, corrupts too. Following this, the discussion will centre on the generality of the power motive and its diverse behavioural correlates and ways of experiencing power. These two themes will cover materials mainly drawn from the motivational and cognitive aspects of power. The third and final theme is to review the concepts of stimulus and power used by Skinner and Heider in their respective analyses of individual behaviour and action.

Power corrupts?

The subject index to the Complete Psychological Works of Sigmund Freud lists only two entries under power. "Power of the ruling class", the first of the two, occurs in a discussion of war wherein Freud bitterly condemned the political power-hunger that characterizes the governing class. The second entry, "Will to power", contains a number of references relating to Freud's disagreement with Adler's formulation of the subject. Lief (1972) suggests three reasons for the neglect by non-Adlerian psychoanalysts of the explicit treatment of power. The first, and most obvious, reason is a deliberate avoidance because Adler made so much of the issue of power. Another reason lies in the very nature of psychoanalytic therapy with its emphasis on the one-to-one relationship in which power is essentially a matter of transference and counter-transference but hardly discussed in terms of power. The third reason is perhaps the most revealing. Bernfeld (Jones, 1954) is quoted as writing that Freud at the age of twelve fantasized that he would become a cabinet minister, but five years later he decided to switch from his desire to wield power over men to a search of power over nature by becoming a scientist. Freud's relations with his colleagues and students, however, give credence to the belief that he never gave up his *earlier* power drive. Despite abundant references to power situations such as the oedipal conflict, toilet training, the reality principle, transference and countertransference, power is not labelled and discussed as such by Freud. For a concrete treatment of power, let us turn to Alfred Adler.

Ansbacher and Ansbacher, editors of Adler (1956), point out that Adler had tended from the beginning toward a theory of the unity and self-consistency of the personality. Such a theory would require a prepotent dynamic force which, in the case of Adler's system, is expressed in the notion of a striving for superiority, that is, from below to above. Every individual is supposed to strive for superiority once the physiological needs have been satisfied. Such a striving, which is postulated as ceaseless and universal, develops in the child as a compensation for his feelings of inferiority which are rooted in his weak constitution and impressions of insecurity and deficiency.

The meaning of superiority, however, has undergone an important change in the writings of Adler. According to Ansbacher and Ansbacher, Adler was initially preoccupied with the neurotic character. When he generalized from the neurotic to the normal person, the latter was pictured as behaving in the same way as the former, only less clearly so and to a lesser degree. In other words, the normal and the neurotic exhibit the same striving for superiority, and differ only in the degree of the striving. Superiority, then, was intended to mean self-enhancement, which in turn was characterized in terms of the drive for power and the enhancement of self-esteem. Adler's conception of power appears for the most part in *Menschenkenntnis*, where he spoke of the goal of power (*Machtziel*) as the most important determinant of behaviour and psychological phenomena.

> Behaviour is determined by a goal, one which shows itself as nothing other than a goal of superiority, of power, of over-powering others . . . All psychological phenomena are united in an inseparable relationship; on the one hand they come under the law of society and on the other hand the striving of the individual for power and superiority. (Adler, 1956, pp. 113-114)

To Adler, the striving for power was as the sexual libido to Freud; and that what Freud found in the unconscious was according to Adler not a mainspring, but a misguided striving for power. In this and other aspects which divided Adler and Freud, Adler had a system of his own which cannot be regarded as a mere distortion of psychoanalysis (cf. Ellenberger, 1970).

Nor did Adler merely replace Freud's libido with Nietzsche's will to power, although at this particular point in the development of his individual psychology, Adler was indeed very much in the shadow of the earlier Nietzsche. It has been pointed out in Chapter 2 that Nietzsche later transformed the will to power into a monistic standard of moral evaluation, and assigned the role of a unitary psychological principle to the will to power. No such transformation occurred in Adler's conception of the striving for power, and Adler continued to use the concept to mean the striving for competitively based superiority. Furthermore, in his later revision of individual psychology, Adler assigned only a secondary role to the striving for power.

In Adler's later revision of individual psychology, the focus was shifted from the neurotic to the normal character. The criteria of normality now consisted of not only a quantitative difference from abnormality, but also a difference in kind. This change was reflected in the new meaning of superiority, which now meant perfection. Thus, the mentally healthy person would still strive for self-enhancement, although he does so to a lesser extent than the neurotic person; beyond that, it is the unique character of the healthy person to strive for perfection. Perfection here refers to the overcoming of internal and external obstacles in the completion of a task, and more importantly, to the furtherance of *social* interests. It transcends self-enhancement in two important ways. Unlike self-enhancement, perfection is not self-centred or self-bound, and is oriented towards social cooperation rather than competition or exploitation. In these two respects, the striving for perfection is in sharp contrast to the striving for power.

From Adler's point of view, physiological drives, the striving for self-enhancement, and the striving for perfection together constitute a hierarchy of dynamic forces ascending in that order. This hierarchical arrangement of drives and strivings, as pointed out by Ansbacher and Ansbacher, was a forerunner of the hierarchy of prepotent motivations which was elaborated later by A. H. Maslow.

The striving for power in the Adlerian sense naturally conflicts with the striving for perfection. The conflict arises from a consideration of the kind of social relations that would obtain when individuals who strive for power interact with one another. Adler reached the conclusion which is identical to the Hobbesian state of nature. The occurrence of group violence and the resulting atrocities were *then* interpreted as resulting from people's striving for power. Such a reasoning involves a dubious logic: individuals striving for power would lead to antagonism and mutual opposition, all antagonism and opposition are then attributed to their striving for power. The sad events of the First World War were seen as the outcome of this striving. In a paper which was probably written soon after World War One and was first translated into English in 1966, Adler (1966) spelt out what he considered to be the false ideal of personal power and its conflict with the highest ideal of social interest: "The striving for personal power is a disastrous delusion and poisons man's living together. Whoever desires the human community must renounce the striving for power over others" (p. 169). Elsewhere, in a discussion of the difference between socialism and Bolshevism, Adler deplored the striving for power in the political arena because of its tendency to abuse social interest. Every intellectual and every religious uprising is said to have been directed against the striving for power. But it has always ended again in the thirst for dominance. Social interest is transformed from an end into a means in the struggle for power. In the case of Bolshevism, it enforced socialism by violence, and its rule was based on the possession of power. "Thus its fate is sealed. While this party and its friends seek ultimate goals which are the same as ours, the intoxication of power has seduced them" (Adler, 1956, p. 457).

Power, as conceived by the later Adler, can only corrupt the individual and the community. A similarly negative view of power is followed by the well-known authoritarian personality studies

(Frenkel-Brunswik, 1948; Adorno *et al.*, 1950). Although these studies did not start from Adler but from Freud, both the empirical characterization and the etiology of the authoritarian personality are more or less replica of Adler's treatment of the striving for power. In a parallel manner, Maslow (1943a) contrasted the drive for power of the authoritarian character with the drive for "strength" of the democratic character. The authoritarian person is one whose basic needs of safety, belongingness, or love have been thwarted and who has come to view the world as a jungle peopled with threatening wild animals. Power would become indispensably important for the authoritarian person both in his dealings with the surrounding world and as the means of assuaging his psychological needs. In contrast to the authoritarian person, the democratic person has no need for power; and when he does have power, he tends to use it less for personal needs and more for the needs of the group over which he has power. He does not seek to have power over people, but "power" over problems. Maslow called the latter capacity for solving problems which are external to a person's psyche "strength".

In a similar vein, Clark (1971) called attention to the pathos of power. As pointed out by Rogow and Lasswell (1963), the complicated "check and balance" system in the American political machinery can at least be partly attributed to a widely-held belief in the corrupting nature of power. Sorokin and Lunden (1959) undertook to demonstrate that power corrupts and absolute power corrupts absolutely. Using historical data from a number of countries, they were able to show that kings, monarchs, popes, and generally, people in positions of power, had left a record of murder and other serious crimes that was many many times more than the crime rate of the population at large — unless their power had been effectively checked. The mock prison experiment by Zimbardo *et al.* (1977) provides a dramatic demonstration of the same theme. In this experiment, volunteer subjects were assigned randomly the role of either a guard or a prisoner. The events which ensued in the mock prison led to the increasingly authoritarian and brutal use of their power by the guards, so much so that the experiment had to be terminated ahead of schedule. On a more modest scale, Kipnis (1972) showed experimentally that when given the power, the experimental subjects became much more active in using it to manipulate their subordinates, and viewed them as less worthy, less interesting, and deserving of their fate.

That power corrupts can hardly be negated. Yet one must at the same time consider the possibility that inasmuch as power corrupts, power also uplifts and enriches life. Furthermore, and no less, powerlessness also corrupts. All these three facets, of course, are basic tenets in Nietzsche's will to power. Having considered the views which bear on the theme that power corrupts, those views pertaining to the other two themes should now be considered.

It would be a mere platitude to refer the positive face of power to the supra-personal or social goal that power serves, and in any case, this point has already been well articulated (e.g. McClelland, 1970). By the positive face of power, I mean something more fundamental. Karen Horney (Kelman, 1972) distinguished the healthy striving for power, which is an expression of inner strength, from the neurotic's compulsive need for power that springs from what she called the basic anxiety. Unlike the later Adler, who dissociated the power striving from the normal character, Horney saw a healthy power striving as part of the normal character. A similar position to Horney's was expressed by McDougall (1948) when he discussed the role of the "self-assertion instinct" in the development of the "self-regarding sentiment". The self-assertion instinct leads a person to search for and establish his superiority within each of the social circles that he successively enters. Every successful realization of self-assertion adds an increment to the person's "positive self-feeling". A negative self-feeling, on the other hand, would be experienced when self-assertion is held in check by a greater power, such as the power of society as a whole. A certain balance in the positive and negative self-feelings would be necessary for the normal development of the self-regarding sentiment which, in turn, would lead to the achievement of self-respect. A self-regarding sentiment containing only positive self-feeling leads to pride, which would prevent the person from achieving a higher form of social conduct. On account of this, McDougall held a cautious view on the self-assertion instinct. He did not, however, denounce the self-assertion instinct; nor did he advocate that the formation of the self-regarding sentiment can be better achieved without self-assertion. His position was more congenial to Horney's than that of the later Adler.

In the following pages, beginning with a discussion of Maslow's self-actualization thesis, it will be argued that power is integral to the notion of psychological health, even though the power concept has rarely been utilized by the psychologists in their formulation of psychological health.

Richard Lowry, editor of a collection of germinal papers by Maslow (Lowry, 1973), has traced Maslow's well-known thesis of self-actualization to Maslow's earlier studies of dominance and self-esteem. Maslow carried out systematic observations of dominance in infra-human primates for his doctoral thesis. The focus then was on dominance *behaviour* and the dominant animal was defined as one whose sexual, feeding, aggressive, and social behaviour patterns are carried out without deference to its associates. Conversely, a subordinate animal is one whose behaviour patterns are suggested, modified, limited, or inhibited by its more dominant associates. Dominance and subordinate behaviours occur only in a social context involving animate objects, particularly members of the same species. The behaviour can be most clearly determined in a situation where there is conflict of interests — the conflict will be resolved in favour of dominance. From this characterization, it can be seen that dominance behaviour is equated with prevailing over the opponent. Its resemblance with Adler's conception of the striving for power is obvious.

Dominance is not necessarily determined by physical size, stronger canines or better fighting ability. These are rather background factors playing a supportive role. Maslow suggested that dominance is determined by a composite of social attitudes, attitudes of aggressiveness, confidence or cockiness. Such an attitude or posture is vital in the "sizing up" process in the first moments of encounter during which the dominance hierarchy is established. It is only when such an attitude is nakedly challenged that physical prowess is called into play. This line of thinking would call into question the adequacy of the prior *behavioural* characterization of a dominant animal.

Maslow (1937) later distinguished between dominance behaviour, dominance-feeling and dominance status, with special reference now to humans. Among the three, dominance-feeling provides the most adequate characterization of what a dominant or subordinate person is. Because of this, dominance-feelings became the focus on which Maslow later developed his conceptualization of psychological health. The initial description of dominance-feeling consisted of thirteen aspects, including self-esteem; self-confidence; high self-respect and evaluation of self; consciousness of "superiority" in a general sense; a feeling of pride; sureness with respect to other people, being able to handle other people; masterfulness and masterly, and a general capacity; as well as an absence of shyness (Maslow, 1937). Obviously, Maslow was full of admiration for the person with high dominance-feeling, just as Christie and Geis (1970b) have ended up admiring their experimental subjects who were high in Machiavellianism.

Dominance-feeling soon became synonymous with self-esteem (Maslow, 1942). Self-esteem was then postulated as one category of vital human needs (Maslow, 1943b). The thwarting of the self-esteem needs would produce feelings of inferiority, weakness, and helplessness, which in turn lead to neurotic behaviour. Their fulfilment, on the other hand, would pave the ground for the emergence of the self-actualization needs, defined as a striving to become what one can become ("What a man *can* be, he *must* be"). Each step forward in self-actualization is a step into the unfamiliar and is possibly dangerous, involves giving up a simpler and less effortful life, and therefore requires "courage, will, choice, and strength in the individual, as well as protection, permission and encouragement from the environment, especially for the child" (Maslow, 1968, p. 204). This would seem to echo Nietzsche's will to power, although there are differences between them. The characteristics of a self-actualizing person do not correspond to the image which Nietzsche held of the person high on the power scale. The will to enjoy, for instance, is lacking in the latter. Nietzsche regarded man as a kind of animal which promises (a faith shared by Maslow), as well as something that must be overcome (which Maslow chose to ignore). Maslow's self-actualization is conceived as the resultant of a dialectic between growth-fostering forces and growth-discouraging forces, whereas Nietzsche's self-overcoming takes the form of a dialectical monism. Maslow has provided a scheme of hierarchical needs specifying the necessary, prepotent, condition for self-actualization to occur. The social implication is that if self-actualization were to be accepted as the ultimate goal of personal development, then Maslow's scheme would provide the blue-print for parents, educators, the government, etc. to discharge their responsibilities. Nietzsche, by contrast, has given no comparable blue-print. He could only exhort people to think and to have faith in the eventuality of conscious and voluntary self-control. In all these aspects, self-actualization and the will to power are different. Yet they both share the basic notion of becoming or uplifting, and put emphasis on an internal mover which, for the lack of a better term, can be described by the philosophical concept of the will. The chain of terms which begins with dominance and ends in self-actualization may have the sem(e)iotical advantage of being more specific than the will to power. However, it has added nothing substantial to what is already contained in the will to power.

Although Maslow rarely used the term power, and when he did use it, he used it in the perjorative sense of authoritarianism, yet his ideas on human psychological health can be shown to originate from a notion which is almost identical with power, namely, dominance. Dominance-feeling, and hence self-esteem, can be described as an assured sense of self power; and self-actualization, as the ceaseless uplifting and enhancement of this self power. It would be totally inconceivable within Maslow's model of psychological health that self-esteem and self actualization could be compatible with powerlessness. The important question is therefore not the elimination of power, or the desire for it, but rather the conditions under which power corrupts or uplifts life. Modern psychology is as silent and unilluminating on this question as Nietzsche. Yet Nietzsche at least saw through the futility of any proposal which is directed at disarming indiscriminantly a person's will to power.

The positiveness of power can be seen on a more fundamental level than either self-actualization or self-esteem. I refer here to the concepts of competence (White, 1959) and personal causation (de Charms, 1968). After reviewing several theories of motivation in animal and psychoanalytic ego psychology which are built upon primary drives, White (1959) lists a number of behaviours that cannot be successfully conceptualized in terms of primary drives. These include visual exploration, grasping, crawling and walking, attention and perception, language and thinking, exploring novel objects and places, manipulating the surroundings, and producing effective changes in the environment. White then proposes that these activities have one common property in that they all form part of the process whereby the animal or child learns to interact effectively with the environment, that is, to become competent. It would appear that competence is used both as a developmental and a relational concept. It refers firstly to the development of inner resources; and secondly, a kind of interaction or transaction which an animal or a child is able to establish with the environment, such that the environmental variables can be brought under the control of these inner resources. As a relational concept, competence becomes synonymous with control over inanimate objects and the self (as for instance sensorimotor coordination). In a later work, White (1963) develops the concept of *social* competence to depict a person's transaction with the social environment. A feeling of social competence is said to build up from the successful experiences of producing intended effects in other people.

The achievement of competence, White (1959) argues, is necessary and functional for biological and evolutionary reasons. Being competent results in the experience of efficacy. A person is able to experience a sense of efficacy from the control and impact which he exerts on himself and the environment, independently of any tangible gain that may accrue – or, *"L'effect c'est moi"*, Nietzsche would have said. Feelings of efficacy are rewarding in themselves. Since the rewarding feeling of efficacy flows from competence, the activities through which competence is achieved are therefore motivated in their own right, and are not prompted by drives. This motivation is called effectance, to be understood as a general, moderate motivation in contradistinction to a drive which is specific and strong. White also suggests, and later elaborates (White, 1960, 1964), that competence is intimately related to self-esteem and personality development.

From the point of view developed by White, it would appear that the achievement of competence and the successful operation of the effectance motivation are the prerequisites of psychological health. In fact, their desirability is assumed by White as a matter of course. The interesting point is that competence and effectance are basically power terms. They bear a close resemblance to Nietzsche's notion of the will to power. The symbols are different, but what is being symbolized is essentially the same. Seen in this way, White's work lends yet another support to our argument that power is integral to psychological health. The third support is provided by de Charms (1968).

De Charms (1968) proposes as a basic postulate of motivation that it is man's primary motivational propensity to be effective in producing changes in his environment, and calls this postulate "personal causation".

> Man strives to be a causal agent, to be the primary locus of causation for, or the origin of, his behaviour; he strives for personal causation. This propensity has its roots in his earliest encounters with his environment, forces him to actively engage his environment thereby testing and deriving valid personal knowledge from it, and is the basis for specific motives. His

> nature commits him to this path, and his very life depends on it. Personal causation is not to be taken as *the motive* for all behaviour, however. It is an overarching or guiding principle upon which specific motives are built. The environment sets different problems (obtaining food, achieving success, gaining friendship, etc.) that may help to define specific motives for individual behaviour patterns. The dimension that underlies all of these is the attempt to overcome the problem through personal causation — the desire to be master of one's fate. (pp. 269-270)

Such a desire cannot be realized in separation from the environment because it is dependent on feedback from changes in the environment that are attributable to one's behaviour. From this point of view, man has a vested interest in engaging in transactions with his environment such that he himself becomes the cause. In this regard, man is like the white-footed mouse, or for that matter, any other animal species, all of which exhibit intrinsic tendencies to modify environmental variables and to avoid or counteract unexpected and nonvolitional environmental changes (Kavanau, 1967).

A person who feels that the locus for producing effects in his environment lies within himself, and that his behaviour is self determined, is called an Origin. A Pawn, on the contrary, feels that the locus for causation lies outside himself, and that causal forces beyond his control determine his behaviour. The feelings of the Origin and the Pawn are equated with the feelings of power and powerlessness respectively (de Charms, 1968, pp. 315-316, 274). These subjective feelings may not be in accord with objective evidence. Nevertheless, they have a directive influence on the person's behaviour, and de Charms has made the claim that they are more important in predicting behaviour than any objective indicator of freedom or coercion.

Like the concepts of competence, self-esteem, and self-actualization, personal causation (Origin) cannot be separated from power. Now, if competence, etc., uplift life, then power must also be credited with the same, even though power also corrupts. The true image of power is therefore Janus-faced. At the general psychological level, power corrupts but also uplifts life. At the sociological level, as we have seen in Chapter 4, power is both integrative and divisive. A society without a power structure is inconceivable, at least not on Earth. Man cannot function with his power motive castrated, at least not as a healthy man. The implicit psychological presumption that power corrupts must be placed in a proper perspective. To add another dimension to such a perspective, the possibility that powerlessness corrupts will now be examined.

The undesirability of powerlessness is already implied in the very concepts of personal causation, efficacy, self-esteem and self-actualization. This, too, is contained in Adler's theory that the striving for power develops as a reaction to the childhood feeling of powerlessness. May (1972) asserts a relation between powerlessness and madness both in the personal sense of enragedness to the point of violence and the psychiatric sense of psychosis. A more impressive demonstration of the undesirable correlates of powerlessness is found in two separate but related research traditions, namely, locus of control and learned helplessness. Though they are not phrased in terms of power, there is a direct bearing between them and powerlessness. Both have been summarized well enough (e.g. Phares, 1976; Seligman, 1975; Kleinke, 1978) to make the following discussion necessarily brief.

A person may perceive that an outcome or reinforcement occurs as a result of his own action. In this case, the person believes that he controls the contingency between behaviour and outcome, and the perceived locus of control is said to be "internal". When the outcome is perceived to be outside personal control (such as due to chance, luck, fate, the influence of powerful others, or forces too complicated to be predicted), an "external" locus of control would obtain. Thus (perceived) locus of control refers to the beliefs or expectancies about the contingency between behaviour and outcome, and not the objective contingency as such. Such expectancies vary in their specificity or generality. An expectancy of internal or external locus of control may be specific and apply to only a particular situation. The laboratory studies on perceived control and stress adaptation reported by Glass and Singer (1972) would fall into this category, and so would the earlier studies on behaviour in skill versus chance situations. Or the expectancy may become generalized and form a general disposition affecting a wide range of situations. The bulk of the studies in locus of control are concerned with locus of control as a personality rather than a situational specific phenomenon. A number of specially designed scales are available which purport to measure individual differences on the internal-external dimension. "Internal" and "external" individuals can then be compared with respect to their personal and social attributes, their reactions to natural or contrived situations, etc.

Both at the situational specific level and the personality level, the results show a number of undesirable correlates of externality. When confronted by a situation in which an individual perceives a lack of personal control over the outcome, he becomes disoriented, shows decrement or maladaptation in learning, and experiences the debilitating effects of anxiety. Compared with internal individuals, external individuals show less personal effectiveness at coping with or attaining mastery over their environments, and exhibit smaller self-control. They are more susceptible to other people's control and influence, being less independent and more reliant on others' judgement. The school achievements of external children are inferior to that of internal children. Moderate but significant correlations have generally been found between externality and anxiety. The last finding should be interpreted with caution because external persons may simply be more willing to admit anxiety or other related personal difficulties than internals. Indeed, one function of externality is its capacity to neutralize the threat of personal inadequacy or failure by attributing the responsibility to external causes. Whether or not such a capacity is adaptive remains debatable, however. Certainly, the findings reviewed in Phares (1976) and Kleinke (1978) strongly indicate that externals are functioning at a lower level than internals. In this sense, externality, both at the situational specific and personality levels, can be said to be corrupting.

Now there is a certain relation between externality and powerlessness. Seeman (1959), in an analysis of the Marxian concept of alienation, lists powerlessness as a major component of alienation and defines the former as arising from the worker's lack of control over the production process. The subsequent development of the concept of internal/external control, of which Seeman was a collaborator at one stage (e.g. Rotter *et al.*, 1962), provides, amongst other things, a way of looking at power and powerlessness (Seeman, 1975; Phares, 1976). To begin with, external locus of control would correspond to powerlessness if externality were defined minimally and purely as the perceived lack of personal control. The conceptual correspondence, however, becomes blurred when externality incorporates certain external sources of control without simultaneously ascertaining the person's belief about them. Apart from *chance*, the other external sources of control (luck, fate, powerful others and complicated events) suggested by Rotter (1966) do not necessarily imply that the person is not in control. Many people believe that fate, luck, and the powerful others are on their side. It is a Christian faith that although events may be unpredictable because of the great complexity of forces surrounding them, somehow God makes them work out to the benefit of His children. Unless these beliefs are totally alien to the American culture, in which most of the locus of control studies have been carried out, there is the possibility that many so-called externals would *not* feel powerless. Because of this, externality would hardly be a full-blown measure of powerlessness. The findings summarized in the preceding paragraph could not have uncovered the full depth of the correlates of powerlessness.

A closer approximate to powerlessness is the concept of learned helplessness (Seligman, 1975). Technically, helplessness is known as outcome independence or uncontrollability, which in turn is defined by the statement that the probability of an outcome is the same whether or not the response of interest occurs. When an animal or a person experiences uncontrollability, he learns or forms an expectation that the outcome is independent of his response. Learned helplessness is thus a pure case of perceived lack of control, and comes closer to powerlessness than externality does. According to Seligman (1975), the expectation of uncontrollability would have motivational, cognitive and emotional consequences such that it "(1) reduces the motivation to control the outcome; (2) interferes with learning that responding controls the outcome; and, if the outcome is traumatic, (3) produces fear for as long as the subject is uncertain of the uncontrollability of the outcome, and then produces depression" (p. 56). Infant and aged humans who are thrust into a state of helplessness (e.g. when the infant is separated from the mother who is sent to prison; an aged person is moved to an old age home), are at risk of being more susceptible to sudden or unexpected death. Powerlessness, whether it is in the form of externality or, more appropriately, helplessness, would seem to have correlates that can be described as damaging.

Internality, externality and helplessness all pertain to a person's belief in or expectancy of the effectiveness of his action. They are linking concepts between behaviour and outcome seen from the person's eyes. As such, they omit another kind of expectancy which concerns the person's ability in producing the behaviour of interest. To distinguish between the two kinds of expectancies, Bandura (1977) has proposed to call them "outcome" and "efficacy" expectancies respectively, and argues that although they are closely related, they should be regarded as orthogonal. Thus, for example, people can give up trying because they lack a sense of self-efficacy in achieving the required behaviour; or they may be assured of their self-efficacy but give up trying either because they expect their actions to have no effect on an unresponsive environment or because they anticipate that their actions will be consistently punished. From this point of view, helplessness coupled with low self-efficacy should correlate with a more profound sense of powerlessness than helplessness *per se*. Added to this the diminution of the will would indeed touch the bottom of powerlessness.

Nietzsche's treatment of the will to power, as outlined in Chapter 2, has led us to expect that power not only has a negative face but also a positive one, and that powerlessness, innocent as it may seem, is in fact psychologically damaging. Once we adopt this perspective and rid us of the one-sided and restrictive presumption that power can only corrupt, a wide range of phenomena at the general psychological level can be meaningfully related to the concept of power. Having reached this position, we can now proceed to a discussion of the experience of power in its diverse forms.

The motive and experience of power

The well known achievement motivation studies by David McClelland and his associates (McClelland, 1961) have two appendages which are less publicized than the n Ach (short for "need for achievement"). They are the n Affiliation and n Power. On the national level, it has been hypothesized that a combination of high n Ach, low n Affiliation and high n Power would form the motivational substratum of an empire building country. Other combinations would correlate with other national aspirations. Apart from this type of postulation, n Power, like n Affiliation, was given little treatment, although Veroff (1957) had made a pioneering study of the power motivation at about the same period. Since then, the study of the power motive has led to a number of major publications. A comprehensive review and exposition of the power motive studies is provided by Winter (1973). A more recent volume by McClelland (1975) outlines a scheme of the psycho-sexual development of the power motive. Unlike Adler, these two writers do not regard the origin of the power motive as problematic enough to require a theoretical explanation. Neither do they feel any need of justifying the postulate of a power motive. Instead, the existence of the power motive is assumed and taken as the point of departure. The initial question of relevance to them becomes one concerning the experimental arousal and measurement of the power motive.

The McClelland-Atkinson research strategy, as outlined in Winter (1973), has been generally used in the arousal and subsequent measurement of the power motive. First, the motive is experimentally aroused by a variety of techniques to be described later. Second, the aroused individuals would view a series of Thematic Appreception Test (TAT) stimulus pictures and are then asked to write fantasy stories on each. These TAT protocols are to be compared with those of a neutral, unaroused group. The observed differences were taken as a measure of the motive. To carry out the comparison would require a coding system that will maximally discriminate between the two sets of protocols. The final coding system is developed by checking the initial *a priori* system against the protocols to yield a revised version which in turn is subjected to further revision until a satisfactory version is crystallized. Obviously this is a painstaking procedure akin to the imposed etic - emic strategy in cross-cultural research. Some theoretical or working notion of the power motive is necessary to guide the arousal of the motive and to provide rationales for constructing and modifying the coding system. Each time the coding system is revised would involve a modification of the preceding conception of the power motive, so that the empirical characterization of the motive arrived at in the final coding system is inevitably a compromise between the researcher's own attribution of power and the informants' phenomenological expression of the aroused power motive.

Winter (1973) has reviewed Veroff's and Uleman's techniques of arousing the power motive. Veroff (1957) had male candidates for student office take a modified TAT while they were awaiting the voting result. This method of arousing the power motive, while in line with Veroff's definition of power as the control of the means of influencing other people, suffered from two drawbacks. It restricted power to the bureaucratic setting of student politics; and by testing the experimental subjects (*S*s) while they were waiting for the polls result, it might have inadvertently incorporated strong elements of anxiety (due to the *S*'s anticipation of failing in public) and uncontrollability (the votes were already cast). Noting these drawbacks, Winter (1973) concluded that the Veroff method was restrictive and over-represented the defensive and avoidance aspects of the power motive. Uleman defined power as direct interpersonal influence and attempted to arouse the power motive by giving the *Ss* a demonstration of hypnosis (Uleman, 1966). Uleman (1972) also used another arousal method by assigning to the *Ss* the role of a psychological experimenter which permitted as well as enabled them to exercise legitimate and successful influence over the other participants. Winter (1973) raised the criticism that the contrived nature of Uleman's second method would not have captured the full range of experience associated with power. His own method (carried out in 1965) was to expose the *Ss* to a film of the 1961 inauguration oath and speech of the late President John Kennedy. He argued that this "seemed an ideal arousal, since the occasion had overtones of each of Weber's types of power: rational-legal (the transfer of elected executive power in a routinized way), traditional (the historic line of presidents since George Washington), and charismatic (the appeal of Kennedy himself)" (62).

In the light of our discussion of Weber's conceptualization of power in Chapter 3, it can be immediately noted that the alleged support from Weber is based on a partial and incorrect understanding of Weber's treatment of power, authority and legitimacy. The triology quoted by Winter do not exhaust the types of power, for they only refer to the types of legitimacy underlying authority which in turn is a subset of power in the Weberian sense. The film captures only part of the whole domain of power which Winter himself has so lucidly portrayed (p. 9). It is a truly fantastic claim that a single film of this sort could arouse the full range of experience associated with power. It is all the more fantastic since Winter has adopted a broad conception of power, namely, that power is *the capacity of producing (consciously or unconsciously) intended effects on people's behaviour or emotion* (p. 5). The nature of the Kennedy film suggests that the heroic, constitutional and lovable aspects of power would have been aroused more than the defensive, avoidance and corrupting aspects. It is no wonder the overall n Power score was more highly correlated with the "Hope of Power" subscore than the "Fear of Power" subscore.

To a certain extent, the necessarily narrow range of the power motive aroused by the film (or by any other technique) can be widened by the variety of the stimulus pictures. Provided that the written language is an efficient medium of expressing the power imageries, and that the *S*s are sufficiently fluent in its use, their fantasy stories should contain a sufficiently wide range of power themes to provide the basis of an empirical characterization of the power motive. Since the researcher has to play the role of deciding which power theme to score and which to omit, such a characterization, as represented by the final scoring system, must also reflect the attribution which the researcher brings to bear on the data. It is a sort of reasoned negotiation. The *a priori* conception of the power motive states that it is a disposition to strive for power (pp. 17-18), with power defined in the manner quoted in the preceding paragraph. Empirically, the power motive is defined as those categories of the thematic appreception that increase under the condition of power arousal. These categories turn out to be actions of, or concern about "establishing, maintaining, or restoring (a person's) power — that is, his impact, control, or influence over another person, group of persons, or the world at large" (p. 250). So that after all the painstaking exercises of arousing and measuring the power motive, the "intend effects" in the *a priori* definition of power can now be empirically specified as "impact, control, or influence". This of course is only a pale reflection of the significant contribution to the understanding of power made by the practitioners of the McClelland-Atkinson research strategy.

The modified TAT stimulus pictures, armed with a standardized coding system, provide a ready tool for measuring the power motive, and thereby help to forge an inroad into the study of human behaviour and experience. A number of general research strategies used in the study can be discerned. One strategy is to treat the power motive as a dependent variable and observe the manner in which certain behaviour alters the motive. A notable example is the experiment showing the effect of drinking on power imageries (McClelland and Wilsnack, 1972). N Power is found to increase linearly with the amount of beer or liquor consumption. Of special interest is the differential effects of the amount of drinking on two types of power imageries, called personalized or p Power and socialized or s Power. Personalized Power refers to those fantasy stories in which the actor strives for a personal goal and contends with an opponent to get it. It is found to increase with moderate drinking and then either levels off or continues to increase with heavy drinking. In s Power, the goal is for the good of other people and the actor shows doubt about his own competence and regards power as deceptive. Like p Power, s Power increases with moderate drinking; but unlike the former, it drops with heavy drinking. Secondly, the power motive can be experimentally manipulated to observe if it has any effect on behaviour. This type of study is rare but an experiment conducted by Davis (1972) provides a close example. He set up power arousing and nuturance arousing conditions and found some tentative evidence indicating that the former led to more heavy drinking than the latter. The third and most widely used strategy is to correlate n Power with the behaviour of interest. A long list of such behaviour has been reviewed by Winter (1973). The variety of behaviour found to correlate with the power motive suggests that the power motive can serve as a unifying principle relating these otherwise quite different behaviour. Alternatively put, there exist various ways for the satisfaction of the power motive. This leads to the innovative scheme proposed by McClelland (1975).

McClelland selects and abstracts four categories of behaviour known to be correlated with the power motive. These are (1) power-oriented reading, such as the "Playboy" and "Sports Illustrated"; (2) accumulating prestigious possessions, e.g. colour television set, rifle or pistol, convertible car; (3) playing competitive sports; and (4) organizational membership. The correlations in question are by no means well established and an earlier study (reported in Winter, 1972) provides only partial evidence. It is the way McClelland conceptualizes the problem that is of interest here. He proposes that the above four categories of behaviour correspond to four modalities of experiencing power (or power orientations) that can be generated by cross-classifying the following two dichotomous dimensions: *source* of power (Self vs outside self, that is, Other) and *object* of power (Self vs Other). Through power-oriented reading, the person exposes himself to power arousing cues from which he derives a vicarious feeling of power. This is a specific instance of the Other - Self (source of power is from outside, self as object) power orientation in which an individual seeks ways for the external environment to act on him to make him feel powerful. McClelland suggests as a primordial instance the infant drawing his strength from the mother through his mouth. Other instances include drawing strength from God or other people or symbol of power. Drug taking and hysteria are regarded as pathological instances. McClelland proposes that this power orientation corresponds

	Source of Power	
Object of power:	Other	Self
SELF (to feel stronger)		
Definition:	"It" (God, my mother, my leader, food) strengthens me	I strengthen, control, direct myself
Action correlate:	Power-oriented reading	Accumulating prestige possessions
Developmental stage:	I. oral: being supported	II. Anal: autonomy, will
Pathology:	Hysteria, drug taking	Obsessive compulsive neurosis
OTHERS (to influence)		
Definition:	It (religion, laws, my group) moves me to service, influence others	I have an impact (influence) on others
Action correlate:	Organizational membership	Competitive sports, arguing
Developmental stage:	IV. Genital mutuality, principled assertion, duty	III. Phallic: assertive action
Pathology:	Messianism	Crime

Fig. 1. A classification of power orientations.
(Reproduced in part from David C. McClelland. "POWER: The Inner Experience". © 1975 by Irvington Publishers, Inc., New York. Reprinted by permission.)

to the oral stage of psychosexual development with dependence as its main characteristic. Figure 1 shown above summarizes the contents of the Other - Self as well as the other three power orientations.

A person accumulating prestigious possessions would incorporate, psychologically, these possessions into his self and thereby expands the self to make it feel stronger. A similar view is expressed by Krech *et al.*, (1962). McClelland proposes that this category of behaviour constitutes an instance of the Self-Self power orientation. The proposal, however, is weak and the accumulation of prestigious possessions does not truly represent the nature of the Self-Self power orientation. The primordial case of the Self-Self orientation is the child who, having successfully learnt to control his bowel movement and urination, thereby gains a feeling of self-generated strength. At the interpersonal level, the Self-Self orientation becomes possible when the child asserts and achieves his autonomy from people whom he used to depend on, and this usually takes the form of saying "No" to the parents. These characteristics, according to McClelland, are indicative of the anal stage of psychosexual development with its emphasis on autonomy and will. Following from this, he cites what seem to be well reasoned instances of the Self-Self orientation, namely, body-building exercises such as yoga and dieting, and in the extreme case, obsessive compulsiveness. How the accumulation of prestigious possessions fits in here is a bit far out.

Akin to the above-quoted body-building exercises are such mind control techniques as *Zen* and *Transcendental Meditation*, which A. Smith (1975) insists are the powers of the right brain (hemisphere). Similar others would include *Ta Chi* and *Kung Fu*. All these, from *Zen* to *Kung Fu*, are Self-Self experiences *par excellence*, and should hence be included together with yoga. Perhaps oriental psychology, or at least part of it, should be approached from the point of view of the Self-Self power orientation. In this regard, it is interesting to note the Buddhist teaching on "Don't hold onto", which means, amongst other things, "Let your desires go from you" and "Don't identify with anybody or symbol". The ability to let desires go, including one's life, brings not only a Self-Self experience. It also frees the person from the social and physical environments that regulate and control the fulfilment of these desires. Because of this, it will unlock the person from the harsh or subtle power that originates from outside the self and thereby enhances the self as a source of power. It provides one way of counteracting the third dimension of power discussed in Chapter 5. As well, it coincides with a social psychological view of power (Swingle, 1976) to be examined in a later chapter. "Not to identify" means enhancing the Self as the source of power *vis-à-vis* Other, and it provides a counterpoint to Kelman's (1961) thesis of identification as a medium of social influence.

Also should be included under the Self - Self orientation are those instances which are generally known as "Self-control", as described by Thoreson and Mahoney (1974). The fundamental of self-control is to know the contingencies that govern one's behaviour and experience and then to bring them under one's wilful control. Instead of playing pawn to external control mediated by the environment, a person doing self-control tries to be the origin. He is acting like a cognitive psychologist managing behaviourally his own little world according to a recipe taken from the Skinnerians and social learning theorists. Professionals who advocate self-control can therefore proclaim power to the person (e.g. Mahoney and Thoresen, 1974; London, 1969). This brand of self-control is unmistakably part of western psychology. Psychologies east and west meet in the Self - Self modality, and their difference is immediately apparent. The east is more concerned with the unity of the body, the mind, and the spirit, and with ways in which the *Gestalt* may move with perfect freedom and equanimity. The west, by comparison, is more enthusiastic in making the mind serve the body better.

The third, Self - Other power orientation is the most common definition that writers assign to power. A person produces intended effects — impact, control, or influences — on another person or the world at large, and in doing so he experiences power. In McClelland's scheme, this modality corresponds to the phallic stage in which the child explores and manipulates the external environment. We usually do not associate this with the power or dominance motive, but rather with others such as effectance. Yet the different symbols only tend to conceal the commonality of what is being symbolized. The reader will recall that as pointed out in the preceding section, the very nature of the self-other relation in effectance behaviour is basically a power relation. As the child grows older, McClelland points out, simple and blunt methods of controlling the environment gradually give way to more subtle ones. The archetype is Don Juan. (Machiavelli, articulate as he was, must be trailing far behind Don Juan.) This development is in part necessitated by the increasingly subtle and more complex nature of the environment into which the child moves. Competitive sports and arguments are typical and relatively more acceptable expressions of the Self - Other orientation; when the expression is otherwise proscribed, it is called a crime. The giving of unsolicited help, such as certain forms of foreign aid, subjects the recipient to a dependence role and is a form of psychological domination of the Self - Other type.

The idea that one source of power lies within the self is, of course, the fundamental tenet which underlies Nietzsche's the will to power and several of the positive aspects of power discussed in the preceding section. The latter include competence, self-actualization, and to a lesser extent, personal causation. This line of thought implies that mankind, like other living species, is endowed with an internal source of power, and has no option but to find some way of dealing with it. McClelland's distinction between the Self-Self and Self-Other modalities points to two directions in which this power may proceed.

Finally, in the Other - Other power orientation, tipped as the most advanced stage of expressing the power motive, the self drops out as a source of power and the person sees himself as an instrument of a higher authority which moves him to try to influence or serve others. The prototype is given by the boy who identifies with his father, incorporates the latter's image and acts out the paternal role. People who join an organization presumably subordinate their personal goals to the higher authority of the organization and act on others on behalf of this authority. The line between an authentic and perverted Other - Other orientation is difficult to draw, because the higher authority may be a structure for domination serving the personal goal of its members. Here, we are reminded of the guards in Zimbardo's mock prison experiment, and the many wars fought under the names of God and Motherland.

With the help of a psychological scale of social emotional maturity, a number of studies have yielded some empirical support for McClelland's hypothesis that a certain correspondence exists between the power orientations and psychosexual development (McClelland, 1975). This indicates that n Power expresses itself in rather different behaviour and experience, depending at least partly on the psychosexual stage or maturity level of the person. Is it possible then to treat one power orientation as if it were morally better than another, depending on their relative maturity levels? The problem of moral evaluation is obviously too complicated to be discussed here. Nevertheless it can be immediately noted that McClelland would find himself in some disagreement with Nietzsche. Nietzsche's distrust of Other as the source of power would confirm the primitive stage of the Other - Self orientation but it also calls into question the ascendancy of the Other - Other orientation in McClelland's scheme. Overcoming self is indicative of a greater inner strength than overcoming other, according to Nietzsche's scale, and hence the relative ranking of Self - Self and Self - Other should be reversed. Application of Nietzsche's scale to the four orientations would result in the Self - Self orientation being put on top of the other three orientations. Conversely, Nietzsche's ideal of self-overcoming would become an anal fixation in McClelland's scheme. Notwithstanding such differences, McClelland and Nietzsche converge on one fundamental premise, namely, the universal nature of the motive of or will to power. In this regard, McClelland and his collaborators have gone beyond Nietzsche by exploring into the power motive in women, something which was not considered by Nietzsche at all.

The ideas examined so far in this section pertain primarily to men.

Women have received far less attention than men in the power motive literature. Two major statements have been advanced regarding the power motive in women. A review of the studies by Winter (1975) indicates firstly that women, like men, are interested in power. Secondly, women's expressions of power are by and large similar to those of men, with the exception that power-motivated women, unlike their male counterpart, do not view sex as a form of power. Results from a study reported in McClelland (1975) indicate an interesting sex difference in the relation between the power motive and the highest stage of maturity. A high n Power makes it more difficult for men to develop mutuality and equality, whereas a high n Power is necessary for women to develop the same. This would mean that while men need to become more gentle before they can move toward mutuality, women would need a dose of assertive training. The reason for this probably lies in the traditional sex roles which accord dominance to the male and subordination to the female. To achieve mutuality and equality between the sexes would require a change first of all in the traditional sex roles. That is to say, men should become less dominant while women should become less submissive.

Power in Skinnerian behaviourism

In a paper presented to the 1973 Walgreen Conference on Education for Human Understanding, Skinner (1973) estimated that forty per cent of his writings were on rats and pigeons. A synopsis of the intellectual development in this forty per cent of his writing activities is given three years later by Skinner himself, in a conference of the New York Academy of Sciences on "The Roots of American Psychology" (Skinner, 1977a). The persistent feature of these activities has been the formulation and development of a general psychological principle of behaviour. In this regard, the focal interest is on the shaping and change of behaviour, that is, behavioural control. At the heart of this general psychological principle of behavioural control are the concepts of stimulus and contingency of reinforcement.

The concept of stimulus has an important place in the intellectual history of the explanation of behaviour. As mentioned in Skinner (1938) and described more fully in Skinner (1953), René Descartes advanced the hypothesis that the behaviour of animals can be traced to an external agent, which is in contrast to the spontaneity hypothesis that regards behaviour as being caused or moved by internal forces such as the "will". The external agent came to be known as a stimulus, and the behaviour controlled by it a response.

The notion of stimulus thus provides a conceptual tool for analysing the ways in which the environment enters into a description of behaviour. An early formulation by Pavlov (1927) assigns to the stimulus a unilateral and autonomous role: the stimulus is said to elicit the response, so that the organism merely responds to environmental events which are independent of and unaffected by the behaviour of the organism. This function of the stimulus is most clearly demonstrated in a physiological reflex. Skinner (1938 and then 1953) identifies the class of behaviour which is under the control of eliciting stimulus as respondent behaviour, which is to be distinguished from operant behaviour. A lot of behaviours are emitted by the organism which cannot be easily traced to an antecedent eliciting stimulus. Instead of reverting back to the spontaneity hypothesis to explain the occurrence of emitted behaviour, Skinner takes the occurrence of behaviour as given, and proceeds to analyse the *rate* or *probability* of its emission. The probability of response replaces the elicitation of response as the basic datum in the experimental study of behaviour. An organism's behaviour, when it occurs, has a certain effect on the environment. When it does so, the behaviour can be said to have operated on the environment, and hence the name of operant behaviour. By acting on the environment, an operant behaviour generates consequences which then influence the probability of a similar behaviour occurring in the future. When the probability is increased in the presence of the consequences, the consequences are called positive reinforcers. If the probability is increased through the absence of the consequences, the latter are called negative reinforcers.

The persistence or otherwise of behaviour can thus be seen as the result of an interchange between the organism and the environment, an interchange in which the environment plays a role that is analogous to natural selection in biological evolution. In this way, it is unnecessary to invoke mentalistic notions such as those necessitated by the principles of hedonism and utilitarianism; and it is still capable of accounting for the data, in an even more precise way. Within the framework of operant analysis, the environment continues to act on the organism, but only after the organism has emitted a response. In respondent behaviour, by contrast, the role of the environment is qualitatively different — the environment controls the behaviour unilaterally and in complete independence of the consequences of the latter.

The most complete formulation of the complex interaction between an organism and its environment, as typified by operant behaviour, is given in Skinner (1969). This formulation specifies (1) the occasion upon which a response occurs, (2) the response itself, and (3) its reinforcing consequences. The first and last entities are conceived as discriminative stimulus and reinforcing stimulus respectively. The interrelationships among the three constitute the contingencies of reinforcement.

Once the contingencies of reinforcement have been ascertained, behavioural control can be effected by making a reinforcing stimulus contingent upon a response. This procedure is technically known as the construction of an operant. As well, the discriminative stimulus can be used to cue the target response without having to provide a reinforcing stimulus, a procedure known as stimulus control. From this body of theoretical knowledge, a technology of behavioural control called behavioural modification is derived and applied with impressive success to several areas of *human* behaviour.

That the concept of stimulus occupies the paramount place in Skinner's experimental analysis of behaviour should be obvious. What is not so explicit is the epistemological affinity between stimulus and power. All behaviour is supposed to be under the control of some stimulus which can or cannot be identified. This epistemological position is well put by Salzinger (1973, p. 583):

> . . . behaviourists no more believe in responses without stimuli than they believe in free will. Behaviourists assume that responses are controlled by stimuli. The control may not always be obvious; it may not always be strong; in terms of today's technology, it may even be impossible to specify the particular stimulation that is controlling a particular response. But stimuli do control responses.

Stated in the above form, stimulus has acquired a role which is more or less identical to the role assigned to power by Russell (1938, pp. 10–11):

> . . . the fundamental concept in social science is Power, in the same sense in which Energy is the fundamental concept in physics . . . . The laws of social dynamics are laws which can only be stated in terms of power . . . .

Others, such as Hawley (1963), have endorsed a similar position. A comparison with Russell is particularly interesting because both he and

Skinner at one time had been genuinely excited by the prospect that the reflex could provide the basic scientific datum for a general principle of behaviour. Russell later gave up the reflex in favour of power, while Skinner, having deserted the same, revitalized the concept of stimulus and has held on to it ever since.

In drawing attention to the epistemological parallel between stimulus and power, I am not suggesting that stimulus should be replaced by power. The point to be made here is that the essence of Skinner's experimental analysis of behaviour *is* concerned with the identification of those powers to which an organism is susceptible and the subsequent transfer of that power into the hands of the experimenter.

This interpretation is by no means alien to Skinner's own image of what the behavioural science is. In "Beyond Freedom and Dignity" (Skinner, 1971), Skinner makes the claim that behavioural science is a science of values. The underlying argument is launched from a distinction made between a thing and its reinforcing effect. The goodness or badness of things, he says, cannot be found in the things themselves. It is simply that good things are positive reinforcers, and bad things are negative reinforcers. The goodness or badness of things is therefore a human value judgement which reflects their reinforcing effects. Now, "Things themselves are studied by physics and biology, usually without reference to their value, but the reinforcing effects of things are the province of behavioural science, which, to the extent that it is concerned with operant reinforcement, is a science of values" (p. 104). Since according to Skinner the behavioural science is a science of values, and values are the reinforcing effects of things, then the behavioural science must also be a science of power. This, I would submit, is the crucial foundation on which rests the other sixty per cent of Skinner's writings, which are concerned with human affairs and the design of culture.

In contrast to his first major work (Skinner, 1938), which is entirely a record of animal pure research, Skinner's second major work, "Walden Two", is a novel (Skinner, 1948). They are however complementary in that the latter is devoted to the propagation of the desirability and efficacy of the wilful design of a new kind of communal living based on the experimental analysis of behaviour contained in the former work. Since then, and certainly from 1953 onwards, Skinner has been expressing his reflections on society in a more direct and serious manner (e.g. Skinner, 1953, 1969, 1971, 1972, 1978).

These reflections are not concerned with the sociological problems of social cohesion, conflict and change, but with the problem of the control of human behaviour. Behaviour control is taken as a given fact and this forms the basic starting point. This fact is for Skinner self-evident in those areas where the individual's behaviour is under the influence of the informal group or controlling agencies such as the government, religion, education, economy and psychotherapy. Self-control is regarded as an exception only on the surface, because self-control itself is a behaviour and as such is the product of controlling variables which originate from outside the individual or are otherwise mediated by the environment. The ultimate source of control is external to the individual (Skinner, 1953). Liberty, as defined by J. S. Mill in the sense of doing what one desires, does not negate the fact of control because the determinants of desire have to be considered; and that there are certain kinds of control under which people feel perfectly free (Skinner, 1971). There is a strong rationalist tendency in such a position.

Since there must always be control, Skinner pleads that a technology for the control of human behaviour should only be evaluated by its efficacy and should not be resisted just on the ground that any control would violate human dignity and freedom. Resistance on such ground would only serve to perpetuate the traditional ways of control, which, argues Skinner, rely excessively on aversive reinforcers, and are ineffectual due to ignorance of the contingencies of reinforcement. As a result they are rapidly endangering the survival of mankind. A better technology of control would operate on the already verified principles of behaviour. Where new problems present themselves, they are to be approached in the manner of operant analysis and in the spirit of experimentation. The main task of this technology is not to control people but to bring people under the control of more effective physical and social environments. The practical guidelines have been portrayed in Skinner (1948) and are reiterated in Skinner (1977b). Here my main concern will be with the relationship between the operation of such a technology and the problem of power.

Skinner makes a distinction between the initiation of the technology and its subsequent routinization. The former requires the deliberate effort of an individual or individuals. This must necessarily imply that some individual is given the power or has acquired the power to do so. Or as Dahrendorf (1968) puts it, control presupposes a power or an authority structure. Looking from the outside, the question of who will control the pioneer controller immediately arises, even though the people inside may not be aware of its relevance. This question will however disappear in a later stage. When the new system of control has settled in, Skinner assures us, the operation of control will become dissociated from the action of any single individual. The claim is made that no cultural practice designed through the application of an experimental analysis of behaviour involves a behaviour modifier who remains in control. This would appear highly credible in the light of Weber's theory of the routinization of charisma, Lukes' three-dimensional view of power, as well as Westergaard and Resler's discussion of the impersonal and anonymous nature of power outlined in Part II. The question of who controls the controller becomes irrelevant because at this stage there is no controller in the form of an identifiable individual. That does not mean other problems associated with power will also disappear. The central question will become one which is concerned with the anonymous power structure in the Utopia, which can be better approached from the three-dimensional view of power than either the one- or two-dimensional view. Where Skinner's psychology of behaviour ends, the sociology of power should begin. People may feel happier and freer in a utopia which observes operant principles. Perhaps they will all acquire the Other - Other power orientation in due course. It remains to be demonstrated whether or not control in such a utopia can dispense with a power or an authority structure.

In "Walden Two" (Skinner, 1948), such a power structure is clearly visible (at least to the reader of "Walden Two") and was frankly admitted by Frazier, who master-minded the Utopia. If Skinner were to construct a *post-Frazian Walden Two* in another novel, it would be most intriguing to find out how he handles the relevance and role of the power structure. Can the orthodox application of operant principles achieve the sociological impossibility, namely, a functioning community which is devoid of a power structure? If it cannot, then the problems of social stratification and conflict, which are inherent in the power structure (see Chapter 4), would certainly remain.

Recognition of the similarity between stimulus and power makes more apparent both the strength and weakness of Skinner's views on society and the design of culture. His views would appear extraordinarily adventurous in the light of our discussion in Chapters 1, 3, 4 and 5 — they represent a long leap from the general animal psychology of power (stimulus) to the human sociology of power. In a sense, Skinner is the modern behavioural science counterpart of Machiavelli. More than Machiavelli, Skinner can lay claim to a brand of science to back up his proposal of how humans can be better governed or not governed. The application of this science, as we have just seen, does not seem to offer any permanent solution to the problems of society. What is critically lacking in this brand of science and its application is the firm understanding of how the locus of power in modern complex societies has shifted away from individual personnels and their decisions or nondecisions. Associated with this lack of perspective is the oversight of the problems which are inherent in the power structure of a society. As a result, Skinner's approach to the problems of society is not unlike Machiavelli's; and it shares with the latter all the pitfalls due to the failure of distinguishing properly between the "ruler" and the "state".

Yet we should not lose sight of an admirable quality of Skinner, namely, his profound and persistent concern with the political and cultural relevance of his work. This quality is all too rare amongst *social* psychologists. For instance, why, the "Walden Two" was not written by a social psychologist?

Power in Heider's naive psychology

In Skinner's radical behaviourism, behaviour is under the control of stimulus which in turn is held to be mediated, in the final analysis, by the external environment. A rather different approach is provided by Heider's (1958) naive psychology, which makes liberal use of the notion of power and turns the latter into an integral part in the analysis of the action of the individual. In a manner which is parallel to Lewin's famous formula, Heider reasons that an individual's action is a joint function of personal and environmental factors. Personal factors include the power of the individual, his intention and how hard he is trying (exertion). Power refers to what "a person *can cause*, either because of his individual physical or intellectual capacities, or because of his position in relation to other people" (p. 238). Defined in this way, power corresponds to its original Latin meaning of "able to" and includes both personal and social power. It is intended as a non-motivational factor in contradistinction to trying, which is a motivational factor. The magnitude of a person's power is inversely proportional to the amount of trying that is required of him to overcome a certain difficulty.

Heider groups the power factor and the effective environmental force together under the concept "can". "Can" and "trying" constitute the two major factors in his discussion of the attribution process. Attribution studies usually operationalize the factor can in terms of ability (an example of Heider's personal power factor) and task difficulty (an environmental factor). The ability may be adequate and inadequate for the task, but in either case, the operationalization sets up a relatively stable power relation between the person and the environment. Within such a relation, the research paradigm looks for variation in the attribution of causality. When, for example, a person "can" achieve a task and yet fails, people would attribute the cause of failure to his not trying hard enough. On the other hand, when he "cannot" but succeeds, the relatively stable power relation implied by "cannot" would induce people to look around and attribute the cause of success to extraneous factors such as luck. Accordingly, if certain categories of people are being stereotyped as "cannot" (e.g. women, subordinate ethnic minorities), their success would be attributed to the imponderable element of luck (Deaux and Emswiller, 1974; Feather and Simon, 1971).

The role of *social* power in attribution received attention from an experiment carried out by Thibaut and Riecken (1955) which examined the effect of power relation on the attribution of locus of causality. It was found that (1) when person Y had high relative power, person X would perceive Y's compliance to X's influence attempt as located inside Y, that is, internally or self-caused; and (2) when person Z had low relative power, X would perceive Z's compliance as located outside Z, that is, as a consequence of coercion by the induced force of X. In short, the experimentally induced power relation provided an important cue to make attributions about the social autonomy of a person.

At this point, two general questions can be raised. When neither the personal nor social power of the stimulus person is defined, will people nevertheless infer it and then use the inferred power for making attributions? Secondly, what is the process underlying the attribution of power? A recent theoretical attempt by Schopler and Layton (1974) provides a promising start in answering the second question at the dyadic level. They generate a framework for predicting attribution of interpersonal power based on two subjective probability estimates which are logically analogous to Dahl's (1957) definition of power. The framework presupposes a closed dyadic system in order to exclude sources of power outside the system from complicating the analysis. This is an unfortunate but apparently necessary restriction, for otherwise many of the shortcomings inherent in Dahl's definition which we have examined in Chapter 5 would operate. Schopler and Layton are then able to illustrate how several classes of phenomena can be interpreted coherently in terms of power attributions, and in this way provide an indirect and partial affirmation to the first question.

Heider has made other interesting and inspiring discussion about the attitude toward power, and the means used in demonstrating personal power. Noting that the attitudes of people toward power/strength and powerlessness/weakness may be both positive, he suggests that the nature of the positive attitudes is different in the two cases. Power, or the strength of a person, evokes "positive evaluation" and "respect"; whereas the positive attitude towards weakness has more to do with "love, pity, sympathy, and with the actions of helping, giving support" (p. 239). A powerless person can therefore activate in another person the social norm of giving help and thereby obliges the latter to help him. From this reasoning it is a short step to the dependence-is-power theories of Berkowitz and Daniels (1963, 1964), and Schopler and Bateson (1965). Studies of new immigrants to Israel by Katz and Danet (1966), and Danet (1973) have also shown how immigrants from traditional backgrounds relied on their apparent powerlessness and dependence in invoking favourable particularistic treatments from the Israeli customs bureaucracy.

An act of harm rather than an act of benefit can serve to demonstrate more convincingly the agent's power. This is because in the case of benefit, its acceptance or rejection depends entirely on the recipient. On the other hand, an agent inflicting harm stands a better chance of getting at the target, for

> Harm provides a more direct and obvious arena for a power contest since [the target] can be counted on to retaliate if he sees a chance of victory . . . Abstention on [the target's] part generally gives recognition to the [agent's] superior power, and defeated revenge reaffirms it. (Heider, 1958, p. 262-263)

In this respect, it is interesting to note that although Heider has explicitly intended power to be a non-motivational personal factor as opposed to the motivational factor of exertion, he comes very near to suggesting a need of power. In view of the close connection between harm on the one hand and aggression and violence on the other, Heider's reasoning that harm serves better than benefit in demonstrating the agent's power has some interesting implication for the study of aggression and violence.

In reviewing a number of approaches to the study of aggression, Tedeschi *et al.* (1974) suggest that aggression can also be conceived as a prima facie instance of coercive power. An understanding of the causes and purposes of aggression would be advanced by uncovering the factors which lead a person to use coercive power. One such factor, according to Tedeschi *et al.* (1972), is the motivational need of the person. Similarly, Raven and Kruglanski (1970) have concluded that the choice of coercive and other forms of power cannot be predicted by assuming only a rational model of man — one must also examine the man's motivational state. What is the motive underlying the exercise of coercive power that inflicts harm on another person? Heider would seem to suggest that it is the actor's needs of demonstrating convincingly his power. It is interesting to note that a number of authors have developed a view similar to Heider's.

McKellar (1977) distinguishes between "hot" and "cold" anger: short-lived, obstacle-removing anger, vs long-enduring, revengeful anger. Hot anger is provoked when the individual's goal-directed behaviour is thwarted, and the purpose of this anger is to remove or destroy the offending obstacle. This type of situation, which McKellar calls the "Need" situation, would seem to fit the frustration-aggression thesis. Cold anger, on the other hand, is provoked when the person is humiliated; and the aim of such anger is to hurt and humiliate in return. McKellar calls this the "Personality" situation. An example will be the motorist who wilfully and forcefully drives his car into another motorist's car in order to return a humiliation, and who considers that the damage which he has done to his own car is worth it. The behaviour of cold anger provoked by the Personality situation illustrates neatly an aggressive act which serves the need of demonstrating or restoring the actor's (threatened) power.

The results of the following experiments indicate that a threat to a person's power would instigate hostility and aggression against the source of the threat, and that aggression apparently serves to restore the person's power. Maslow (1941) has suggested that goal-blocking (i.e. frustration) alone will not lead to aggression or hostility, threat is also necessary. The idea was taken up by Horwitz (1958), who operationalized threat in terms of the reduction of a person's expected social power. In one experiment, reduction of expected social power was implemented by usurping, illegitimately, the power (votes) initially assigned to the experimental subjects. He found that the subjects expressed greater hostility following a frustration that reduced their expected social power as compared to a frustration which did not reduce their power. Another experiment showed that hostility increased progressively over three treatment levels which involved increasing degrees of power reduction. The main effect due to power reduction therefore could not be entirely attributed to illegitimacy, and the results of the second experiment would support the contention that hostility was at least partly instigated by the reduction of a person's expected social power. However, there was no evidence in these experiments to show that the subjects' sense of power was indeed restored after their expression of aggression.

A recent experiment by Worchel *et al.* (1978) showed a significant main effect on the use of aggression (administering electric shock to another person) due to the subjects being insulted by the target person. The operationalization of the insult was intended to constitute a threat to or a decrease in the self-esteem of the subjects. Such a decrease in the subjects' self-esteem was taken by the authors to be equivalent to a reduction in the subjects' sense of personal power. The experimental results strongly suggest that the use of aggression by the subjects served to restore the latter's sense of power. Again, as in Horwitz's (op. cit.) experiments, there was no independent evidence to show that the use of aggression had actually enhanced the subjects' power. A clear-cut experiment remains to be carried out.

Fanon (1967) recommends violence to the "wretched of the earth", suggesting that the use of violence against their colonial master would cleanse and free them from inferiority, despair and inaction, and make them fearless and restore their self-respect. The development of an intergroup relation characterized by the use of violence, or other non-violent but equally direct and coercive power such as a crippling industrial strike or sit-in, may indeed serve a certain need of power. Violence and other forms of coercive power can provide a dramatic and swift means of producing immediate impact, thus altering the perception of personal causality from one of the Pawn to one of the Origin. It should be noted that no causal relationship between power motivation and interpersonal or intergroup relation is implied here. What is intended is the suggestion that the use of coercive power may, under certain situations, enhance the feeling of power; and that the power motivation may be a contributing factor to the use of coercion.

The above line of reasoning can be related to our earlier discussion (see Chapter 4) on the reciprocal relationship between power comparison and conflict. Conflict is often the most effective way of ascertaining the relative power of the parties. The power comparison established through conflict and its subsequent acceptance by the parties would make further conflict unnecessary. Peace returns and would last until the existent power comparison becomes unstable once again. Added to this idea that coercive power can demonstrate convincingly the actor's power would explain partly why conflict is often associated with violent or non-violent coercion.

At this point we are already branching out into the power relation between people, a topic which will be taken up in the following chapter.

7 Psychological Views of Social Power

This chapter will be concerned with the power relation between people, that is, social power. In social psychology, field-theory and social exchange theory are most heavily involved with this topic. The contributions made by these and other theoretical systems in social psychology have been broadly reviewed by Schopler (1965), and Collins and Raven (1969). In so far as the theoretical analysis of social power is concerned, neither field-theory nor social exchange theory has made any advancement of significance since around 1964, even though they have been elaborated and have influenced much of the empirical research. My discussion on the field-theoretical analysis of social power will focus on the postulated relationship between power, influence and dependence.

Power and dependence are key theoretical constructs in the study of social influence, leading to what Moscovici (1976) has called the conformity bias. The theoretical role of power as postulated by field-theory has been flatly rejected by Moscovici, who has seriously proposed to disband the concept of power from the study of social influence in general, and from the study of minority influence in particular. This proposal deserves careful consideration, and I shall make an attempt to that end. It seems to me that between the conformity bias and the active minority, there is still a place for power.

The third and final section is devoted to a critical examination of the social exchange analyses of power and power change. I shall try to point out an implicit assumption of *laissez faire* liberalizm behind the social exchange analyses, and how this assumption is reflected in the selective treatment of power change.

Field-theoretical conception of power and influence

Lewin (1944) regards power as one important field-theoretical construct which is dynamically related to other constructs. A basic construct is *position*, defined as a spatial relation of regions (e.g. occupational position). The relation of positions at different times is *locomotion*. The tendency to locomotion is *force*, and the possibility of inducing forces of a certain magnitude on another person is *power*. It is interesting to note the way Lewin distinguishes between *goal* and *values*. A goal has the conceptual dimension of a force field where all forces point toward the same region. A goal is therefore a positive valence. Values, on the other hand, do not have the character of a goal. They merely influence behaviour by determining which activity has a positive and which has a negative valence for a person. They are not force fields but they induce force fields. In this way, values are constructs which have the same psychological dimension as power fields. Power is formally defined in a discussion of "organizational" dependence and unity. A's power over B equals the quotient of the maximum force which A can induce on B, and the maximum resistance which B can offer (Lewin, 1941). Note that in both the 1941 and 1944 statements, power refers to induced force, not *change* as such. The maximum change which can be induced by A in B defines B's organizational *dependence* on A. B's dependence on A will be equivalent to A's power over B when it is assumed that there is a close relation between induced change and induced force, an assumption which Lewin (1941) regards as "reasonable". Analytically, it is important to keep the distinction between force and change, and hence power and dependence.

Lewin then relates the concept of power to the organizational unity of a whole and the ease with which change can be induced. In a dynamic whole, a leading region which has a greater relative power over the led region is called a "head". The greater the power of the head over the led region, the easier it is for the head to induce change. The organizational unity of a whole is then defined as equal to the power of the strongest head over the rest of the whole. If the whole is composed of equal power parts, organizational unity will be small. This happens during development when the whole differentiates into more and more parts, leading toward regression or disorganization. With the emergence of a predominant head or a new higher head which assigns the previous heads the role of subheads, organizational unity will increase. In the latter case, the degree of hierarchical organization of the whole is also increasing. Note that "whole" refers to the topological representation of a field in general, and is not confined to a person.

Later development in the analysis of power by field theorists grew out of their concern with the study of social influence processes, which have remained a dominant topic in social psychology. The manner in which social influence is construed, as described by Cartwright and Zander (1968a), is more or less a re-statement of Lewin's concept of organizational dependence in the active voice.

> In examining specific instances of influence, we shall be concerned with *acts* performed by O and with changes in states of P. If O performs an act that results in a change in a particular state of P, we shall say that O *influences* P with respect to that state. (p. 215)

Power continues to be defined in the Lewinian manner, except that it is no longer expressed as the quotient of induced force and resistance, but as the difference between them (Cartwright, 1959; French and Raven, 1959). It is thus inevitable that influence is intimately related to power, just as Lewin has said that it is reasonable to expect a close relation between induced change and induced force. Specifically, power is potential influence, and influence is power in action. The analysis of influence must hence necessarily require an analysis of power. And the way to do it, at the dyadic level, is to start at the source of power and influence, namely, an act performed by the agent, which usually takes the form of a communication, either intentionally or unintentionally.

In keeping with the distinction between induced force and induced change, a power relation need neither be asymmetric nor controlling. A and B may have equal reciprocal power on one another, a relation which is different from a non-power relation wherein neither A nor B has power over the other. In an asymmetric power relation, A may or may not control the behaviour of B. From the view-point of political behaviourism (see Chapter 5), both the symmetric equal-power relation and the asymmetrical but non-controlling power relation would not qualify as power relations at all because there are no observable effects. Both are regarded as proper power relations in field theory because here power, being defined as potential influence, is a variable rather than a none-or-all relation. This becomes clear in the distinction drawn between power and control (French and Raven, 1959; Cartwright, 1959b). When A is able to activate forces acting on B but unable to change B's behaviour, A is said to have power over B but cannot control him.

The insistence among field theorists on coordinating power to specific acts is largely dictated by their own terms of reference which is with interpersonal influence in dyadic relationships. Undoubtedly, the important role of "agent" in the language of field theory, and the orientation of locating changes in the acts of agents are also responsible for the manifestation of this type of behaviourism and methodological individualism. The over-riding factor, however, seems to be the interpersonal level of analysis. Thus, it is apparent that before field theorists turned their attention from the power of a group over its members to interpersonal power, that power was not coordinated to the acts of individual agents, but to group cohesiveness (Festinger *et al.*, 1950).

Whereas the source of interpersonal power is said to originate from an act performed by the influencing agent, the *bases* or *resources* of power lie elsewhere. The best known typology of power bases is the one produced by Raven and his associates, which has been used in a large number of empirical research in laboratory experiments and ongoing social relationships. French and Raven (1959) initially listed five bases of power, each giving rise to one type of power: reward, coercive, legitimate, referent and expert power. Informational influence, which is based on the content of the communication, was distinguished from expert power, which is based on the credibililty of the agents. Information was not referred to as a type of power. The five types of power fall into two classes, depending on whether or not the induced change brought about by the agent requires surveillance for its continuance. Reward and coercive powers would require surveillance while the others do not. Raven (1965) added information as the sixth type of power on the basis that it is uniquely different from expert and other types of power. The induced change as a result of information is internalized by the person and its continuance becomes independent from the agent, whereas the change brought about by the other types of power continues to depend on the agent although it may or may not require surveillance. This three-way classification is important in that it pushes the analysis of power beyond the mere identification of induced change and examines the stability of the change. It also provides a good match with Kelman's (1961) three processes of social influence (Raven, 1974).

Empirical research leaves little doubt that each type of power can be successfully operationalized to effect some change in the influencee.

Grouping of the six types into three classes also helps to illuminate the consequence of power beyond the immediate induction of change. What is lacking in the conceptual exercise is a scheme that would delineate the functional and sequential relationships between the various types or classes of power. Since informational power is more effective than the others, why is it that the latter still continue to exist? Is it because information presupposes a certain normative order which originates outside information and requires other forms of power for its maintenance? Since reward is uneconomical and coercion is ultimately self-defeating, would they not tend to transform into other types of power that are more economical and productive? If one type of power were more primary than another, at what stage in the influence process would they differentiate or merge? Questions concerning the relationships between types of power are as important as the classification of power, and they immediately arise when one wants to know the power process in on-going social interactions.

The six types of power are often discussed and used to guide research in such a manner as if it were only the kind or type of power that will matter. The quantitative variable of the power differential between agent and influence has been largely ignored. As pointed out by Mauk Mulder, whose work we shall examine in a later chapter, the quantitative variable is not just another variable but is one of fundamental importance in all power relations, including the power relation between the agent and influencee. As a matter of fact, an unpublished report by Raven *et al.* (1962) contains an argument with supporting data indicating the importance of this quantative variable. They examined and found an interesting interaction between referent and expert powers. The defining character of expert power is the possession of a certain superior characteristic. Such a characteristic, by virtue of its superiority, simultaneously distinguishes the expert from the influencee, who is a lesser expert or non-expert. In other words, expertise means difference, and the greater the expertise, the greater would be the difference separating the agent from the influencee. Referent power, on the other hand, presupposes certain similarity on which the influencee bases his identification with the agent. When such a similarity comes into conflict with the difference on which expert power is based, an agent will find his referent and expert powers pulling in opposite directions. He cannot wield maximum referent power and maximum expert power at the same time. When he is too great an expert, he loses his referent power. To increase his referent power, he must let go some of his expert power.

As far as interpersonal power in the face-to-face setting is concerned, the agent is in a direct relationship with the influencee, and hence referent power is always present although it may vary both in degrees as well as in valence. This indicates that other types of power cannot operate in isolation from referent power. They must necessarily interact with referent power. Their effects should therefore be considered in conjunction with their interaction with referent power. The reasoning put forward in the preceding paragraph concerning the inverse relation between expert and referent powers indicates that it is the amount of power that is the critical element in ascertaining the interaction. From this it would follow that the quantitative variable of the differential between the power of the agent and the influencee, *wherever this is quantifiable*, is as important as the qualitative nature of the type of power in the social influence process. A full discussion of the power differential variable will be presented in Chapter 8.

The causal relation between power and influence as advocated by Lewin and his students has dominated the American social psychological thinking on social influence. It has left a deep mark in the experimental paradigm used in conformity research, as well as in the theoretical interpretation of conformity and normalization. A recent attempt by Tedeschi and his associates to formulate a general theory of the social influence processes bears the same mark, although it also takes into account certain elements from social exchange theory and is couched in the language of decision-making. The following discussion will centre first on Tedeschi's theory and then conformity.

The attempt by Tedeschi and his associates has resulted in the Subjective Expected Value Theory (Tedeschi *et al.*, 1972) and the Subjective Expected Utility Theory of social influence (Tedeschi *et al.*, 1973). Both are behavioural decision theories which assume that the decision-maker will act so as to maximize the subjective expected value (SEV) or the subjective expected utility (SUE). SEV is the mathematical product of the *objective* value of an outcome and the probability of its occurrence. SEV does not take into account idiosyncratic perceptions of objective value which are influenced by such personal factors as need and satiation. The concept of utility takes care of that and is defined as the *subjective* value of an outcome for a particular individual. Apart from this theoretical distinction. SEU also differs from SEV in that the probability component is now used to refer to the subjective estimation of the chance of the occurrence of an outcome. The SEU therefore requires psychological measurements rather than a straightforward computation of objective data. However, it has been further assumed that in experiments "the average of the subjects' utilities and subjective probabilities should approximate the objective values and probabilities" (Tedeschi *et al.*, 1973, p. 59). The basic syntax of the two theories remains identical despite the above two theoretical distinctions. In the schematic overview of the SEU Theory (Tedeschi *et al.*, 1973, p. 67), for instance, the term "utility" has replaced "value" in the previous overview of the SEV Theory (Tedeschi *et al.*, 1972, p. 357), but otherwise the two overviews are exactly identical.

The SEU Theory purports to explain a number of influence outcomes (the Dependent Variables), which include compliance, conformity, attitude change, response frequency and imitation. These are to be traced back ultimately to five Independent Variables. Four of the latter variables refer to the characteristics of the agent (which constitute the "source factor") and the fifth one to the credibility and utilitarian implication of the communication issued by the agent ("message factor"). The Independent Variables, when perceived by the influencee, would induce certain cognitions in the mind of the influencee (Target Cognition). On the basis of Target Cognition, the influencee infers the subjective expected utilities of the influence message as well as decision alternatives, which constitute the Predictor Variables for predicting the Dependent Variables.

The variables comprising the source factor refer to the power bases of the agent. With the exception of information power, all the types of power listed by French and Raven are present and are partly recombined in a novel way. Reward and coercive power also play a role in the message factor by backing up the agent's communication to the influencee.

Four types of communications or messages have been distinguished: threats, promises, warnings and mendations (Tedeschi *et al.*, 1972). The difference between threats and promises on the one hand, and warnings and mendations on the other, depends on whether the agent mediates or does not mediate the reward and punishment. Thus a threat refers to the agent's prediction of a contingency between the influencee's behaviour and an unfavourable outcome, where the outcome is controlled by the agent. Where the outcome is not controlled or affected by the agent, a threat becomes a warning. Similarly, a mendation is to a promise as a warning is to a threat. These four types of messages convey openly the agent's wish and constitute the open influence modes, to be distinguished from manipulative modes in which the agent operates clandestinely and disguises his intentions (Tedeschi *et al.*, 1972).

The relation between power and influence in the SEU Theory is clear: influence is ultimately derived from the power of the agent and the manner in which he communicates to the influencee. The influencee is assigned an active cognitive role busily processing the message and his cognitions of the power base of the agent. As well, the influencee weighs various decision alternatives against one another. At the end, he decides what to do with the message.

The concept of utility and the inclusion of decision alternatives reflect the "influence" of social exchange theory. Tedeschi's social influence theory in general is a combination of the field-theoretical and social exchange conceptions of power linked together by the language of decision-making. A similar approach which focuses on the perceptions and decisions of the actors has also been proposed by Pollard and Mitchell (1972). Tedeschi rejects the inclusive view of power which identifies power with all instances of interpersonal causation. He is less explicit with regard to what he would accept as the necessary components of a delimited concept of power. My impression is that he favours the view which regards power as the ability in the employment of sanctions and rewards in situations involving certain conflict of interests. The exercise of power would necessarily involve the overcoming of resistance. His views on power, as distinct from that of social influence in general, resemble closely the two-dimensional view of Bachrach and Baratz. (This impression is mainly based on Tedeschi and Bonoma, 1972, pp. 2–8; Tedeschi *et al.*, 1977, pp. 314–322; Tedeschi *et al.*, 1973, pp. 28–32.)

Between the conformity bias and the active minority

Normalization arises from reciprocal influence (Sherif, 1936), and conformity, from majority influence (Asch, 1951). These are well-known enough to make any summary unnecessary. Our point of departure is Moscovici's (1976) critique of what he calls the conformity bias and his reinterpretation of conformity and normalization.

Conformity is the change induced by the majority on a minority towards the majority's position or norm. In the conformity paradigm, influence is (1) regarded as flowing unilaterally from the majority to the minority who is (2) seen as reacting passively to the influence. This paradigm, Moscovici (1976) argues, presents a partial and biased approach to social influence when it is judged from the perspective of the "genetic point of view". From the latter point of view, influence is bilateral or reciprocal, and can be generated by the minority as well as the majority. Accordingly, a broader conception of social influence should include not only majority influence, but also reciprocal influence and minority influence. Successful minority influence leads to innovation and change, the very opposites of conformity and the preservation of the status quo that arise from majority influence.

At a deeper level, the conformity bias is embodied in (3) the theoretical position that influence stems from power, and from this, (4) the explanation of conformity in terms of the minority's dependence on the majority. It would be apparent that (3) coincides with the position advocated by field theory. The trouble with such a position, Moscovici asserts, is that influence and power are being confounded to the point where other, non-power, sources of influence cannot be visualized. As a consequence, it is hard to envisage that a minority can influence the majority unless the minority has first achieved some sort of superior power. Indeed, Hollander's (1960) attempt to investigate the influence of an individual minority on the group, as formulated in the thesis of idiosyncrasy credit, is premised on the individual's first gaining status through conforming. The underlying assumption of this thesis is that minority influence can only be staged from the top, and not by one who remains at the bottom.

Whereas (3) looks at the influence process from the point of view of the agent by uncovering his power base or the lack of it, (4) provides a complementary view by examining the relative powerlessness of the influencee, which is manifested in his dependence on the agent. Two kinds of dependence have been advanced (Jones and Gerard, 1967; Deutsch and Gerard, 1955). A minority depends on the majority for information about the nature of social reality (information dependence), as well as for their role in the direct mediation of outcomes for the satisfaction of needs (effect or normative dependence). Information dependence is activated when a person is uncertain about his opinion. The two types of dependence help to illuminate and elaborate Lewin's concept of organizational dependence. Information dependence, in particular, converges with Sherif's postulate of the need for a stable perceptual frame of reference to reduce uncertainty. More than effect dependence, it has been regarded as basic to the general influence process. However, as far as the basic premise concerning the relation amongst dependence, power, and influence is concerned, not much new theoretical ground has been broken since Lewin's 1941 statement. This remark, it should be noted, is not Moscovici's. His remarks are more far-reaching and embracing. For the present purpose, I will examine only Moscovici's proposal to disband power from the social influence process, a proposal which Moscovici on another occasion (Moscovici, 1975) has maintained as one of the two basic truths upheld by the active minority approach to social influence.

In social interaction, influence of various kinds occurs. A social psychology that concerns itself with social interaction must therefore allow a central place for influence. As we have just noted, students of influence in the Lewinian tradition identify influence with the overt expression of power; while Moscovici, as we shall soon discover, insists that there is an important divergence and a fundamental practical and theoretical difference between influence and power. The issue raised by Moscovici is clearly not merely one of terminological nuance. It cuts deeply into the theoretical construction of what constitutes and produces influence. The basic questions which Moscovici raises in the study of minority influence have all helped to bring the issue into sharp focus.

In a series of experiments, Moscovici and his associates are able to demonstrate that a minority (usually of two) can influence the majority on a perceptual task, such as in inducing the majority to say "green" to a blue slide. The minority have no "power" over the majority in these experiments, since the majority do not fall into either an information or effect dependence on the minority. This is particularly true in those experiments involving a nomic majority, that is, a majority who possess a common norm or dominant response of their own. The major factor of the success of the minority is their behavioural styles. The behavioural style that has received the most attention and which seems to be the most decisive one is consistency. This refers to the consistency between the minority members, as well as the consistency in the relation between the position which they advocate and the changes in the stimulus field. Consistency alone is not sufficient. At the same time, the minority must present their position in a distinctive and certain manner, and with an aura of autonomy, investment and fairness. Armed with these behavioural styles, the minority not only can induce a change in the majority which is comparable to that found in majority influence, but can also influence to a deeper level than the majority (Moscovici and Lage, 1976). As well, an experiment by Wahrman and Pugh (1972) shows that contrary to Hollander's idiosyncrasy credit hypothesis, a minority who first tried to gain status through conformity before adopting a deviant position had less influence than a nonconforming minority. The import of these experiments is that behavioural styles replace power as the main factor in bringing about influence.

On the theoretical side, Moscovici formulates the thesis that the influence process is directly related to the production and resolution of conflict, in which inter-individual dynamics take precedence over intra-individual dynamics. According to this thesis, conformity is a means of *resolving* the conflict presented by the contradiction between the majority and minority's positions. Normalization enables both sides to *avoid* the impending conflict in which neither side wants to engage. Innovation, finally, is mediated by the conflict which the minority *create* for the majority. This conflict explanation provides an alternative to the information dependence explanation currently in use to interpret conformity and normalization. In contrast to the conflict explanation, the latter relies on the postulate of some intra-individual dynamics in the reduction of uncertainty. Dependence, and hence power, become unnecessary not only for the successful instigation of influence, but also for the purpose of interpreting the influence. Moscovici states:

> By insisting on power and influence as interchangeable concepts, focusing on dependence and neglecting behavioural styles, many social psychologists have worked hard to build scientific knowledge around phenomena which, as far as we know, raise no problems and require no explanation. Or at least, they took as their starting-point a perspective that was unproblematic, and therefore raised questions which needed no answers. (1976, p. 151)

To rectify the failure of the conformity bias, Moscovici advocates the separation of influence from power, and argues that power cannot be the cause but is rather the result of influence. "Only by rejecting the present exclusive and overwhelming preoccupation with dependence and the model of social relations which is built around it, shall we be able to extend our vision" (Moscovici, 1976, p. 62). The success of the study of minority influence speaks for itself, and there is reason to believe that Moscovici's insistence on the divorce of influence from power has been instrumental to the success. With this, there can be no quarrel. The questions which I want to raise are of a more general nature.

The aim of research in social influence is not so trivial as to content itself with only demonstrating how some people can be induced to say "green" to a blue slide, or "long" to a short line in the laboratory setting. The aim, or at least the avowed aim, is to understand the general process of influence. Experimental findings are only one link for such an understanding to be extended, albeit a vital link. Where laboratory experimentation ends, social analysis should begin. Or rather: before experimentation, social analysis should have begun, such that where experimentation ends, social analysis will continue. The two statements are not contradictory, they rather point to two complementary roles of experimentation. Thus it is pertinent to examine Moscovici's proposal of separating influence from power on a more general level. After all, he himself has pitched the discussion of the relation between influence and power on a macro level. Since, too, Nemeth (1975) has pleaded that the contribution of the active minority studies should be discussed in relation to the more general process which these studies try to illuminate.

Let us forget field theory for the moment and raise the naive question of what is meant by influence. Moscovici (1974) has warned us that it is futile to give a dictionary definition of influence because such a definition would be misleading and inadequate for covering the facts that he has subsumed under this term. A sample of these facts includes the creation or preservation of social relations, socialization, and the establishment of rules. In fact, influence is said to be inherent in the dialectical relation between the individual and the group or society, and can be found even in the mere copresence of two persons. "Each individual's judgements, behaviours, and perceptions take place in the copresence of, or in relation to, other persons, whose judgements, behaviours and perceptions interfere with his own" (Moscovici, 1974, p. 181). And later, "It is my contention that influence is the central process of social psychology, upon which all other processes depend. As such, it could serve as the principle which could integrate all the facts and all the theories of social psychologists. Without recognition of this, there can be no progress in theoretical and empirical knowledge. This will remain true at least as long as interaction is assumed to be the main concern of social psychology

— something that has tended to be overlooked recently" (Moscovici, 1976, pp. 6–7). It becomes obvious that what Moscovici means by influence coincides with induced change, and hence influence, in field theory.

Instead of assuming that influence is an extension of power, Moscovici demarcates between influence and power. In Moscovici (1974), he does this by distinguishing two kinds of social pressures: institutional and inferential pressures. Institutional pressures are exerted by legitimate institutions and the social agents for the purpose of maintaining the cohesion of the group or society as a whole. These pressures are based on the agents' formal positions, and their control over resources and the means of reward and punishment. Inferential pressures are of a moral or spiritual nature. They are rooted in the cognitions, values and symbols shared by the members of groups and society. Their existence provides greater coherence and predictability for social interaction, as well as an increased awareness of interdependence and group goals. Between these two kinds of pressures, Moscovici states, "There is an important divergence and a fundamental practical and theoretical difference" (p. 188). This divergence or difference arises because institutional pressures represent a power relation, whereas inferential pressures reflect influence relations.

> (In a power relation) the convergence or submission is due to the domination of A over B . . . through the means at A's disposal to compel B to obey his orders, without necessarily referring to the intrinsic properties of this opinion. What makes B change his position is not necessarily a genuine modification of his judgement or preference as a result of what A says; B changes his position because of the satisfactions A can grant him and the punishment A is authorized to inflict on him. (Moscovici, 1974, pp. 188-189)

And,

> (In an influence relation) the convergence of judgements or opinions results from the capacity of the group or individuals to express the values, the point of view usually shared, making it convincing and alive . . . Inferential pressures . . . force the individual to go beyond his action; they appeal to his internal frame of reference, his beliefs, and draw a conclusion between his actions and beliefs, thus giving a meaning to what he does or thinks. The appeal to the sense of guilt, to humaneness, or to loyalty, always represents such a pressure, a very effective one. (p. 189)

It becomes apparent from the above quotations that Moscovici holds a consensual view of influence while endorsing a coercive view of power. The distinction he makes between influence and power coincides with Friedrich's distinction between authority and power (see Chapter 4). Influence, or inferential pressure, coincides with Friedrich's definition of authority as reasoned communal elaboration. Our discussion in Chapter 4 of Friedrich and the controversies surrounding the rationalist and Utopian conceptions of power would suggest that any clear-cut demarcation between power and influence beyond the "ideal type" of distinction in Weber's sense would serve only to produce a partial and superficial analysis of either "power" or "influence". At the *sociological* level, the conclusion drawn by Moscovici that, "The exertion of influence does not require power. If one has power, he does not need to exert influence" (1974, p. 189), is as naive as it is short-sighted. A more penetrating analysis of "power" and "influence" can be served by regarding them as the extreme ends of a power continuum in the Weberian sense. "Power" then corresponds to the coercive end while "influence" would correspond to the consensual end of power.

In Moscovici (1976), he goes further and presents an analysis of the relation between power and influence with the conclusion that "Therefore, if power presupposes influence, and is in part a result of influence, we cannot possibly consider it as the cause of influence" (p. 62). The conclusion is reached by raising the intriguing question: what is the origin of power? This question is approached first by making a distinction between "coercive power" (coercion and reward) and "normative power" (expertise and legitimation). Only "normative power" is then included in the analysis. (It would serve no useful purpose to ask if the above conclusion can apply to "coercive power" as well, which it obviously cannot.) The ensuing analysis is simple and straightforward. "Normative power" requires for its operation the precondition of a certain value consensus. The sharing and attribution of values are contingent on individuals having been previously influenced (i.e. not coerced or in any other way). From this the above conclusion is drawn.

That the influence process, in Moscovici's sense, becomes heavily involved in the establishment of a consensus does not mean that the analysis should stop there. Inasmuch as one should ask about the origin of power, one must also query the origin of influence. Not to ask the latter question serves only to foreshadow the conclusion that "power" is the result of "influence". Even if we accepted Moscovici's thesis concerning the effectiveness of the minority's behavioural styles, it does not follow that all the important events of influence in society can only be instigated by active minorities who are outside the power system. What can happen does not mean that it usually happens that way. The combined strength of the social psychological analysis of influence, from the failure of the conformity bias to the success of minority influence, does not warrant the generalization of the autonomous and unique status of behavioural styles in the laboratory to the influence process in the world at large, much less to the origin of power.

The citation by Moscovici of the exemplary careers of such successful active minorities as Copernicus and Freud does not in itself provide any more convincing argument than that given by Machiavelli in his citation of the careers of *unsuccessful* active minorities, which points to the opposite conclusion. If the active minorities in the cultural and political history of, say, China, were to be counted and sorted out into those who were successful and those who were not, the probability of Moscovici being supported would be pretty low. Then one must not make the strong assumption of relying on recorded history alone, because unsuccessful active minorities are less likely than their successful counterparts to be given a place in history. The gentlemen who wrote the history books, and the political and ideological conditions under which they did their writing, must also be kept in mind in the assessment of how history was made by active minorities. The dictum that every new idea begins in a minority of one, as quoted by Moscovici, cannot be falsified because it must be true by the definition "new". Innovation and change are undoubtedly topics of immense significance, but to take as the starting point the behavioural styles of the active minorities may not carry the analysis far enough. Men make their own history, Karl Marx said, but they do not make it as they please. The assessment of the role of the behavioural styles should be carried out in relation to the role of other factors, and this should perhaps be undertaken in a sounder framework such as that provided by the sociology of knowledge (e.g. Berger and Luckmann, 1967).

There are good reasons to end this discussion by suggesting that power should now be invited back to the study of minority influence. Minorities do not refer to their numbers but to their subordinate position in a power hierarchy (Moscovici, 1976, p. 19). The influence exerted by an individual who is in a position of power, according to the above definition, is not an instance of minority influence. The general tenor of Moscovici's argument suggests that this kind of regular influence which stems directly from power is so obvious that it hardly raises any problem requiring an explanation. It certainly sounds more challenging to explain the influence from below than from above. The point is, however, that the two cannot be neatly separated unless one is confined to dealing with the minority's influence on a mere collection of unrelated individuals, in which case it is no longer an instance of *minority* influence. What is unproblematic about influence from the top constitutes a problem for influence from below. In other words, the more efficient social control is, the more difficult minority influence would become. It is precisely because minority influence does not take place in a power vacuum that somewhere in the line of its analysis, power will move to the foreground.

One can, along with Weber's analysis of charisma, begin the analysis of minority influence in terms of legitimacy (see Chapter 3). An active minority need not accumulate enough legitimacy or idiosyncrasy credit before they can start influencing. *The nature of the influence attempt can be seen as the very base of the legitimacy of a charismatic kind.* The reader will recall that in Weber's treatment of the subject, charismatic legitimacy lies in its being a revolutionary force. The charismatic leader, like Moscovici's active minority, always starts out as a true minority outside the existent power system. His legitimacy is derived from the very conflict which he creates with the institutional order. He converts and wields influence over his followers by his conscious and distinctive opposition to some established aspects of society or the group, and by revealing a new or different normative pattern. The fundamental resemblance between charismatic legitimacy and Moscovici's conflict theory should be abundantly clear. This is the more remarkable since they were formulated independently and at different levels. What separates them are their respective starting points. Moscovici starts from behavioural styles; and Weber, from the emancipatory effect produced by the charismatic leader's new claim to legitimacy.

Of course it may not be possible to analyse minority influence in the laboratory setting in terms of charismatic legitimacy. The existent experimental paradigm for the study of minority influence simply allows no place for this kind of analysis. It is only when the attention shifts to the on-going social process of minority influence that the relevance of Weber's analysis will become apparent. It is with such a possible development in the study of minority influence in mind that I venture to make the above — and the following — suggestions.

Moscovici has distinguished a group which has a norm or a code of its own from one which has none, and calls them nomic and anomic respectively. For reasons that should be obvious enough, the two kinds of groups present different problems to the active minority. If one adopted the rationalist image of society and the Janus-faced view of power outlined in Chapter 3, one can easily visualize a third type of group which, for the lack of a better term, may be called pseudo-nomic. By this I mean a group whose norm originated from an outside group and reflects the latter's interests. In general, the subordinate group in an intergroup relation can be viewed as a pseudo-nomic group with respect to those dominant norms, values, or models of proper behaviour imposed upon them by the superordinate group. The pseudo-nomic group may or may not fully identify with the imposed norm, but in either case, the norm would embody the interests of an external superordinate group that is otherwise absent in the norm of a nomic group. Because of this, the situation presented to the active minority by the pseudo-nomic group has two problems which are absent in the situation presented by a nomic group.

To influence a pseudo-nomic group, the active minority must first of all differentiate between the norm and the group members, and direct their attack on the former but not the latter. Mugny's (1975) experiment represents a similar line of thinking and remains important because of the basic questions it tries to illuminate. All revolutionary leaders, regardless of their ideology, take great pains to differentiate (and persuade others to do the same) between the existent oppressive government, which has to be overthrown, and the oppressed people, who need to be won over. While the relation between the active minority and the pseudo-nomic group members may not be one of power, (and indeed it is advantageous to the former to persuade the latter that their relation will never be a power one), the relation between the active minority and the pseudo-nomic group on one hand, and the target norm on the other, is a power relation in the final analysis. This leads to the second additional problem facing the active minority who try to influence a pseudo-nomic group. It is over this latter problem that the full range of power will move more and more to the foreground.

In the eyes of the outside group which impose the norm, the stirring signs of the active minority would appear more likely to be acts of "power" than either acts of "influence" (following Moscovici's distinction) or mere exhibition of behavioural styles. To the extent they do so, they would define the relation between them and the active minority as one of "power", not "influence". This definition of the situation, of course, may not always be sufficient to cause the active minority to reciprocate. So let us assume for a while that the latter continue their influence attempt in the manner after Moscovici.

Now, in keeping with Moscovici's (1976, p. 223) recommendation, we ought to take a long-range view of the influence process, and pay particular attention to the later phases. The later phases are concerned with the translation of the private acceptance of the minority's position to public acceptance. As soon as the translation begins, if not before, the outside group, finding their "influence" over the pseudo-nomic group being eroded and threatened, would resort to "power". The "influence relation" between the outside group and the pseudo-nomic group will transform overnight into a "power relation". At this stage of the influence process, what can the active minority do?

If the active minority still could and wanted to remain active, then more likely than not, they will begin to talk power. Whether they will converse in the language of the Holy Bible, Gandi's satyagraha (Bondurant, 1958), Machiavelli's "The Prince" upside down (Alinsky, 1971), or the complete works of Marx, Lenin and Mao, power to them will acquire a more positive meaning and a more generic term of reference than what have been intended by Moscovici. Some of them may of course continue defining the situation as one of "influence", much to the confusion of the pseudo-nomic group members. But regardless of the contradictory viewpoints which the three sides may bring to bear on the situation, and despite the diversity of viewpoints that may exist within each side, one can begin to analyse the situation only by bringing power back into the analysis. Our discussion of power in Part II will provide a lead in this direction, and I invite my fellow social psychologists to go further. It serves no useful purpose to regard power and behavioural styles as competing viewpoints, now that the earlier bias of power has been recognized. Instead they are complementary.

Social exchange and power

Social influence, whether it is in the form of normalization, conformity, or innovation, is identified by the change which the agent induces in the influencee. Since social influence is integral to social interaction, induced change is therefore a pervasive element of social interaction. From this point of view, a social psychology of social interaction is about induced changes. From the point of view of Thibaut and Kelley (1959), however, the concern of a social psychology of social interaction becomes something rather different.

Thibaut and Kelley (op. cit.) look at social interaction from a social exchange and reinforcement perspective. The participants in social interaction provide certain outcomes for one another. Depending on the nature and contingency of these outcomes, social interaction will take its course. Interaction can thus be seen as an on-going social exchange in which the behaviours of the participants are interdependent. A particular behaviour of one participant affects, and is itself affected by, the behaviour of the other participant. The pairing of the two behaviours yields an outcome to which the participants attach their respective subjective utilities. Since the outcome is a joint product of the behaviour of both participants, their behaviours are interdependent. Interaction proceeds as each participant selects from his own repertoire of behavioural sequences the optimal ones to match those of his counterpart. Both participants are assumed to be rational utilitarians and are capable of governing their behavioural sequences by reinforcement principles.

Such a perspective enables the student of social interaction focus on why the participants behave the way they do, including why they stay in or leave the relationship. The question of induced change becomes secondary. Theoretically, each participant can affect another's behaviour because the outcome is jointly determined and he can choose between different behaviours and thereby alter the outcome. The ability to elicit the desired behaviour from the partner depends on the extent to which the outcome accruing to the latter can be altered. Thibaut and Kelley (op. cit.) designate such an ability "power" and define it as the range of outcomes that can be moved. The greater the range of person B's outcomes which can be moved by A's behaviour, the greater will be A's power over B. In short, power consists in the control of outcome. Defined in this manner, power would be continuously exercised throughout the course of interaction, except when the participants enter into a trading agreement, such that they mutually agree to a certain course of action leading to the optimal outcome.

Though controlling person B's outcomes, person A may, under certain conditions, have fate or behaviour control over B. Person A has fate control over person B when his response completely determines B's outcome regardless of the response of B. Behaviour control refers to A's ability to elicit the required response from B. Fate control is not identical with behaviour control, since fate control by itself cannot produce the required response. From a political behaviourist's point of view, fate control is therefore not a form of power. It qualifies as an instance of a power relation in the Weberian or Russellian sense if the control of B's fate *per se* is A's will or intention. Since, too, A can convert his fate control into behaviour control by rewarding B for a particular response. It should be noted that both the operation of behavioural control and the conversion of fate control into behaviour control presuppose that the less powerful person is sensitive to the contingency and allows his behaviour to be governed by reinforcement principles.

Social interaction in general, and the mutual exercise of power in particular, presuppose the existence of a dyadic relationship in the sense that interaction and the exercise of power would cease as soon as one of the persons leaves the relationship. So the question of what keeps the relationship becomes important. For this purpose, Thibaut and Kelley introduce the concept of "comparison level for alternatives", defined as the lowest level of outcomes that a person will accept in the light of alternative outcomes available elsewhere. Person B will remain in the relationship so long as the outcome of the relationship is superior to that provided by his best alternative relationship, otherwise he will make exit and enter the latter instead. The general tenor of Thibaut and Kelley's reasoning concerning the formation and termination of a dyadic relationship conveys the assumption of a kind of *laissez faire* liberalism which fits the classical capitalist market and the modern American marriage market better than a power relation. Is it not the unique characteristic of a *power* relation which renders exit from the relationship a matter of problem for the *emigre* rather than just a matter of voluntary choice? Does exit from a power relation not require some greater effort than just saying "Good-bye"? It is perhaps only appropriate that America – the land of apparently limitless individual opportunities and freedom – should have championed the role of a modern advocate for the generalization of *laissez faire* liberalism to the analysis of power. This mode of thought characterizes all the major social exchange analyses of power, themselves a distinctively American contribution to psychology, by Thibaut and Kelley as well as by Blau (1964). These analyses make such a strong assumption of the availability of external alternatives and the exit option as to place only secondary importance on what Hirschman (1970) has called the voice mode of reaction, that is, the demand for change in the relative power positions of the existing relationship. I will amplify this point in the last part of this section; for the moment I will point out Jones and Gerard's (1967) attempt to subsume Thibaut and Kelley's analysis of power under a broader typology and how such an attempt reflects the strong influence of Lewin on the one hand and Skinner on the other.

Jones and Gerard (1967) provide a concise summary of Thibaut and Kelley's analysis of power by relating A's control over B to B's dependence on A. The precondition of any power relation, as already noted, is that B is being kept in the relation with A through the lack of a better outside alternative, as expressed by the concept of comparison level for alternatives. B's dependence on the relationship gives A *contact control* over B, a term suggested by Jones and Gerard (op. cit.). Corresponding to A's fate control over B is B's *total* dependence on A's responses. Similarly, A's behaviour control means that B is *contingently* dependent on A's responses. What is control to A is dependence to B. This mode of conceptualizing power is a direct legacy of the field theoretical conception of power and its relation with dependence. The legacy is complete when Jones and Gerard further suggest that the analysis given by Thibaut and Kelley is confined to *outcome* control, as distinguished from *cue* control, and that corresponding to these two kinds of control are effect dependence and information dependence respectively. Lewin's shadow is indeed long and lasting.

In the case of outcome control, the controlling person is seen to be in possession of resources desired or dreaded by the other person. The provision of these resources then enables the provider to control the behaviour of the recipient by making the provision contingent upon the production of the desired behaviour. In the case of cue control, no resources of a materialistic nature are necessary. The controlling person need only provide a cue which from knowledge about the previously learned contingencies of the target person would trigger certain responses in the latter. Expressed in these forms, outcome control and cue control would correspond to Skinner's concepts of a reinforcing and a discriminative stimulus respectively, which we have outlined in Chapter 6.

Between reinforcement and field theories, is there any room for the notion of exchange? Jones and Gerard (op. cit.) provide an answer by stating that "power (outcome control) almost inevitably confronts counterpower and that therefore the application of power usually involves compromise through a kind of fair-exchange principle", and that cue control, on the other hand, "is not directly hemmed in by any such exchange principle" (p. 535).

Another social exchange analysis of power is the one presented by Blau. Blau's (1964) general aim is to explain how social life becomes organized into increasingly complex structures of associations. He makes a distinction between a micro- and a macro-structure. The principles of social associations can be most vividly analysed in a micro-structure, that is, a face-to-face small group. These principles, Blau believes, are equally applicable to complex structures, although there are emergent properties in the transition from a micro- to a macro-structure which would require additional assumptions. Such an approach to the problem makes Blau, himself an eminent sociologist, bent on constructing a general explanation of social associations which is based on the pyschological principle of the small group. It is for this reason that Blau's analysis of power is discussed under a psychological rather than a sociological heading. In this regard, he shares a similar belief with Thibaut and Kelley (1959), who state that "At this point in the development of social theory it seems unwise to rely too heavily upon social stratification as a model for small group status system or to test hypotheses about these systems by reference to evidence from larger aggregates" (p. 223). Advocating from a similar platform are Homans (1961) and Emerson (1972), who, as much as Blau, are excited by the notion of social exchange. Chadwick-Jones (1976) has written a thorough volume on social exchange theory. My concern here, as in the preceding discussion of Thibaut and Kelley's work, is with the social exchange analysis of power.

Social association, Blau (op. cit.) argues, is prompted by social attraction, which includes both intrinsic and extrinsic rewards. The forces of social attraction stimulate exchange transactions which under certain conditions will give rise to the differentiation of power. Note that Blau is here primarily concerned with explaining the emergence of power relations, or more accurately, the genesis of power relations with the exception of coercive force. The latter is regarded as a special case. With the exception of this special case, power has its origin in the unilateral provision of service under the following limiting conditions concerning the recipient. The recipient cannot do without the services; cannot obtain the services elsewhere at a lower cost; cannot obtain the services by force; and is unable to reciprocate through a lack of exchangeable services. To repay the provider, the recipient subordinates himself to and complies with the provider's wishes, that is, to reward the provider with power over himself (the recipient). This however is not in accord with the rational egoistic assumption which underlines the notion of exchange because an egoistic recipient would feel no reason to repay a past debt unless he sees his future as dependent on his debt being cleared. Blau removes this difficulty in his reasoning by saying that the recipient rewards the provider with power as an inducement for the latter to provide the needed services. In this way, power balances an imbalance of exchange.

At this point, it can be noted that Blau's explanation of the etiology of a power relation (but not coercive force, which is being excluded) contains the assumption that power functions as a medium of exchange. A disadvantaged recipient who behaves according to the expectation of Blau is in effect transferring a certain part of the power over himself to the provider in an amount which is equivalent to the imbalance of exchange. Power become a kind of money. As such, Blau's view of power up to this point would add another dimension to Parsons' monetary model of power. We have seen in Chapter 4 how Parsons regards power as a nonzero-sum generalized medium which the *power wielder* can put to use for the betterment of all parties. Blau is saying here that a person who is later subordinated to another person does so voluntarily and is *himself* trading off his power, so to speak, for his own betterment. Blau's emphasis on the rationality of the *weaker* person also constitutes a point of difference between his view and the view of Thibaut and Kelley. The latter, as we have noted, looks at power through the eyes of the stronger person by uncovering the range of outcomes and their contingency which this person can bring to bear on the weaker person.

So far Blau has based his analysis on the face-to-face small group. The exclusion of coercive force from the analysis is not so much due to coercive force being irrelevant to the small group as to its incompatibility with the assumption of voluntariness in social exchange which Blau has made. The point is, however, that a similar incompatibility can be shown to exist in those power relations which Blau has endeavoured to explain in social exchange terms. This is because the decision a person makes between alternatives is not necessarily a voluntary choice — he may have to make a choice which he does not want to make. A person who chooses to give up his money in exchange for being spared of his life is no more voluntary or involuntary than the recipient who chooses to reward the provider with power under those limiting conditions which Blau has specified. The common element in both situations of exchange is that the person has made a decision based on a rational choice of the best alternative that is available. If voluntariness were a necessary logical assumption of social exchange analysis, then the only power relation which is amenable to social exchange analysis would be the one in which exit from the relation is always possible and profitable. However, Blau's explanation of the emergence of a power relation stipulates an exit which is unprofitable. His explanation is therefore contradicted by the very assumption he has made concerning the nature of social exchange. Such an assumption, as pointed out by Lively (1976) and Birnbaum (1976), is logically unnecessary for a social exchange analysis to proceed. All that is required are the conditions of reciprocity and rationality. The real function served by inserting a voluntary assumption into social exchange is, according to the above two authors, to provide a *justificatory* theory of social exchange in general, and through this, the differentiation of power. The depiction of the bargain as one made of free choice would consequently entail a moral obligation to obey.

Even granting that the voluntary assumption which Blau has introduced can be removed from causing an inconsistency in Blau's explanation of the emergence of a power relation, the explanation offered by Blau can hardly be said to have explained what it purports to explain. This is because the question about the resources which the parties possess *before* entering the exchange relation has not been answered. In a small group with random membership and no formal hierarchy, it may be inappropriate to require an explanation to answer the question concerning the differential possession of resources by the members. This does not justify, however, that the same question can continue to be unanswered when the differential distribution of resources becomes a regular pattern, or when there exist certain particularistic norms which favour some people more than the others. Under these situations, the emergence of a power relation would be predetermined by factors other than those involved in the process of social exchange.

The limitation of the social exchange analysis of power reveals itself clearly in the situation where the power relation is unaccompanied by any direct social exchange between the parties. Another situation which casts doubt on the generality of the social exchange analysis arises over the continuation of power.

In a small group or a macro-structure with a formal power hierarchy, the process of social exchange examined thus far seems irrelevant to the understanding of how and why some members have power over the others. Under these circumstances, the power relation amongst the group members is governed by the positions they hold which bear no direct relation of social exchange with one another. Blau attempts to overcome this difficulty by introducing the notion of *indirect* exchange on the one side, and by appealing to an entirely different mode of explanation on the other, namely, the role of shared norms. It is difficult to establish, nevertheless, the correspondence between the relative power of the members on the one hand, and the respective services they provide through the long chains of indirect social transactions.

Blau notes that the continuation of a power relation, once it has been established, is no longer related to social exchange. Instead, it is maintained by making others increasingly dependent, by controlling the socialization process and supporting those values which legitimize the existent pattern of dominance. Such an explanation runs directly counter to the account of the genesis of interpersonal power, which is formulated in terms of free social exchange. As well, it casts doubt on the relevance of exchange theory to the explanation of the continuity of power relations. The criticism in question is succinctly stated by Lively (1976, p. 7): "At most it (the social exchange theory) could perhaps explain how power differentials ever arose in the first instance. If so, it seems a flight into a historical anthropology as much beyond empirical verification as Locke's state of nature — to which Blau's small group bears a close resemblance". Indeed, as noted by Chadwick-Jones (1976), Thibaut and Kelley (1959) are reluctant to use the term "exchange theory" because of their concern with many power relationships where no exchange occurs.

Homans seldom mentions power in his work (Homans, 1961). When he does, he uses the term loosely in conjunction with leadership and authority, all of which refer to the situation where an individual often and regularly influences several others at a time. The logic of the analysis, as revealed in his discussion of authority, is simple in an elegant way. At the outset he makes it explicit that since he is interested in elementary social behaviour, he is more concerned with persons who acquire authority by their own actions than with persons who have it handed to them by appointment or inheritance. He makes no claim that an answer to the former would be equally applicable to the latter. The problem is then posed in a manner which already foreshadows the nature of the analysis he subsequently undertakes: how does a man *earn* authority? The answer is adequately summarized by Homans as follows.

> A man earns authority by acquiring esteem, and he acquires esteem by rewarding others. What he does for them often takes the form of giving them advice that, when taken, they find rewarding. Accordingly they come to recognize him as a man compliance with whose instructions is apt to be rewarding, and they get to be all the more prepared to comply with his instructions on some new occasion. This allows him the opportunity of giving them instructions when they have not asked for them, particularly instructions that, if obeyed, coordinate their activities toward the attainment of some group goal. (Homans, 1961, p. 314)

There can be no doubt that the situation depicted above does occur, somewhere, and that the stated sequence of events has solid support from the principles of reinforcement and generalization. It is a more scientifically based formulation of authority than Friedrich's idea of authority as communal reasoned elaboration (Chapter 4). This notwithstanding, the analysis which Homans has provided is too restricted in its applicability. For an even more thoroughly Skinnerian analysis of authority, the reader is referred to Adams and Romney (1959).

In the remaining part of this section, I wish to point out several characteristics in the social exchange analysis of power change. The kind of power change which social exchange theorists are most interested in is the maximization of outcomes on the part of the disadvantaged party and the resistance to it put up by the advantaged party. There has been little interest in changes concerning the relative power positions of the parties. In other words, the focus has been on competitive behaviours which alter the outcomes but do not affect the given power relation itself. Thibaut and Kelley's (1959) discussion of power strategies refers mostly to the manoeuvres which the members of a power relation may carry out to maximize their outcomes. The closest they get to the problem of a change in the power relation is when a member opts out of the relationship. Underlying this selective choice of emphases is their belief that men are often simply enjoying or consuming whatever rewards or satisfactions which they can find in a relationship. This belief and the selective choice of emphases are clearly expressed in Kelley and Thibaut (1969).

Noting the distinction made by Jones and Gerard (1967) between outcome dependence and information dependence, Kelley and Thibaut (1969) propose that the comparison level for outcomes marks the dividing line between two different orientations. When the lowest outcome obtainable from the existent relationship is above the comparison level, the person would act simply and directly to enjoy his outcomes. "He is generally satisfied with them, but he will, of course, make adjustments of a minor or 'local' sort in order to attain the better ones among them" (p. 10). When the outcomes drop below the comparison level, the person would adopt an information-seeking and -processing set to maximize information in order to increase the long-run gains. In the latter situation, there would seem to be at least three options of which Kelley and Thibaut discuss only the first two. Firstly, the person may begin to doubt whether the original comparison level for outcomes is realistic or not. He may then lower his aspiration and come to terms with what he can obtain from the relationship. In the process of readjusting the comparison level for outcomes, this level may come close to the comparison level for alternatives. When this happens, the second option, namely, choosing among the available alternatives, will be adopted. What Kelley and

Thibaut have not seriously considered is the option that the disadvantaged person may try to change his power position *vis-à-vis* the other person. The reason for neglecting the last option seems to lie in an implicit belief that a disadvantaged member can always opt out of the existent relationship and find satisfaction elsewhere.

Another characteristic of the social exchange analysis of power change is the emphasis on the role of the availability of alternatives outside the power relationship. This is clearly illustrated by the research on the development of contractual norms in a power relation (Thibaut and Faucheux, 1965). In an unequal dyadic power relation where there is no attractive alternative available to the less powerful person, he will appeal to norms of equity and fair sharing in order to protect himself against the more powerful person's exploitative use of power. To make appeals for the invocation of norms would not be sufficient to inhibit the more powerful person from using his superior power. Anticipating this inadequacy, Thibaut and Faucheux (op. cit.) supplied the less powerful person with an attractive external alternative. The experimental results confirm their expectation that such an alternative would enable the less powerful person to improve his share of the outcomes. Faced with a less powerful person who threatened to opt for the external alternative, the more powerful person appealed to norms of loyalty and group spirit while agreeing to a more equal share of the outcomes. The result was a tendency leading towards the development of a contract. Later studies (e.g. Murdoch, 1967; Thibaut, 1968; Thibaut and Gruder, 1969) have similarly made use of the presence of an external alternative to create an effective "counter power" for the less powerful person.

Apfelbaum (1974) in her stimulating review of the gaming experiments on conflicts and bargaining cites a large number of experiments which have incorporated the use of an alternative in their designs. This is not surprising since most of these gaming experiments are conceptualized within the social exchange framework which logically admits only two categories of power: differential control of outcomes or resources on the one hand, and the availability and profitability of external alternatives. When the former category of power has been utilized in the operationalization of the basic or initial power relation, the outcomes which are originally determined by this power relation can only be altered either by terminating the very power relation or by confronting this power relation with the latter category of power, that is, an external alternative. On a random expectation basis alone, half of the experiments would be expected to make use of an external alternative. Since, too, it would be more enlightening to uncover how *different* categories of power interact.

Emerson (1962) derives four power balancing operations which together would exhaust the logical possibilities that can be offered by the social exchange analysis of power change. The power of person A over person B, according to Emerson, equals B's dependence on A. B's dependence on A is directly proportional to B's motivational investment in goals mediated by A, and inversely proportional to the availability of goals from alternative sources outside the relationship. The power relation would be balanced when there is equal and reciprocal dependence. It would be unbalanced when the dependence is unequal. Up to here, the similarity of Emerson's formulation and Thibaut and Kelley's (1959) is obvious. Emerson then postulates that unbalanced power relations are inherently unstable and would generate one or more balancing operations to redress the balance. Logically, these operations would change the imbalance of either the motivational investments or the outside alternatives. Person B, the more dependent and hence less powerful member, may decrease his motivational investment in A by *withdrawal*; increase the availability of goals outside the relationship through *extension of the power network* by forming new relationships; increase the motivational investment of A in him by giving *status* to A; or decrease A's alternatives by *coalition formation*.

In a provocative discussion of the locus of social power, Swingle (1976) raises a number of points which have some bearing on the social exchange analysis of power in general, and Emerson's (op. cit.) power balancing operations in particular. The first point Swingle raises is that psychologists generally are given to claiming that power resides in the power wielder (the Source) by virtue of that person's ability to marshal greater resources. The second and third points pertain respectively to Swingle's assertion that power should be considered to reside in the Target and the audience. Superior resources enable the Source to gain an edge of power only because the Target desires these resources or dreads the consequence of being deprived of them. Quoting Reich's proposal for a Consciousness III revolution, Swingle reasons that if and when the Target repudiates the values and desires which make the Target dependent on the Source's resources, the power of the Source will cease. This reasoning is reminiscent of Lukes' (1974) comment on the role played by power in the inculcation and shaping of desires and values, and is a direct echo of the Buddhist teaching that men should not hold onto their desires. In a way, Swingle's argument that power resides in the Target rather than the Source is already anticipated by the notion of dependence which figures so prominently in both the field-theoretical and social exchange analyses of power. The main thrust of this notion is that power should not be viewed only from the strength of the Source, but also from the subjective and objective states of the Target. It is thus logically possible for Emerson (1962) to deduce the *withdrawal* mode of power balancing operation from his analysis of power based on dependence.

The third point raised by Swingle (op. cit.), that power resides in the audience, has great relevance to power change which occurs in the presence of a third party. If a losing side in a conflict situation can expand or change the forum by such means as demonstration and mass media report, there is the chance of gaining new and additional support from outside the immediate power relation. From this point of view, effective power resides less in the possession of superior resources and more in the ability to control the scope or limits of the conflict to a safe forum. The idea of forum highlights an important area where an effective external alternative may be created or utilized. It helps to bring to the fore the power network extension and coalition formation operations identified by Emerson (1962).

The importance of an external alternative to the achievement of power change, particularly from the point of view of the less powerful person or group, cannot be underestimated. This indeed is one of the valuable contributions made by the social exchange analysis of power. Furthermore, as Apfelbaum (1974) has remarked, choosing an alternative may well be the only way that an individual can reject or challenge the rules governing the social system. We can only agree with her suggestion that it is important to know how such alternatives appear within the cognitive field of the person and the functions they play, as well as how socially powerless individuals can search for and discover new alternatives. However, it is all too easy to overestimate the availability of external alternatives to people who are disadvantaged and powerless. When the choice of an alternative takes the form of making exit from the existent power relationship, the realization of this choice may be particularly difficult since it would threaten the power relationship at its very root. Even if exit were possible, the advantage (from the point of view of the less powerful) that can be derived from it pertains more to the dyadic relation and less to the intergroup relation. For unless the less powerful group can make exit *en masse*, the successful exit of individual members may well have the adverse effect of deflating the group's discontent and preventing the discontent from mobilizing the group members to act in unison (Gamson, 1968).

An analogous situation is the one created by individual social mobility, that is, the exit of the individual members of the disadvantaged group to the advantaged group. To the extent that the rate of social mobility can be regulated by the advantaged group, the prospect of successful social mobility would entice the disadvantaged group members to act more in terms of individual than of a group as a whole. Through this and the requirement that the upwardly mobile individual must first of all have achieved a certain standard laid down by the advantaged group, social mobility functions as a mechanism of social control and preserves the *intergroup* relation.

It is all too easy for the experimenter to set up an exit and an attractive alternative in the laboratory. What is easy for the experimenter becomes problematic for the disadvantaged group members in the world outside the laboratory. We need not look too far back into history in order to gain an appreciation of the problem facing people who search for an exit and/or an alternative. If exit were nonproblematic, then the path of the Scottish, Welsh, Irish and French Canadian nationals would have been less thorny. And many more European Jews would have survived the holocaust. If an external alternative were easy to come by, many of the "boat-people" who were forced out of Indo-China would not have ended up at the bottom of the ocean; nor would their cry "Receive us" have fallen on deaf ears.

As Blau (1964) has pointed out, Emerson's (1962) assumption that an unbalanced power relation is unstable and tends towards balance is one-sided and oversimplified. Inasmuch as the less powerful party is interested in redressing the imbalance, the more powerful party wants to keep the imbalance. The study of power change, which will be taken up in the next two chapters, is more complicated than social exchange theory would imply.

IV

A Study in Power Change

> As I review this last section, where I have functioned as a self-appointed consultant to those in low power, I am struck by how little of what I have said is well grounded in systematic research or theory.
>
> Morton Deutsch (1973)

8

Power Differentiation and the Power Distance Mechanisms

Introduction

It is all too obvious to state that in order to characterize fully a power relation, one must delineate what kind of power is involved as well as how large is the power inequality. Both the qualitative and quantitative elements must necessarily be present in any power relation. There is no lack of discussion about the former, in psychology as well as sociology and politics. One need only recall the painstaking exercises which social scientists have performed in the classification of various types of power, and the fine distinctions they put forward between power and other related concepts such as authority, influence, force and coercion. These efforts are necessary not only because of the different shades of opinions which the students of power have formed around the concept, but also because of the intricate interrelationship between one "type" of power and another. The transformation of one type of power into another is the major reason favouring an inclusive, holistic, or three-dimensional view of power. Such a view enables a reflexive attitude toward the conceptual controversies which are in abundance in the literature. These controversies, we must note again, are not trivial terminological quarrels. They are as we have already seen, basic to a number of important theoretical formulations in sociology, politics, and general as well as social psychology.

On the other hand, discussion of the power inequality between the units in a power relation has been relatively less enthusiastic. Indeed, is it not implied in the very notion of a power relation? Why bother at all to attend to the power inequality? What difference would it make whether the power inequality is large or small, as long as the units are hierarchically related in a superordination — subordination relation? In the following pages, an attempt will be made to develop an argument which will provide a positive answer to the importance of the power inequality variable. Before proceeding to an examination of the argument, it would be useful to establish clearly what is intended by the power inequality variable and how this variable will help us focus on a question of considerable importance.

Field theory (discussed in Chapter 7) provides a useful vocabulary for this immediate task. The field-theoretical conception of power in terms of induced force, as distinct from induced change, makes it possible to regard power as a continuous variable rather than an all-or-none discrete factor. A power relation can be symmetrical or asymmetrical. In a symmetrical power relation, the units have equal power on one another. The power they have over one another can vary from high to low. Thibaut and Kelley (1959) have shown from their own analysis how high mutual power is associated with higher interdependence and cohesiveness than low mutual power. In the limiting case where the units have no power over one another, the symmetrical relation ceases to be a power relation. In the latter, neither one of the units can activate any force to bear on the other. When the units have unequal power over one another, the power relation is asymmetrical. The magnitude of this inequality can vary from high to low. In a hypothetical case, somewhere along the variation scale, there is a critical region in which the amount of power inequality is just sufficient to enable the superordinate unit to induce change in the subordinate unit. This is where influence in field theory is said to occur. A power inequality greater than this critical value would enable the superordinate unit to have control over the behaviour of the subordinate unit, and not just power over the latter. This corresponds approximately to what Thibaut and Kelley (1959) have called usable power. A power inequality less than the critical value, on the other hand, would not result in control, and the superordinate unit is said to have power over but cannot control the subordinate unit. In the following discussion, the power inequality variable will be used in its broad sense to refer to any inequality of power between the units, regardless of whether the inequality will result in control or not. When it results in control, it will be specified as a controlling power inequality; when it does not result in control, it will be known as a non-controlling power inequality.

Seen in this context, the power inequality variable refers only to an asymmetrical power relation. It helps to highlight the variations in the magnitude of the inequality of power between the units in an asymmetrical power relation. Because of this, the power inequality variable enables us to raise two varieties of questions. (1) How do people within an asymmetrical power relation go about changing the power inequality relative to one another? and (2) under what conditions will they do so? These questions are of the same kind, in that they all address to power change. The concept of power inequality provides us with a general operational definition of power change: a change in the existent power inequality would constitute an instance of power change. The greater the power inequality is changed, the more radical will be the power change. Of course, power change is not only about a change in the power inequality, and a radical or a conservative power change cannot be judged solely in terms of the size of the inequality that has been reduced. There are dimensions other than the inequality of power that must also be considered, such as the social structure of the group and the contents of the ideology that provide the definition of what is proper and desirable. A social psychology of power change cannot be complete until these dimensions are coherently articulated together with the inequality of power. The concept of power inequality offers no more than a beginning in the development of the social psychological study of power change. Such a beginning, as I hope I shall be able to demonstrate, is a fruitful one. It will become apparent later that in trying to achieve this, I shall rely heavily on the foundation work laid by Mauk Mulder and his associates in the Netherlands. Before we turn to their work, a few words need to be said about the existence of power inequality which is part of social life.

Power inequality

The existence of power inequality can be examined at various levels. At the societal level, one can take as a universal fact, at least among modern industrial societies, that the distribution of power in society is unequal. The unequal distribution of power is concretely expressed in social stratification, which is highly correlated with the division of labour and ownership of private property. As we have examined in Chapter 4, there is reason to believe that power inequality exists, or will exist, as long as social control remains as a basic problem for society. And society is impossible without social control, even though the kind of social control may vary from time to time and according to the circumstances. Thus there is always a limit to the extent to which power change can equalize the distribution of power in society. It is precisely because no power change can be complete, or remains complete for too long, that further power change is always a real possibility.

The prevalence of power inequality in society does not imply, of course, that all interpersonal relationships, and every single incidence of social interaction, must necessarily involve an inequality of power between the parties. This is because power is circumscribed in its range and scope, so that there is always some possibility for an individual person to choose to associate and interact with his equals. The relative salience of power inequality in interpersonal relations is difficult to assess with any degree of accuracy more than a statistical abstraction. Triandis (1977) has reviewed a number of empirical studies of interpersonal relations carried out in several cultures. Factor analysis reveals a few common components, one of which is superordination — subordination. Power inequality does emerge as a relevant and important component in the mosaic of interpersonal relations. Indeed, it would be more difficult to show the absence than the presence of power inequality in interpersonal relations. In such intimate relations as the marital and parent-child relations, power inequality abounds (Herbst, 1952; Blood and Wolfe, 1960; Goode, 1963; Rollins and Thomas, 1974).

A meaningful approach to the question of the extent of power inequality at the group level is through analysis of the process of small group interaction. Here we shall put aside the transient and amorphous episodes of social encounter and attend only to those interactions which proceed over a relatively longer span of time. Small group research around the 1950s clearly indicates the development of a hierarchical structure as a result of group interaction. One such indication is the differentiation of leadership roles reported by Bales and his associates (Bales, 1950). Whatever else a leadership role may stand for, it marks off a power inequality between the leader(s) and the ordinary members. The differentiation of leadership roles can thus be seen as a kind of power change in reverse, that is, the development of power inequality. Later discussion of Bales' work has emphasized the differentiation of expressive (social-emotional) leadership from instrumental (task) leadership, much to the neglect of the lower part of the hierarchical structure, and through this, has blurred the inequality of power as an important feature in the development of group structure. Contrary to this, it is noteworthy that Bales has placed considerable emphasis on the hierarchical nature of group structure.

In a paper titled "Developmental Trends in the Structure of Small Groups", Heinicke and Bales (1953) described in detail the structural change that occurred in the course of group interaction. Ratings by the group members and observation were the main sources of data. The "degree of structure" of a group was defined as the extent to which the group members agreed on their relative ranking in the following areas. (1) Idea ranking: who had the best ideas. (2) Guidance ranking: who did the most to guide the group. (3) Leadership ranking: who stood out most definitely as leader. Not all the ratings were collected at the end of every group interaction session, and sometimes the leadership ranking was based on the observer rating rather than member rating. The available data yielded a high positive intercorrelation among the three rankings, indicating that the measures were all tapping the same broad factor which the authors called "status". The above three rankings would therefore constitute a composite index of the status hierarchy of the group. Among the groups with a high degree of structure, the members who were rated highly on the status hierarchy were better able to get their groups to accept their suggestions. This behavioural correlate seemed to indicate a close relation between status and power. The close relation was further supported by the structural changes occurring in the groups.

Of the ten groups under observation only four had attained a high degree of structure. At first sight, the large proportion of groups which attained only a low degree of structure may indicate that the process of status differentiation is not a basic process after all. A closer examination of the developmental trends in the High and Low groups enabled the authors to argue that the reason why the Low groups did not achieve a higher degree of structure was because of certain additional difficulties which they encountered – and not because the process of status differentiation was weak or absent amongst the Low groups. The data showed that whereas the status struggle was settled at the end of the second session among the High groups, it lasted to the end of the final, sixth session in the Low groups. Among the High groups, the status struggle, as indicated by the social emotional conflict between the members, reached its peak during the second session and from then on dropped to a low level. The resultant consensual status hierarchy then facilitated the making of decisions on task problems; and the members of a High group were in general more satisfied than their counterparts in a Low group. In the Low groups, the status hierarchy which emerged at the end of the first session was challenged in the second session. The new hierarchy, in turn, became the target of revision in the following session, and so on. The content and style of member interaction in the Low groups left little doubt that much of the activities were revolved around the claims and counter-claims to status. The lack of a stable status hierarchy in the Low groups reflected, paradoxically, the significance of what was lacking. The retarded development in the Low groups, together with the high frequency of social emotional conflict among the members, strongly suggests that the mechanism of social control was somehow absent or was otherwise weak. It would then appear that what Heinicke and Bales have named the status hierarchy was also responsible for maintaining control of the group activities. In view of this, and despite the authors' softly softly characterization of status (ideas, guidance and leadership), the process of status differentiation must embody a certain element of power differentiation. In a more recent article, Bales (1968) proposes a three-dimensional space by means of which the interaction process at a particular stage of its development can be characterized and located. One of the dimensions, known as dominance-submission, expresses more explicitly the differentiation of power during interaction.

Indeed, we may well ask if the differentiation of power is not a necessary characteristic which distinguishes a group from a collection of unrelated individuals. In an introductory chapter to their authoritative book on group dynamics, Cartwright and Zander (1968b) offers a minimal definition of social groups which is in line with Lewin's conceptualization of a social group. Simply put, this definition states that a collection of individuals will develop into a group when the relations between them become "interdependent". Other additional defining attributes can be introduced to characterize different kinds of groups or the degree of groupness. Of these additional attributes, the authors have reviewed no less than ten. But none of these attributes touch on any sort of power dimension. In view of this, it is a great surprise, and a pleasant one too, to find that of the six major parts that comprise their book, one is wholely devoted to power. What is more surprising — this time it is a surprise which causes an unpleasant dissonance — is that they make no mention of power when they discuss those elements which are important for the understanding of groups. In their introductory chapter to the final part which discusses the structural properties of groups, the following statement is found.

> It appears to be almost impossible to describe what happens in groups without using terms that indicate the 'place' of members with respect to one another. Various words have been employed, but the most common are position, status, rank, office, role, part, clique, and subgroup. Although these do not all convey intuitively quite the same meaning, all do refer to the fact that individual members of a group can be located in relation to other members according to some criterion of placement. The prevalence of such terms in the literature on groups, moreover, suggests that such placement of individuals is important for understanding what happens in and to groups. (Cartwright and Zander, 1968c, p. 486)

The "place" of members in a group forms an integral part, expressed as the differentiation of statuses, in Sherif's (1962) definition of a social group. The other defining attributes of a group are interdependence and norm. By status, Sherif means primarily power, which in turn is defined in the Weberian sense. The following statement by Sherif contrasts very well with the above statement by Cartwright and Zander.

> In seeking perspectives on special areas of intergroup relations through consideration of the systems of which they are parts, we immediately encounter the *power* dimension, which has been one of the most neglected aspects of small group research . . . . The differentiated statuses which define any organization from an operational point of view are positions in a power dimension, whatever else they may be. As such, every group is a power group, even though means and instrumentalities of sanctions do differ in formal and informal organizations. (Sherif, 1962, pp. 16-17. Original italics)

The groups observed by Bales and his associates were laboratory discussion groups. The group members met and interacted for several sessions spread over a period of time. It is unlikely that this kind of group setting would have constituted an important part of the members' social life. Even then, the groups showed signs of power differentiation. In two studies involving twenty-four groups of boys and eight groups of girls who lived in camps that lasted the same double four-week sessions, Lippett *et al.* (1952) were able to show even more clearly the differentiation of power amongst the group members. The children in the first study were found to have no difficulty in naming the top and bottom members of their group with regard to "who is best at getting the others to do what he (she) wants them to do". In the second study, the children (all boys) were asked to rank every group member, including themselves, on the above criterion. The ranking received by each child indicated his power position in the group as perceived or attributed by other members (attributed power). It was found that the attributed power correlated highly with the child's rating of own power position. The high degree of consensus on the relative power positions of the group members indicates the subjective reality of power differentiation in group life. At the behavioural level, the children who received higher attributed power made more frequent attempts to influence the behaviours of others, were more directive and successful in their influence attempts. There was also other evidence which further corroborated the validity of power differentiation. Thus high power boys were found to have physical superiority and expertise in camp craft. The group members liked them better and identified more with them than low power members.

Other observation of Lippitt *et al.*'s studies, reported separately by Rosen (1959), uncovered certain variations in the differentiation of power. In one of the camps made up of boys from middle class homes and who were well adjusted, group consensus on the relative power positions of the members was reached at an earlier stage than it was in another camp which consisted of boys from a lower socioeconomic class and who were maladjusted in their social relationships. Boys in the former camp were also more accurate in perceiving their own power positions than boys in the latter camp.

Gold (1958) carried out a study which demonstrated the existence of power inequality in the classroom. Each child was asked to rate his classmates on "how often he (the classmate) could get him to do something for him". The results of the relative power positions of the class members showed a great deal of stability and consensus. Each child was then presented with a pair of pictures showing a high power and a low power child, and was asked to distinguish them with regard to the possession of resources which have previously been found to be important to the school children ("expertness", "coerciveness", "social-emotional" and "associational"). It was found that the possession of each kind of resource was upheld by the children as more characteristic of the high power child than of the low power child. This lent some support to the discriminatory validity of the operational definition of power relation in the classroom. Gold's study confirmed what had been found earlier by Haufmann (1935) and Thomas and Thomas (1928), namely, that the children's world is full of power inequalities.

When a group comes into contact with another group, the intra-group differentiation of power begins to adapt to the particular relation between the two groups. The pressures generated by intergroup competition call for greater and more efficient social control within each group. It is in association with intergroup competition, and particularly with intergroup conflict, that the power *some* group members have over the others will be more acutely felt by both the power wielders as well as the members who are subjected to it. The classical intergroup field experiments conducted by Sherif and his associates (summary in Sherif, 1966), together with the participant observational study of the street corner society of Italian immigrants in the United States carried out by Whyte (1945), give vivid and ample illustrations of the intra-group power differentiation under conditions of intergroup competition and conflict.

So far we have been concerned with groups no more than the size of a school class. These groups are all informal groups in that they lack a formalized organizational structure such as that found in formal groups or organizations. Power differentiation in informal groups remains personalized and implicit. It is implicit since there are no formal offices or titles to give it a concrete identity, and it is personalized since the power relation among the group members has no existence independent of the current set of members. There is no impersonal niche out there which a member can occupy and thereby maintains his power over the other members. The position of power achieved by a member remains personal. The power he wields cannot be transmitted. What is more, he can only maintain his position of power through continual interaction with the other group members. In a study of nursery school children, Merei (1949) introduced a change in the hierarchy of dominance among the children by separating from the groups those children who had been found to be dominant and allowing the other docile children to play together. In the course of their interaction, the docile children developed their own rules and patterns of play. When the previously dominant children were brought back to their respective groups, it was found that they had to re-establish their power positions all over again. In the process of reestablishing their power positions, the behavioural styles of these children made a great difference to how successfully they regained their dominance. Those children who immediately attempted to assert themselves and insisted on the legacy of their foregone power were generally unsuccessful in reestablishing themselves. More success came to those who first worked within the established norms of the group, and then gradually achieved dominance.

Quite apart from these empirical observations, there is a persuasive theoretical argument leading to the conclusion that the process of power differentiation is basic to group interaction, and that therefore power inequality is a basic group phenomenon. The argument has already been cited at the beginning of the present chapter, and is based on the problem presented by social control. In Chapter 4, we examined Dahrendorf's (1968) argument that society is possible only when the behaviours of its members are regulated. The regulation of behaviours is vested in the mechanism of social control, and social control must necessarily assume a power or an authority structure. Dahrendorf's argument would be applicable to groups, both small and large, unless the problem of social control in groups has been rendered unnecessary either as a result of the members becoming uninterested in their membership, or because of the transient nature of some of the groups. In a similar vein, Koestler (1967) and Milgram (1974) have argued that hierarchical structuring is necessary for the coordination and control of the individual's activities in society or a group.

An alternative explanation of power differentiation in groups would be that the power inequality which becomes established in association with group interaction is the result of individual differences of the group members. Such an explanation can take several forms. Certain personality traits, such as dominance and submissiveness, may be postulated as predisposing a person to take on a dominant or a submissive role. There is not much point in this form of the explanation that seeks the answer to the social process of power differentiation in psychometric tests. In view of the generally low explanatory power of personality traits (Mischel, 1968), and the ill-fated personality trait approach to leadership (Gibb, 1969), such an explanation can be safely set aside.

What is more noteworthy are two other explanations which highlight the role of individual differences in the process of power differentiation, although they do not account for why power differentiation is necessary. One of the explanations is that certain status characteristics, such as a middle class background or a professional occupation, may be carried over by a person to enable him to establish a relatively higher power position *vis-à-vis* others who possess inferior status characteristics. The third version is in terms of the differential possession of valued resources by the group members. According to social exchange theory (Chapter 7), a member who provides the group with valued resources during group interaction will gain power in return. These two explanations are similar in that the individual differences of the members held to be responsible for power differentiation are not the direct outcome of stable personality traits, as in the preceding explanation, but are socially determined and related to the functional requirements of the group. They would complement the social control explanation in the following way. Group interaction requires social control, and hence power differentiation will inevitably occur. Which of the group members will occupy a higher or lower power position is left unaccounted for by the social control explanation. The explanations in terms of status characteristics and valued resources would do just that — but no more, since neither superior status characteristics nor the provision of valued resources can explain why a power hierarchy would be necessary for group interaction.

The import of the social control explanation, together with the explanations of status characteristics and valued resources, is to lend credence to the argument that power inequality is a basic attribute of groups by showing why power inequality is necessary and how it can become a reality. (This, of course, does not imply that power inequality is therefore desirable.) The fact of power inequality, and the reasons behind it, are even more obvious in formal groups and organizations.

Russell (1938), as we have seen in Chapter 1, examines at great length the power wielded by and through organizations. Apart from their influence on society at large, organizations have great practical relevance to adult human beings. More and more of the working population are dependent on organizations for their gainful employment. The possibility of occupational mobility and the competitive demands for personnel offered by the organizations, do not alter the fact that the employability of the vast majority of working men and women is confined to those jobs provided by one organization or another. It has been estimated that in 1910, 23% of the American labour force were self-employed workers. Half a century later, the figure decreased to 15%, and nearly half of of the corporate wealth was in the hand of 200 large corporations (Etzioni, 1964). As pointed out by the same author, large complex organizations had existed long before the Industrial Revolution: the Catholic Church, complex commercial organizations in the Italian city-states, universities in medieval Europe, and state bureaucracies in ancient Egypt, imperial China and Byzantium. Yet it was with the rise of industrialization and modernization that organizations have increased in number as well as have become more formalized. Etzioni calls this phenomenon the "organizational revolution". Prethus (1962) characterizes modern complex societies as "organizational" societies, while Whyte (1956) speaks of the "organization man".

The enmeshment of more and more of the working population in organizations makes it highly relevant to examine the kind of power inequality existing in the organizational context. Division of labour is a commonly used technical device to rationalize the work process. This is largely necessitated by the nature and scale of the task which an organization has to solve (Steiner, 1972). When the task consists of component parts which require different operations or skills, it can be more efficiently solved if there were division of labour based on these operations, in which case there will be functional/role specialization. Specialization, or horizontal differentiation as it is commonly called, produces heterogeneity which requires coordination such that the extent of heterogeneity will be progressively reduced at successive levels of coordination. The progress of horizontal differentiation therefore necessitates vertical differentiation, which means control through a hierarchical structure (Blau, 1970, 1972). Building on the works of Merton (1957) and Gouldner (1954), Katz and Kahn (1966) propose that a hierarchical structure is a necessary device to guarantee reliability of performance and stability of socially patterned behaviour through the formulation and enforcement of rules. These rules are elaborated in great detail in order to iron out any uncertainty (Crozier, 1964). There is control to the very detail. A hierarchical structure may take various forms. The most prevalent form adopted by modern complex organizatior, is an authority structure which approximates Weber's (1948) ideal type of bureaucracy.

The existence of an authority hierarchy in the organization means power inequality among the employees. This type of power inequality is of a different kind from that in an informal group. As discussed above, the latter remains personal and implicit. In an organization, the power inequality becomes explicit and impersonal. There are offices and titles to mark off the power positions from one another, and the existence of these positions is independent of their current incumbents. The personnel may change their place and some may leave the organization, but the authority hierarchy would still remain. A person who joins an organization is automatically locked into the authority hierarchy and finds himself being placed in a power relation *vis-à-vis* the other members. Of course there is always an informal side which may be incongruent with the formal hierarchy (e.g. "The captain is a coward, but look, the lieutenant is brave"). The formal hierarchy may have left some glaring lacunae of uncertainty for the more adventurous members to move in and establish their extra or para-formal authority (e.g. as chairpersons of new committees). There also will be some members, new and old, who for one reason or another try to be out of place. The incongruity, conflict and bitterness that ensue are regular phenomena frequent enough to suggest the inadequacy of this kind of hierarchical structure. Merton (1957), among others, has shown the other, more pathological side of bureaucracy. Despite these deficiencies and pathology, a formal authority hierarchy has certain advantages which recommend it to the power holder as an organizational principle.

Chief among these advantages is that remote or absent control becomes a real possibility. The boss need not to be physically present. He can be the boss of several geographically dispersed organizations. When a top executive is on leave from the organization, provided that he retains his title, life on his return will be less turbulent than that of Merei's (1949) dominant children when they were returned from exile. The same advantage filters down the hierarchy and the rank and file members can take leave without fear of losing their positions. From the point of view of the power holder, another major advantage created by a formal authority hierarchy is an increase in the liquidity of his power (Blau, 1974). The chain of command in a company, for example, makes power cumulative by giving successive managerial ranks authoritative control over an increasingly larger number of subordinate employees. The limited power of many low-level managers can be accumulated into a greater power vested in the hands of the top executives. Since the formal power hierarchy is impersonal and the personnels are replaceable, the entire "power" of an organization can be literally transferred to enhance the power of another organization, as for instance through the merging or consolidation of departments or companies.

Whatever the reasons that might have promoted the adoption of the bureaucratic authority as an organizational principle, whether these are due to the need for control arising from division of labour, or the advantages which the bureaucratic authority offers to the power-holder, or the collapse of the feudal system in Europe (Bendix, 1945; cf. Coleman, 1973), the so-called bureaucratization phenomenon has left a deep mark in the developed countries. A longitudinal study of the bureaucratization of industrial organizations was undertaken by Bendix (1956), using the numerical ratio of administrative employees to production employees as an index of the internal bureaucratization of the organizations. This index reflects the number of hierarchical levels in an organization. The results showed that internal bureaucratization had trebled since the turn of this century in U.S.A., Great Britain, Germany and Sweden. In France, the increase had been comparatively slight — only because the level of French bureaucratization was already high to begin with.

Frisbie (1975) has constructed a composite index of a society's overall bureaucratization. It consisted of four inter-related dimensions one of which was "hierarchical authority", operationalized as the ratio of administrative, executive, and managerial workers to the total labour force. When this index was applied to 71 countries where the necessary information was available, it produced a rank order of these countries according to their degree of bureaucratization. The rank order showed that developed countries are mostly above the median while developing countries are mostly below the median. It was also found that the rank order correlated highly with per capita energy consumption. Together, the results indicated that a higher level of bureaucratization is associated with social development.

Never in human history before have so many men and women — in absolute as well as proportional terms — been so engulfed in formal organizations upon which they depend for their livelihood. From the first job he takes up to the last one before he retires, for about forty hours a week he is enmeshed in a network of social relations which are in one way or another, either directly or indirectly, the outgrowth of a formal power order. He takes and carries out orders which are passed down to him, nicely or rudely, as a matter of course. He tries hard in his career to get into a position, one after another, such that he can give more and more and receive less and less orders. Or as Simon (1947) has put it, to participate more in deciding what others should do, and less in actual performance.

The above brief discourse into the inequality of power is not intended as an objective appraisal of the extent of power inequality in social life. On the one hand, I have ignored those instances involving a symmetrical power relation or no power relation at all. On the other hand, I have made no mention of the power inequality between the races, castes, generations, national states, and the sexes. In one sense, the above discussion is redundant because power inequality would necessarily follow from the fact of power; and there is no lack of writers who have already alerted us to the latter fact. The existence of power inequality seems obvious enough. At the same time, it has also been taken for granted. For this reason, the existence of power inequality should be emphasized. With this said, we shall proceed to an examination of power change which involves the alteration of the power inequality amongst individuals.

The upward and downward power distance mechanisms

Mulder accepts the will to power as a basic and primitive general motivation which cannot be derived from other motives. For Descartes: I think, therefore I am; for Mulder: I exercise power, therefore I am (Mulder, 1974). Power to Mulder is a genotypic concept which is generally defined to refer to the ability (possibility) of determining or directing to some extent someone's behaviour (Mulder, 1971, p. 10). The main concept that he uses in the study of power change is "power distance", by which is meant the inequality existing between two persons or units on some power dimension. This is similar to power inequality, and the two terms will be used interchangeably in the following discussion.

Since power is intended as a genotypic concept, there are diverse ways in which power can be expressed and operationalized. Accordingly, power distance can be operationalized in terms of a number of power dimensions. A sample of these dimensions would include: rewards and punishment (Mulder *et al.*, 1966), scope of decision-making and/or frequency of compliance elicited (Mulder *et al.*, 1973; Veen, 1972), formal positions in a simulated group (Mulder and Veen, 1970; Mulder *et al.*, 1971) or an organization (Mulder *et al.*, 1967; Mulder *et al.*, 1970), and expertise and information (Mulder and Wilke, 1970).

In Chapter 7 we have seen some indication of the role of power inequality or distance. Referent power interacts with other types of power to produce an effect which can only be understood in terms of the power distance between the agent and the influencee. The change induced by, say, expert power would not vary linearly with the amount of expertise because the greater the expertise, the greater will be the power distance, and hence the smaller will be the referent power. This reasoning is based on the nature of referent power.

A special attempt was made by Mulder and his associates to compare the respective effects of the quantitative (power distance) and qualitative elements of power. Raven and French (1958) have found, in accord with common sense, that a leader who wielded legitimate power received more favourable attitudes than a leader whose power was illegitimately based. Mulder *et al.* (1966) suggested an alternative explanation in terms of power distance. On the basis of their power distance reduction theory, which we shall examine later in this chapter, it was possible to hypothesize that the smaller the power distance between the leader and the group members, the more favourable would be the latter's attitudes toward the leader. They argued that in Raven and French's experiment the person who successfully, albeit illegitimately, usurped the leadership (illegitimate power) might have been perceived by the group members as more powerful than the legitimate leader. Consequently, as compared to their counterparts in the legitimate power condition, the group members in the illegitimate power condition might have perceived a larger power distance from their leader. If this were true, then the unfavourable attitudes found by Raven and French in the illegitimate power condition could be interpreted as a result of the larger power distance perceived by the members. In Mulder *et al.*'s experiment, when the power distance variable was held constant, the previous difference found between the legitimate and illegitimate power conditions disappeared. It was also found that the members' attitude was less favourable in the large power distance condition than in the small power distance condition, regardless of the legitimacy or illegitimacy of the leader. These results suggest that power distance is a more basic variable than legitimacy/illegitimacy. A similar comparison between power distance and the other types of power remains to be carried out, however.

Results from other studies indicate that power distance is a unitary variable in the sense that the experimental conditions of large and small power distance have been found to lead to contrasting phenomena which are consistent across different types of power. The types of power may be different, but the power distance *per se* is accompanied by similar results. The relevant studies have been pulled together in a key paper by Mulder (1974). What follows is a digest of the findings.

Earlier studies on small group communication showed a preponderance of communications directed by low status persons to high status persons. Mulder (1959) suggested that this phenomenon could be regarded as indicative of a tendency on the part of the low status persons to reduce the power distance between themselves and the high status persons. Similarly, the positive attitudes held by the lows toward the highs were taken as another indication of the former's tendency to reduce their power distance. These two categories of behaviours illustrate, on an indirect and post hoc basis, the operation of power distance reduction on the level of irreality (Mulder, 1965), non-reality (Mulder *et al.*, 1973), or low reality (Mulder, 1974), so called because they are substitutive behaviours which do not result in the actual reduction of the power distance.

Experiments have been set up to observe the operation of power distance reduction at the non-reality level and the manner in which this phenomenon is related to the power distance variable. In these experiments (Mulder, 1959; Mulder *et al.*, 1966), the power distance variable was manipulated to give a small and a large power distance condition. In the small power distance condition, the power inequality between the experimental subjects and the more powerful person was smaller compared with that in the large power distance condition. It was found that the subjects in the small power distance condition, as compared with their counterparts in the large power distance condition, showed more liking of and a more favourable attitude toward the more powerful person. If liking and a favourable attitude can be interpreted as the expressions of vicarious power distance reduction, then the results would indicate an inverse relation between the power distance variable and the vicarious reduction of power inequality. Such an interpretation must be treated with caution because the exact nature of power distance reduction at the non-reality level has not been clearly formulated. While liking and a favourable attitude may have the psychoanalytic meaning of reducing the power distance from the more powerful person, the meaning of a dislike and an unfavourable attitude is more ambiguous. Are they indicative of a low tendency to reduce, pyschologically, the large power distance? Or do they reflect a high tendency to reduce the power distance, but in a rather different phenomenological sense from that of liking and a favourable attitude? When the people rebel against the authority and riot with cruelty, what do their hatred and dislike indicate — a high or a low tendency to reduce the power inequality? Perhaps it is the intensity of an attitude, rather than its positive or negative valence, that is more indicative of the degree of power distance reduction at the non-reality level.

More relevant to the study of power change is the reduction of power distance at the reality level. That is, the actual taking-over of the superordinate position by a subordinate member. The findings from a variety of studies indicate that power distance reduction at the reality level bears a similar inverse relation with the power distance variable. These studies include observational studies of workers' councils in Holland and Yugoslavia, field experiments involving hockey teams, and controlled laboratory experiments. They have been summarized by Mulder (1974). The following discussion will focus on laboratory experiments.

The basic experimental paradigm was a hierarchically structured group consisting of either two or three ranks or tiers. Only one experimental subject was assigned to a group, the other group members were confederates of the experimenter. The subject was recruited on a voluntary basis and led to believe that he and two other recruits were going to work on a real-life project under the auspices of a firm. A representative from the firm would act as the group supervisor. Three experimental conditions were set up. (1) Large power distance condition: the subject and the other two members occupied the same, bottom rank in the group. (2) Small power distance condition: the supervisor would appoint in a haphazard manner one member (the subject) as his assistant in supervising the other two members. The subject in this condition would hence occupy an intermediate rank between the supervisors and the other members. Compared to (1), the power distance between the subject and the supervisor in (2) was said to be smaller for the reason that whereas the subject in (2) had some power over two people, his counterpart in (1) had none. (3) Small power distance due to achievement condition: this condition was identical to (2) except that the subject was promoted to the assistant's rank on the basis of his (supposedly) superior performance during the first part of the project.

After the project had begun for two hours, the supervisor was called away to attend to some urgent business in the firm. This resulted in an emergency situation for the group and created an opportunity for one of the group members to take over the top position. Before leaving the group, the supervisor sent a message to the group members asking them to indicate their intention of taking his position to supervise the group during the remaining one hour of the project. The message was supposed to circulate among the members with the subject knowing that he was actually the last person to receive it. Upon receiving the message, the subject found that all the other members had already indicated how strongly they would like to take over. Since the top position would go to the person with the strongest intention, and since the subject was the last person to decide, the subject was put in a situation such that he could either take over the top position or leave it to the member who had shown the strongest intention. In this way, the subject's decision would constitute a measure of his power distance reduction tendency on the reality level.

The results were fairly consistent. In two experiments (Mulder *et al.*, 1973), the numbers of subjects taking over the top position in the two small power distance conditions were very much alike (no significant difference), but each one of them was substantially larger than that in the large power distance condition (the differences were significant in the first experiment at the 0·01 level or better; and were approaching the 0·05 level in the second experiment).

The almost identical results in the two small power distance conditions are as important as the differences found between them on the one hand, and the large power distance condition on the other. They seem to show that upward mobility due to achievement had no significant *additional* effect on the power distance reduction tendency. "We conclude . . . that power distance as such, is a sufficient cause of power-distance reduction tendencies . . . on a level of reality as demonstrated in Experiments 1 and 2" (*ibid.* p. 95). The same conclusion was maintained in a later summary paper (Mulder, 1974, p. 21).

It should be noted that Mulder *et al.*'s operationalization of the two small power distance conditions might not be as clear cut as they would have intended. In the "pure" small power distance condition [condition (2)], the subject's appointment to the assistant's rank was not completely determined by chance. He might have privately inferred that his appointment was at least partly due to certain qualities which made him stand out in the eyes of the supervisor. There was no manipulation check in Mulder *et al.*'s experiments to establish the intended difference between the two small power distance conditions. However, even though the "pure" small power distance condition might have been inadvertently contaminated by an achievement or a personal factor, the main effect of the power distance variable has been replicated under conditions where the confounding effect of achievement has been further reduced (Mulder *et al.*, 1971; Ng, 1977a).

A hypothesis stating the inverse relation between the power distance variable and the power distance reduction tendency was put forward by Mulder in 1958 (quoted in Mulder, 1974). The hypothesis acquired the name of a "gradient hypotheses" in Mulder *et al.* (1973). In an earlier publication (Mulder *et al.*, 1971), the same hypothesis was aptly phrased as the "addiction theory", a term which has become more commonly used in Mulder's more recent work (Mulder, 1974, 1975). It is not the least powerful persons who would display the keenest power distance reduction tendencies, but those who already have some power. The tendency to reduce the power distance is hence the reverse of the tendency to reduce such physiological needs as hunger, which increases with greater deprivation. The consumption of food would decrease the tendency to consume more; but the "consumption" of power would intensify the desire for more. Power can therefore be compared with drugs: one can become addicted to power.

A more or less identical version of the Addiction Theory can be found elsewhere. Lasswell and Kaplan (1952) have proposed that "the amount of power tends to increase till limited by other power holders" (p. 94), and that the "forms of power and influence are agglutinative: those who with some forms tend to acquire other forms also" (p. 97). Before them, Russell (1938, p. 8) has commented that a little more power would lead to the desire for more. And before Russell, there was

Hobbes whose statement on the "general inclination of all mankind", namely, a perpetual and restless desire for power after power that ceaseth only in death, has already been noted in Chapter 1.

As for the explanation of the Addiction Theory, Hobbes (1651, Chap. 11, p. 161) suggested that the acquisition of more and more power is the only means of preserving what a person has already gained. Russell's (1938) explanation is that power is inherently insatiable. The account given by Lasswell and Kaplan is more complex. Their basic argument is that "positions in different value patterns tend to approximate one another", hence for instance, "a person of high wealth position might exercise ecopolitical power, and through it further increase his wealth. Through wealth, he may tend to acquire respect, and thereby councillorship as well. On the basis of both wealth and respect, he may influence other values than power — for instance, enlightenment, and transmit his political perspectives through authoritativeness as well as paid publicity" (1952, p. 97). Mulder, on the other hand, has suggested a variety of explanations.

On the level of personality and general motivation, it has been suggested that the power distance reduction tendency is positively correlated with self-confidence or individual prominence (Mulder, 1965). This kind of explanation, however, cannot account for the main effect of the power distance variable, which is a situational or contextual variable. Two other interpretations have been advanced. One is based on "Appetite Theory", another is on "Cognitive Theory" (Mulder *et al.*, 1973). Both have been further developed in Mulder *et al.* (1971). The Appetite Theory postulates that the actual experience of exercising power in the small distance condition brings satisfaction which in turn motivates the person to aspire for more. The exact reasoning of the Cognitive Theory is difficult to pin down. It includes the following arguments. The person in the small power distance condition knows from experience that when he has exercised power, he would wish for more. The perceived small power distance between the person and the top position gives him a right to lay claim to the latter; encourages in him a feeling of responsibility for answering the requirements of the crisis situation; or it may function as a pressure to close a gestalt (all from Mulder *et al.*, 1973; Mulder, 1971).

Of the two theories, the Appetite Theory is closer to the notion of addiction, whereas the Cognitive Theory represents a "minimum" theory in the sense that it does not require any assumption about the motivational effect arising from the *experience* of exercising power. In the two experiments discussed above, all the subjects actually lived through the situation. Those in the small power distance conditions had actually exercised some degree of power over the other two group members, however short the duration might have been, before the opportunity for power distance reduction was introduced. So apart from cognizing the power distance between themselves and the top position, the subjects in the small and large power distance conditions had different experiences in the exercise of power. The results would lend support to the Appetite Theory but they cannot shed light on the Cognitive Theory because the experiential and cognitive factors were confounded.

As a first step to test the Cognitive Theory, Mulder *et al.* (1971) reformulated the Cognitive Theory into a "Minimal Cognitive Explanation". The Minimal Cognitive Explanation states that the mere cognitive representation of a power structure which consists of a top position, an intermediate position occupied by the subject, and one or more lower positions will be sufficient to activate the power distance reduction tendency on the part of the subject. It asserts that the cognitive process alone is sufficient to cause the power distance reduction tendency, and it explicitly denies the experiential element as a necessary condition.

The Minimal Cognitive Explanation was then subjected to an experimental test. The subjects were given a detailed written report of the project situation in the previous two experiments. Instead of actually participating in the project, the subjects in the present experiment were instructed to role-play their participation in the project situation. In this way, the three power distance conditions were set up purely at the cognitve level. The situation described in the scenario culminated in the supervisor's leave, whereupon the subjects were asked to indicate how strongly they would like to take over the supervisor's position.

The results fell into the same pattern as in the "actual" experiments. The percentages of subjects who decided to take over in the large power distance, small power distance, and the small power distance due to achievement conditions were respectively 35, 51 and 57% (the respective numbers of subjects were 40, 41 and 39). The figures in the two small power distance conditions were not significantly different from each other: but when they were combined, the average was significantly greater than the figure in the large power distance condition. Results pertaining to the power distance reduction tendency on the non-reality level were also successfully replicated. The conclusion was that the actual experience of exercising power was not necessary to activate the power distance reduction tendencies – a purely cognitive representation of the situation would be sufficient. The results lend support to the Minimal Cognitive Explanation, which was later renamed as the Minimum Representation Theory by Mulder (1974). The Minimum Representation Theory has remained, to the best of my knowledge, the most advanced version of the power distance reduction theory.

Thus far only one side of the power distance has been considered, namely, the *reduction* of the power distance with respect to the more powerful or superordinate position. This can be called the upward power distance mechanism. The other side is concerned with "keeping a power distance from less powerful persons" (Mulder, 1974), or alternatively put, the "downward power distance mechanisms" (Mulder, 1975).

In empirical research, it is difficult to separate the individual effects of the upward and downward power distance mechanisms, because a reduction of the power distance with respect to the more powerful person would imply an increase in the power distance with respect to the less powerful person, and vice versa. Theoretically, both mechanisms can be present in all the group members except the one who has reached the very top position. For the person in the top position, his power distance mechanism is unique in that it can only be directed downward. (His counterpart will be the lowest person of a group, whose power mechanism can operate only in the upward direction.) For all the other members, the taking-over of power may embody one or more of the following concerns. (1) A primary interest in the intrinsic quality of that power. (2) To increase the power distance with respect to the less powerful persons. (3) To dissociate from and establish a power distance with respect to one's former peers. (4) The apprehension that unless one takes over the top position, one will be deprived relative to the person who successfully takes over the top position. The last consideration stems from the very fact that as soon as the top position opens up, the existing power relation among those members who remain in the group will become unstable and is vulnerable to change unless the top position is filled by somebody else from outside the group. It would be interesting to look into the relative salience of the upward and downward power distance mechanisms.

The downward power distance mechanism presents a similar picture to the upward power distance mechanism except that it is now of course in the reverse direction. A person will display a tendency to increase or at least to keep the power distance from the less powerful persons. This tendency is reflected in the avoidance of social intercourse with, and negative feelings about, the less powerful. An increase in the power of the less powerful would be regarded as a threat to the person's own relative power position. Furthermore, as in the upward mechanism, the strength of this downward mechanism is said to be inversely related to the power distance variable, so that when the power distance becomes smaller, the person will tend to give in to reality and to accept the intruders into his power realm. Indirect evidence was cited from communication studies (Mulder, 1959), and anecdotal illustrations were quoted from the observation of the interactions between company executives or board members on the one hand, and staff members of various ranks on the other (Mulder, 1975). No systematic study has yet been conducted to test the inverse relation postulated between the power distance variable and the downward power distance mechanism.

At the theoretical level, it requires only a moment of thought to arrive at the conclusion that the upward and downward mechanisms would strengthen one another. This has been well put by Mulder (1975, p. 8).

> The stronger power distance reduction tendency of the more powerful meets weak resistance from the powerful, but the already weaker power distance reduction tendency from the less powerful is confronted with the hardest resistence. Thus it appears that the feasibility of effective power distance reduction by the least powerful is pretty low, and a trend may be anticipated toward the development of two classes of power within our social systems, the powerful and the powerless.

This raises at least two questions of considerable importance. One pertains to the problem of how to motivate the "powerless" to reduce the power distance between themselves and the "powerful". I shall return to this question later in the next chapter. Another question concerns the formation of a power elite circle, which will be briefly discussed below.

Consider the case of the upwardly mobile persons, in peace time as well as in "revolutions". The upward power distance mechanism implies that these people will become even more oriented in an upward direction, try to join the levels above them and tend to develop positive attitudes toward the more powerful. The downward power distance mechanism suggests that they would tend to dissociate more and more from those people with whom they previously had shared the same power position. There is thus a tendency for the upwardly mobile persons to be absorbed into the elitist circle, and for the successful revolutionaries to form, sooner or later, into a stratum at a large power distance from the mass. The former is illustrated in the "passing for white", and the latter, in the development of a power elite in the post-revolutionary Yugoslav system. Djilas (1959) has called attention to the development of a new class in Yugoslavia, and Mulder (1975) quotes the results of one study which showed that 703 out of the 708 Yugoslav activists each fulfilled 6·4 functions.

In the work carried out by Mulder and his associates, the concept of power distance serves both as an independent and dependent variable. As a dependent variable, power distance provides an index for power change. Depending on the hierarchical structure of the group and the hierarchical level at which the power change is initiated, a change in the power distance can have a more or a less radical consequence for the group. I shall return to the problem of radical and conservative power change in the next chapter. As an independent variable, power distance has been generally shown to be inversely related to the upward power distance mechanism both at the non-reality as well as the reality levels. A similar inverse relation has been predicted between power distance and the downward power distance mechanism. This prediction has yet to be investigated systematically.

Structural and non-structural parameters of power distance reduction

The concept of power distance, as we have just seen, provides us with a focal point for looking at power change. Power differentiation, the downward power distance mechanism, and the upward power mechanism are all instances of power change in so far as they involve a certain change in the power distance between the units. Power differentiation and the downward power distance mechanism are similar in that they all result in an increase in the power distance. They differ according to whether the initial power distance is zero (in which case power differentiation is said to have occurred) or not zero (the downward power distance mechanism). The upward power distance mechanism, on the other hand, would result in a reduction of the power distance. Space and the current state of my interest permit me only to have a closer look at the upward power distance mechanism in the following discussion. This will admittedly produce a very partial picture of power change through ignoring the downward power distance mechanism. I must therefore ask the reader to regard the following discussion as no more than the beginning of a study of power change. In this study, Mulder's Minimum Representation Theory will serve as the point of departure.

It has been noted that the power distance variable is intended by Mulder and his associates as a unitary variable. They emphasize (for example, Mulder *et al.*, 1973) that it would be more fruitful to treat power distance as a genotypic variable than to search around among phenotypic variables. Such a position appears to be based on an induction of the empirical facts such as those mentioned above. The various ways of operationalizing the power distance variable reported by Mulder and his associates seem to be straightforward enough to lend credence to their validity. This is largely due to their choice of unidimensional indices such as the relative amounts of expertise, reward and punishment. For each of these indices, the manipulation of the power distance variable can be carried out in a nonambiguous manner. When other slightly more complex indices are used, it is not always clear what exactly are the parameters in these indices that contributed to the size of the power distance. The case in point is the nature of the power relations between the naive subject, other working members and the group supervisor in the two sets of experiments described in the preceding section. In these work groups, what are the parameters which differentiate the small and the large power distance conditions? To be able to identify more clearly these parameters would sharpen our understanding of how the instigation of power change can be facilitated or inhibited, particularly in a context which approximates a formal organization.

Mulder and his associates have proposed two rationales which are both derived from certain characteristics in the power structure of the work groups. In the small power distance condition, as the reader will recall, the work group has an inverted-Y power structure in which the subject occupies an intermediate position between a more powerful person and two less powerful persons. In the large power distance condition, the work group has a two-tiered spoke-like power structure in which the subject and the other two members occupy the same bottom rank under a more powerful person. The first rationale said to differentiate the two conditions is that whereas the subject in the inverted-Y structure has control over two persons, his counterpart in the spoke structure has none. This would lead the former subject to perceive a smaller power distance from the top than the latter subject. The second rationale is less easy to comprehend, however. In contrast to the spoke structure, the inverted-Y structure is "Interpreted by us as a primitive (in the mathematical sense), that is, as a basic, general figure, not itself derivative but one from which other constructions (behaviours) are derived" (Mulder *et al.*, 1971, p. 111; cf. Mulder, 1974, p. 32); and that "The 'primitive' is a component of our culture" (Mulder, 1974, p. 33).

It can be shown that these two rationales, suggestive as they are, do not adequately cover the parameters which are inherent in the power structure, nor are they precise enough to pinpoint the relationship between power structure and power distance. Ng (1977a) proposes four parameters which would provide a more adequate and precise model of power distance reduction in a work group.* Three of the parameters specify the structural aspects of the power relation amongst the units in a group. These include the total number of tiers or ranks in the group, the number of rank differentials separating a unit from the top (target) position, and the size (that is, the number of incumbents) of each rank. The fourth parameter is a non-structural parameter.

The first and the third parameters would distinguish one type of power structure from another. Take for instance the inverted-Y and the spoke structures. The former has three ranks, with one incumbent of each of the two upper ranks and two incumbents of the bottom rank. The spoke structure has two ranks, with one incumbent of the top rank and three incumbents of the bottom rank. Knowledge of the second (rank differential) and third (rank size) parameters concerning a subordinate unit would specify its structural position in the power structure. Thus for the subject who occupies the intermediate position

* The experiments reported in Ng (1977a), and those in Ng (1978) which will be discussed in the next chapter, were part of the present author's Ph.D. thesis (Ng, 1977b).

in the inverted-Y structure (small power distance condition), there is one rank differential with respect to the target and the rank size is one. Such an information makes it obvious that this subject is the most senior subordinate member of the group. From knowledge of the first parameter, it can then be inferred that there is a third rank below the subject; and by knowing the size of this rank, an inference can be made about the amount of control that has been delegated to the subject. As for the subject who occupies the bottom rank in the spoke structure (large power distance condition), there is also one rank differential with respect to the target but the rank size here is three. Thus this subject is not the most senior subordinate member of the group; and furthermore, since there are only two ranks in the group, there is no other person under his control. In this way, the three structural parameters provide more adequate and precise information of the formal power relations amongst the units. At the same time, they provide a basis on which the amount of control, if any, can be inferred.

The fourth parameter, known as the inter-rank latitude, is a non-structural parameter to take into consideration the power inequality between two different ranking units which is unaccounted for by the structural parameters. The power inequality between the head and his deputy may vary from one group to another, even though the structural parameters are identical in both groups. The variation may arise, for instance, from the fact that the headship in one group is more highly esteemed and carries greater influence outside than the other. Or the variation may be due to a difference in the absolute size of the power between the two structurally identical groups. Ten fish in a big pond may have a more spacious power distance than ten fish in a small pond.

Only the rank differential, rank size, and non-structural parameters were tested by Ng (1977a). The predictions concerning the main effects of these three parameters on the power distance reduction tendency were generated by two considerations. The first consideration was to establish the relation between these parameters and the power distance variable. Once this was done, Mulder's Minimum Representation Theory could be invoked in making the hypotheses. A moment of thought would make it clear that the rank differential and the non-structural parameters are each directly related to the power distance variable, and consequently they should be inversely related to the power distance reduction tendency. The rank size parameter presents a more complicated but uniquely interesting problem. Consider a three-tiered power structure in which the subject occupies the intermediate rank. Two opposite predictions can be made depending on whether the subject acts in terms of self or in terms of a subgroup of similar others within the power structure. In the latter case, the larger the subject's rank size, the larger will be the subgroup of similar others, and hence the greater will be the subgroup's power relative to the target. Consequently, a larger rank size will mean a smaller power distance with respect to the target. The prediction will be a *direct and linear* relation between the subject's rank size and his power distance reduction tendency. In a later discussion on social and political categorization, I will follow up the case in which the subject acts in terms of a certain subgroup within the power structure.

In the case where the subject acts in terms of self, as he does in both Ng's (1977a) and Mulder's experiments, two slightly different predictions can be derived. A larger rank size means less control for the subject, individually, over the bottom rank. According to Mulder's reasoning behind the control rationale, the rank size should be *inversely and linearly* related to the power distance reduction tendency. From the point of view of the social comparison theory (Festinger, 1954), however, the matter is slightly different in an interesting way. An important tenet of the social comparison theory is that people tend to use similar others for comparison. Since people on the same rank are more similar to one another and less similar to people on a different rank, it follows that when the rank size exceeds one, similar-others comparison will be possible and salient. In the case where the subject acts in terms of self, similar-others comparison would highlight perceived competition for the top position from his peer(s). When the rank size is one, similar-others comparison is impossible. Two consequences may follow. One is that there is no comparable perceived competition. The second consequence can be expressed as follows. While the social comparison theory states that upward comparison is preferable to downward comparison in providing a stable evaluation of one's ability, downward comparison may be preferred if we assume that comparison serves *self-enhancing* as well as self-evaluating functions. For by comparing downward with someone slightly worse off would make the ego feel better. So that when the rank size is one and similar-others comparison is *ergo* impossible, there would be a *relatively* greater tendency for downward comparison than when the rank size exceeds one. By downward comparison, the subject who alone occupies the intermediate rank would have an inflated sense of power which would reduce his perceived power distance from the target. It can be concluded from these two consequences that the power distance reduction tendency would be high when the rank size is one, and low when the rank size is two *or* more. The inverse relation between the rank size and the power distance reduction tendency is, from the perspective of social comparison, dichotomous and not linear.

The above consideration revolves around the relations between the parameters and the power distance variable. This consideration provides only one point of view. There is the possibility that another class of intervening variable may also impinge on power change in the work group situation. Given the prevalence of bureaucratic authority as an organizational principle in society at large, one would expect that the bureaucratic rules concerning power change would also have some bearing on the work group situation. Note that the power change in question is necessitated through the departure of the head of the group who actually initiates the change. It is not a kind of change which is being *forced* from below. Under the circumstances, the seniority rule becomes relevant, according to which the prospect of getting the top position is in inverse proportion firstly to the rank differential parameter and secondly to the rank size parameter. For these two structural parameters, the predictions based on the seniority rule would be congruent with those based on the reasoning which Mulder has provided. The non-structural parameter, on the other hand, invites a divergent prediction. Within the term of reference of the seniority rule, the non-structural parameter is an irrelevant factor since this parameter does not impinge at all on the relative seniority of the subordinate members, which is determined by the rank differential and rank size parameters. The second fish, whether it is in a large or a small pond, should always take over from the first fish.

The two experiments reported in Ng (1977a) were modelled on Mulder *et al.*'s (1971) cognitive representation method. The predicted main effects of the rank differential, rank size and non-structural (inter-rank latitude) parameters were tested by systematically varying one parameter at a time. Each parameter was varied to yield a large and a small condition. In the first experiment, the 48 subjects were randomly and equally assigned to the six conditions, with eight subjects per condition. Each subject indicated firstly on a 10 cm scale how strongly he would like to take over the top position; and secondly, whether he would definitely take over or not. There were thus two indices of the subjects' power distance reduction tendencies. The results of both indices showed that, for each parameter, the small condition was associated with a greater power distance reduction tendency than the large condition. None of the differences were significant at the 0·05 level, however. In general, the main effect of each of the two structural parameters was greater than that of the non-structural parameter. This was especially true in terms of the second index. Thus, only two subjects would definitely take over in the large rank differential and rank size conditions, whereas as many as six subjects did so in the small conditions. The corresponding figures in the two non-structural parameter conditions were three and five.

As discussed in Ng (1977a), the six vignettes used in the first experiment to set up the experimental conditions were not entirely successful. They conveyed accurately the intended manipulation to less than a half of the subjects. This faulty procedure was overcome in the second experiment by presenting to the subject a diagram of the relative ranking of the group members. The diagram enabled the subject to identify correctly his position in the power system. The second experiment also differed from the first one in two other aspects. Four vignettes were used instead of six; and each subject (n = 40) responded to all the four vignettes instead of only one. The overall experimental design was a balanced replicated Latin square design. Fig. 1 shows the four power systems contained in the vignettes.

The structural and non-structural parameters of the four power systems, as summarized in Fig. 2 below, were varied in such a way as to enable their main effects to be tested. The tests were carried out by planned comparisons of the power systems in the following manner. (1) Rank differential effect: System 51 with two rank differentials (large rank differential condition) was to be compared with System 21, which has one rank differential (small rank differential condition). (2) Rank size effect: System 61 with a rank size of three was to be compared with System 22, which has a rank size of one. (3) Inter-rank latitude effect: System 21, which has a large inter-rank latitude, was to be compared with System 61, which has a smaller inter-rank latitude. In each comparison, the parameters other than the one being tested were held constant across the two power systems.

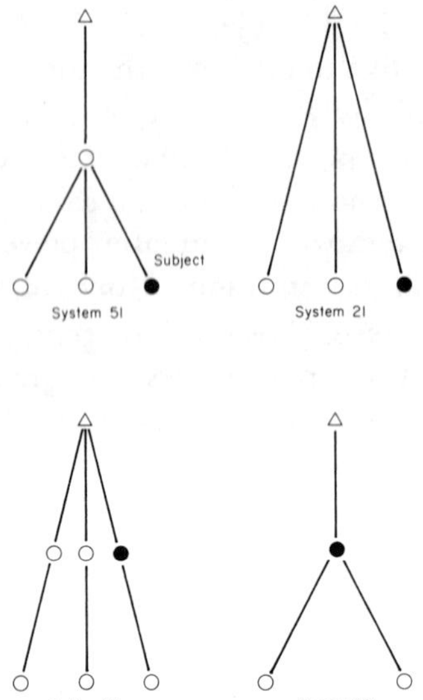

Fig. 1. Diagram showing the four Power Systems

Power system	Rank differential	Rank size	Inter-rank latitude
51	2	3	Large
21	1	3	Large
61	1	3	Small
22	1	1	Small

Fig. 2. Summary of the structural and non-structural parameters of the power systems.

The main results are summarized in Table 1. More subjects in the small rank differential condition (System 21) than the large rank differential condition (System 51) stated that they would definitely take over. Similarly, more subjects in the small rank size condition (System 22) than the large rank size condition (System 61) decided to take over. McNemar tests showed that the difference between the two rank differential conditions was significant at the 0·05 level, and that the difference between the two rank size conditions was significant at the 0·001 level. The difference between the two inter-rank latitude conditions was small and non-significant. As far as the first index of the power distance reduction tendency is concerned, each of the three pairs of means was compared by a statistical formula which would correct for the Error Rate Experimentwise (which increases with the number of comparisons made) for planned *unorthogonal* comparisons. The comparison pertaining to the rank size parameter was significant at the 0·05 level, others were not.

TABLE 1
Summary of the results of the second experiment

	Power system			
	51	21	61	22
Power distance reduction tendency				
1st index	51	56	63	73
2nd index	10	18	15	30
Expectation to take over	42	53	59	67
Perceived opposition	59	50	53	43

The 2nd index of power distance reduction tendency gives the number of subjects (out of 40) who would definitely take over the top position. The other three sets of results were obtained on a 99 mm scale.

Each subject was also asked to indicate how much he thought he should take over the top position, and how strongly the other members in the power system would oppose his taking over the top position. It can be seen from Table 1 that the smaller the two structural parameters, the greater was the reported amount of expectation to take over, and the smaller was the amount of perceived opposition. The effect due to the rank differential parameter was significant at the 0·05 level in both cases; while that of the rank size parameter was significant only in the case of perceived opposition. The inter-rank latitude parameter, on the other hand, did not lead to consistent or significant changes in either the amount of expectation or perceived opposition.

The overall results provided some support for the main effects of the two structural parameters. There was no support for the effect of the non-structural parameter. These results strongly indicate that the power distance variable can only alter the power distance reduction tendency in the work group situation in so far as the manipulation of this variable involves the structural parameters. A change in the power distance variable without a concomitant change in the power structure would have no effect on the power distance reduction tendency.

It is interesting to note that the findings of an experiment by Mulder *et al.* (1973) also support the above conclusion. In this experiment, the power distance variable was operationalized by varying the relative decision-making power of the subjects and their target without changing the structural parameters (the subjects occupied the intermediate position regardless of the power distance conditions). This operationalization involved only the non-structural parameter. The results showed no difference between the large and the small power distance conditions, just as in the case of the non-structural parameter.

Thus in order to understand power distance reduction in a work group, it is not enough to know the power distance variable without knowing also the structural and non-structural background of this variable. The structural parameters of rank differential and rank size are able to regulate the power distance reduction tendencies of the group members to a remarkably large degree. The reasons for this are not only that the two structural parameters are directly and inextricably related to the power distance variable (the non-structural parameter has this property too), but also because they activate the bureaucratic seniority rule which appears to have a bearing on this kind of power change. The latter reason holds as long as the subject is acting in terms of self. When the subject acts in terms of a subgroup, the situation will become rather different, as we shall examine in a later chapter.

As discussed in Ng (1977a), the rank differential and rank size parameters are essential components of a power structure, and hence the experimental variation of any one parameter must always occur in a structure which comprises the parameter in question and also the other parameter. In this way, the individual effects of the two structural parameters are necessarily mediated by the total power structure and consequently they cannot be directly generalized. The effect of the rank differential parameter would be reduced if the rank size parameter is large. Similarly, the effect of rank size would decrease when the rank differential is large. As far as the power distance reduction tendency is concerned, what is important is not the individual structural parameter in isolation, but the configuration of these parameters. This leads to two conclusions which are both supported by the experimental data. One is that the greatest power distance reduction tendency will occur where the structural parameters are minimal and the non-structural parameter is not too large. The small power distance condition in Mulder's inverted-Y power structure can be exactly characterized by the above statement. There is nothing intriguing about this "Primitive" inverted-Y structure — it is simply one which contains a position with minimal structural parameters and a not too formidably large non-structural parameter. We shall call this position the "Neck" in later discussion.

The second conclusion is that when the structural parameters are large (regardless of the size of the non-structural parameter), the power distance reduction tendency will be minimal. Such a condition is obtained when the subject is assigned the bottom rank in a three-tiered power system (i.e. System 51 in Fig. 1). In later discussion, this position will be known as the "Bottom".

The Bottom differs from Mulder's large power distance condition (as represented by System 21) in having a larger rank differential. As the results have shown, the power distance reduction tendency of the Bottom is even smaller than Mulder's large power distance condition. For the purpose of comparison with the Neck, the Bottom is a more extreme opposite than Mulder's large power distance condition. Partly because of this reason, the Bottom will replace Mulder's large power distance condition in the subsequent experiments reported in the next chapter. The experiments will be focused on the question of how to identify the new conditions under which power change may be instigated by people who occupy the lowest position in a power system. In this respect, the Bottom will pose a greater challenge than the large power distance condition. Another reason for replacing the large power distance condition by the Bottom is that the situation of the Bottom seems more realistic because groups are more often stratified with an intermediate layer than without one.

9

Do the Powerless Always Stay Put?

Step-by-step power equalization

The inverse relation observed between the upward power distance mechanism and the power distance variable has a certain important practical implication which can best be seen against the background of what Mulder has called the world-wide democratization process. In Holland and some other European countries, particularly Yugoslavia, democratization programmes aiming at worker participation and power equalization have been set up in various work councils. In reviewing the contributions made by the social scientists toward this democratization movement, Mulder and Wilke (1970) and Mulder (1971) observed a strong trend amongst the social scientists in the second half of the 1960s favouring this movement. The general belief was that power would be achieved through worker participation.

Mulder challenged this belief with a two-pronged argument. Quoting a number of field studies of work councils in Holland and Yugoslavia, Mulder (1971) pointed out that the vast majority of workers were simply not motivated to participate in high-level decision-making. To buttress this point, Mulder (ibid.) cited the experimental finding concerning the inverse relation between the power distance variable and the power distance reduction tendency. When the experimental studies on power distance reduction tendency are brought to bear on the observation of worker apathy, they lend credence to the suggestion that the unmotivated workers are after all obeying a scientifically established law.

Quite apart from the problem of motivating the apathetic workers, there is also the problem of ensuring that worker participation would indeed lead towards power equalization between the workers and the management. Mulder and Wilke (1970) argued that far from contributing to power equalization, worker participation on the basis of the existing power inequality between labour and management would actually increase the power inequality. Participation on the basis of power inequality would expose the less powerful party to the influence of the more powerful party. The larger the existing power inequality, the greater would be this influence; and the greater the participation, the greater the workers would be exposed to such an influence. The results of three experiments reported by Mulder and Wilke (1970) supported their reasoning. The conclusion was that

> power equalization between 'haves' and 'have-nots' cannot be realized through and after participation as such. When equality in relevant knowledge, in ability, in motivation strength, etc., is not realized before the participation process, the power differential will not decrease but, on the contrary, will increase still further. (Mulder and Wilke, 1970, p. 446)

In place of the participation solution to power equalization, which is regarded as neither feasible nor workable, Mulder recommends a "step-by-step" learning programme of effective participation. A situation is said to offer the most favourable climate for learning how to participate "if it allows people to get more power *step by step*, taking up a higher position with more power at a small distance from their former position" (Mulder, 1972, p. 13, original italics). Power change in a stepwise manner is deemed to be the only feasible method in view of the inhibitory effect due to the large power distance between the workers and the management. It is also held to be a more effective means of power equalization than the alternative all-at-once method of worker participation. It is clear that the power distance reduction theory has played an integral part behind this contemporary social psychological proposition of gradual power change. In a paper presented in a conference on organizational theory, Mulder concludes, "from the p.d.r. (power distance reduction) theory, it follows: the learning to effectively reduce power distance should be, in general, *step-wise*" (Mulder, 1975, p. 19, original italics).

While accepting Mulder's argument that participation under a large power inequality would in fact increase the power differential instead of decreasing it, there are reasons to doubt the generality of the motivational argument. It is true that the workers are by and large highly unmotivated to participate in decision-making. Against this fact, we have to remind ourselves that workers have played an active part in the labour movement, that industrial strikes are still happening, and that men at the bottom stratum of society did and do involve themselves in rebellions and revolutions. In order to substantiate the counter argument that people who are socially powerless can be highly motivated to reduce the power inequality, let us examine how often or seldom men have rebelled. In this regard, Gurr (1970) has already summarized much of the relevant data.

Gurr (1970) distinguishes three types of political violence according to their scale (size of participation), degree of organization and focus of violence. These are turmoils, conspiracies and internal wars. Turmoils are relatively spontaneous, unorganized political violence with massive participation, such as political strikes and riots. Conspiracies are highly organized political violence with limited participation, which include political assassinations, *coups d'état*, small-scale terrorism and guerilla wars. Finally, internal wars are highly organized political violence with widespread participation designed to overthrow the regime. If the powerless were unmotivated in power change, then there would be no turmoils or internal wars, only conspiracies. However, of the 1003 identified events of political violence in 114 nations between 1961 and 1965, 653 (or 65%) were turmoils, 55 were internal wars, and 295 (or 29%) were conspiracies. The high frequency of civil strifes involving the mass of the population does not in itself show that the participants were seeking for power change. Some indication of their motives would be necessary. In this respect, Gurr (op. cit.) has showed that the motives behind these turmoils and internal wars were more political than either economic or social. Political motives, as opposed to economic or social motives, were defined as including demands on or opposition to the regime, its incumbents and policies, foreign governments, or competing political groups (Gurr, op cit., p. 178). Expressed in percentages, 90% of all the turmoils had political motives, and the corresponding figures for internal wars and conspiracies were 98% and 93% respectively.

There is no reason to believe that the first half of the 1960s was more violent than the rest of human history. Quoting Sorokin, Gurr (op. cit.) states that 24 centuries of European history have averaged only four peaceful years for each year of violent disturbances. Based on the "Chinese Chronicle" (1976), I have counted no less than 80 major peasant uprisings, totalling over 200 years, in China from the year of her unification (221 B.C.) to the end of the nineteenth century. Uprisings occurring during the same period were counted as one. On the average, there was one year of violence to every ten years of peace, and one major uprising every 27 years.

Furthermore, Gurr (1970) has proposed that there has been a historical trend toward what he calls the politicization of collective violence, that is, the focusing of violence on political objects or the political system. He suggests that two characteristics of contemporary societies have contributed to this politicization. First, the origin of many deprivations is ambiguous; second, the scope of government responsibility is widening, and people expect their government to be involved in the solving of conflicts and provision of new values. When this politicization trend is superimposed onto man's long historical shadow of violence, one can hardly brush aside the politically violent acts of people with minimal power in society as exception rather than the norm, or as apolitical rather than concerned with power. There is no convincing reason to believe in either a theory of *economic* deprivation or a theory of relative power *affluence* as holding the only key to the understanding of power change.

Even in a simulated experiment in which the volunteer subjects act out roles with the full realization that it is merely an experiment, the power inequality created among the subjects can lead to fierce revolt on the part of the subordinate or less powerful subjects. The prisoner subjects in the Stanford mock prison revolted, albeit unsuccessfully in a disastrous way, on the second day of the experiment (Zimbardo *et al.*, 1977; Zimbardo, 1975). Brown (1978) described the experience in a simulated three-tiered miniature society consisting of the Elites (who control and have easy access to all resources), the Ins (who have access to some of the resources and have control over a few resources), and the Outs (who neither have access to nor control over any resource). The Elites formulated in advance a detailed plan to preserve the three classes by spying on the Ins to keep them from becoming too well organized and by placing the Outs under the control of the Ins. When the Outs arrived at the site the day after the other two groups, they "almost immediately recognized their status and began to discuss their potential for a united front against the rest of the system" (p. 167). Unlike the prison guards, the Elites had no monopoly control over the use of coercion. This allowed the Outs to use physical violence and harassment against the outnumbered Elites. The Ins, weakened by the Elites, could not hold the line and utterly failed in keeping the Outs to work for the system. Instead, they were torn by the Elite vs Outs conflict and became the target of exploitation and betrayal by both ends of the society. Unable to control the Outs, and increasingly fearful of them, the Elites surreptitiously left the site.

As the simulation drew to a close, the Outs laboured to entice the Ins into

> an alliance against the Elites. The Ins . . . finally agreed to participate in a "new society", granted assurances that their separate identity would be preserved. When the Elites finally returned, they were greeted by a united front that wanted to try them for their "crimes against humanity", though it was also agreed there should be some place for them in the "new society". The revolution was complete. (Brown, 1978, p. 168)

Furthermore, as we have examined in Chapter 4, there are strong theoretical reasons to expect power inequality to be associated with conflict between those who hold power and others who are subjected to that power. For these and the above reasons, it is difficult to fully endorse the *generality* of Mulder's contention that people who are at a large power distance are not motivated in power change. Leaving aside the question of worker apathy, let us take a closer look at the inverse relation hitherto observed between the power distance reduction tendency and the initial power distance. A suggestion can be made that far from being an invariant fact, the inverse relation in question may be a function of the particular set of conditions under which the observations were made.

In making this suggestion, the ultimate aim is to generate questions which would lead to a broader perspective of the general process of power change. There is no convincing reason to suppose that the study of power change is reaching its end once the inverse relation between the power distance reduction tendency and the power distance or power parameters variable has been established. Another, more immediate aim, is to show that Mulder's stepwise proposal is based on a scientific model of power change which is inherently conservative and individualistic. The strongest tendency to take over the top position comes from the person who is nearest to it. The result is therefore a minimal change, since the power distance that is being reduced is the smallest of all the power distances existing below the top position. As well, the pattern of dominance will remain unchanged since the Neck will continue to be in a dominant position relative to the Bottom. In these two respects, the resulting power change is conservative when compared with the change brought about by the Bottom. In the latter event, not only will a larger power inequality be reduced, but there will be also a reversal in the power relation between the Neck and the Bottom. The conservative element contained in the experimental discovery of the inverse relation between power distance reduction tendency and the power distance variable is closely related to the individualistic nature of the experimental context, as I will try to show below.

In all the experimental studies on power distance reduction discussed so far, the reduction of power distance (or its absence) took place on an individual basis. Each of the positions in the power structure was filled by a single individual, and within this multi-individual system the subject understood that he was to act purely in terms of self. If the multiindividual system were to be replaced by a multigroup system, and if the new situation now requires the Bottom member to act in terms of his membership group instead of self, would the Bottom member be activated to reduce the power distance of his group?

By posing the question in this way, we bring in what seems to us to be an important distinction of social behaviour. There are situations in which an individual acts in terms of self, and others in which he does so in terms of his membership and/or reference group. Parents who expose themselves to danger in order to protect their children are acting in terms of self. Patriots who fight against the foreign invaders are acting in terms of their beloved country. A philanthropist who gives his fortune away to individuals in need is acting in terms of self. A group leader who distributes rewards to the group members does so in terms of the group. The self/group distinction is not meant to be dichotomous. The modes of behaviour which we call "self" and "group" form the extremes of a continuum of social behaviour. There are also behaviour which contain a mixture of both elements, as for instance, when a local manufacturer supports the consumers' movement of boycotting foreign goods.

A lot of events which do not normally occur near the "self" end of the continuum can occur with greater frequency and intensity near the "group" end, and vice versa. As we have noted in Chapter 4, Georg Simmel pointed out that when a person enters into conflict in the name of a group, the latter will fight all the more courageously and steadfastly. For the present, we are concerned with the group mode of behaviour and its possible effect on raising the power distance reduction tendency of the Bottom member. We shall concentrate only on one variant of the group mode of behaviour which will be discussed in the remaining part of this section. The occurrence of power change under the influence of this particular variant of the group mode of behaviour will be dealt with in the next section.

There are at least two variants of the group mode of behaviour which should be distinguished. The distinction is based on whether the actor (who is acting in terms of the group) is acting towards an ingroup or an outgroup member. The former overlaps partly with intragroup behaviour, while the latter is identical to intergroup behaviour. Note that not every instance of intragroup behaviour exhibits the group mode of behaviour; much of intragroup interaction takes place in which the members relate to one another in terms of self. On the other hand, every instance of intergroup behaviour is by definition (see below) a group mode of behaviour. It is on intergroup behaviour that we shall focus our discussion.

Along with Tajfel (1978a, p. 28), whose work forms the basis of the present discussion, we adopt Sherif's definition of intergroup behaviour: "Whenever individuals belonging to one group interact, collectively or individually, with another group or its members in terms of their group identification, we have an instance of intergroup behaviour". Tajfel (1978a) has summarized three types of situations in which the experimenter may expect to obtain intergroup behaviour.* The first, and obvious, type is the interaction between "natural" groups. Secondly, the experimenter can cultivate two collections of individuals into two realistic, full-blown groups; and then brings them into interaction in situations wherein the group divisions are further accentuated, as for instance in Sherif's classical intergroup experiments. The third type of situation is exemplified by the minimal social categorization experiments in which the individuals are informed privately by the experimenter that on the basis of some trivial criterion they are classified as members of one group or another. Subsequently, each individual is required to allot monetary points to two other anonymous members who are designated as belonging either to the same group as the individual or to the other group; or one of them is said to belong to one group and the other, to another group.

Of the three types of situations, the last two are possible options for the experimental creation of intergroup behaviour. The degree of imposition by the experimenter of an explicit intergroup division in the third type of situation is minimal compared to that in the second type of situation. As will be reviewed briefly later, the induction of minimal social categorization has led to intergroup behaviour in several

*Tajfel also mentioned a fourth type of situation in which intergroup behaviour occurs even though the experimenter either does *not* predict it, or even tries to prevent it.

experiments. It seems unnecessary to invoke the second type of full-scale intergroup division in order to induce intergroup behaviour. Furthermore, as pointed out by Billig (1976), there was clear evidence in Sherif's intergroup experiments that prior to the institutionalization of intergroup competition, intergroup behaviour had already occurred. In fact, intergroup behaviour (defined according to Sherif's definition) in the Robbers Cave Experiment (the third of Sherif's intergroup experiments) occurred as soon as the boys in one camp discovered the presence of the other boys. Of course, the kind of intergroup behaviour occurring prior to intergroup competition was different from that after the competitions; and that the relation between the two camps of boys might never have developed into full-blown conflict had the experimenters not deliberately guided the camp activities to revolve round the competitions. Because of this, the third type of situation (as induced by the minimal social categorization procedure) may not be able to replace the second type of situation (as induced by Sherif's procedure). It complements the latter by bringing to the fore some of the "subjective" elements (namely, social identity, intergroup social comparison, and the process of categorization) which are not dealt with in any detail by the latter (see Tajfel and Turner, 1979; and the next section).

We have chosen to adapt the minimal social categorization procedure to the study of power change partly because of its relative simplicity over Sherif's procedure. This admittedly is a bad reason because Sherif's procedure may in fact be a more effective means of achieving our end. The most important reason for us is that the social categorization procedure is more suitable than Sherif's (or any other) procedure for the experimental identification of the minimal condition(s) which would raise the power distance reduction tendency of the Bottom member. As the next section will show, the minimal social categorization procedure by itself is insufficient to increase the Bottom's power distance reduction tendency. Yet the procedure has the potential of being further developed because other variable(s) can be easily inserted into it. One such variable is derived from the literature on rank equilibration. As noted in Chapter 4 when discussing the effects of dimensional incongruency as a result of social stratification, the idea of rank equilibration can be traced back to the work of Benoit-Smullyan (1944), and through him, to Weber's multi-dimensional model of social stratification. A combination of the ideas of rank equilibration and social categorization leads to what will be called "political categorization". The final section will report some experimental evidence which shows that political categorization under certain conditions did raise the power distance reduction tendency of the Bottom.

Power change through social categorization

The research on social categorization provides us with a method of inducing the intergroup mode of behaviour as well as a theory of explaining how the particular behaviour is brought about. Most of the research attention has been focused on one class of behaviour, namely, intergroup discrimination, otherwise known as intergroup bias. This refers to discrimination mainly in two areas: firstly, the differential evaluation of ingroup members and their performance *vis-à-vis* the outgroup; and secondly, the differential allocation of monetary rewards to the ingroup and outgroup. Expressed in the language of social stratification (see Chapter 4), these two areas would correspond to aspects of the social-evaluative and economic dimensions respectively. Behaviour which has direct political consequence, such as power change attempt, has not been covered except in relation to the interesting development of sociolinguistic studies (e.g. Giles, 1978). The occurrence of intergroup discrimination, particularly with regard to the discriminatory distribution of money, provides a clear indicator that the subjects are acting in terms of their membership group *vis-à-vis* the outgroup. Before the implication of social categorization for the study of power change is examined, a brief review of the social categorization literature is in order.

The procedure of setting up social categorization was described by Tajfel (1970), and more fully by Tajfel *et al.* (1971). Subjects in a typical social categorization experiment are (randomly) divided into groups on some *ad hoc* and trivial criterion. Group membership is anonymous, and within each group, members are designated by individual code numbers. Each subject knows only his own group membership and membership number, but not the others'. There are no intragroup or intergroup interaction and no utilitarian value to be gained from group affiliation. The procedure ensures that the resulting groups are "minimal groups"; in fact, the "groups" are no more than cognitive categories set up in the minds of the subjects.

After the induction of social categorization, each subject would allocate monetary points to two anonymous group members other than himself. The two recipients are designated by individual code numbers and labelled either as all belonging to the same group as the subject, or all belonging to the outgroup; or belonging to different groups (one from the ingroup and the other from the outgroup). The subject realizes that just as he is allotting money to some unknown persons in the experiment, he is being allotted money by some other unidentifiable persons. He is informed that like the other participants in the experiment, he will receive at the end of the experiment the total amount of money allotted to him anonymously by the others. Under this anonymous situation, the money he receives is completely unrelated to the money he allots to the others; and reciprocity is beyond the question.

Several point matrices are provided for each subject to indicate his decisions. They are designed and combined in such a way that the subject can choose among four strategies in allotting the monetary points. He can choose to increase the maximum joint profit of both recipients (the Maximum Joint Profit choice); or to increase the profit of one recipient only; or to maximize the relative difference in favour of one recipient (the Maximum Difference choice); or to allot the same number of points to both recipients (the Fairness choice). Note that the four types of choices are not discrete choices which can be made in isolation from one another. Each type of choice represented in a particular point matrix is combined with one or more of the other types of choice. The combination is inevitable because of the very nature of the point matrix, and because of this, the strength or "pull" of one type of choice can only be stated in relation to that of the other choice(s) which is also represented in the matrix.

The total results are therefore complex, but the evidence for intergroup discrimination is clear-cut. When one of the recipients is an ingroup member and the other an outgroup member, the predominant choice is for the subjects to maximize the relative difference in favour of the ingroup recipient, even though this may in some instances mean a decrease in the absolute amounts of awards that could be allotted to the ingroup recipient. It looks as if it is more important (for whatever reason) to the subjects to establish a comparative superiority than to secure the maximum amount of awards for the ingroup; and when the above two motives are incompatible with one another, it is the former which tends to guide the choices. The feeling here is analogous to that of a vintage car owner who painted the following on the *back* of his or her car: "I AM SLOW BUT I AM AHEAD OF YOU".

There is another, more subtle way in which intergroup discrimination is manifested. When the two recipients are both ingroup members, the amounts awarded to them are significantly nearer to the Maximum Joint Profit end of the matrices than the amounts awarded to two outgroup recipients. Since the two choices are made on separate matrices, giving more to the ingroup recipients does not mean one has to give less to the outgroup recipients — nevertheless one does so.

The induction of "minimal" social categorization (that is, the mere perception that people are divided into groups) is therefore sufficient to trigger off intergroup discrimination when the opportunity to allocate rewards to other ingroup members and outgroup members presents itself. This finding is in sharp contrast to an earlier negative finding reported by Rabbie and Horwitz (1969). The latter, as pointed out by Tajfel *et al.* (1971), was a reflection of the irrelevance of the social categorization variable to the dependent variable rather than a disconfirmation of the effect of social categorization. Later studies (e.g. Doise and Sinclair, 1973) have successfully replicated the occurrence of intergroup discrimination as a result of minimal social categorization. The same result was obtained when the extraneous factor of familiarity/unfamiliarity was controlled (Tajfel and Billig, 1974). That is to say, the effect of minimal social categorization cannot be attributed to the unfamiliarity of the experimental situation.

In the above social categorization experiments, the "groups" into which the subjects were categorized were not entirely minimal. Group membership was determined by the possession of a similar attribute which, however trivial it might be, would lead to a certain perceived similarity by the subjects in the same group. It is not possible to tell from these experiments whether the observed social categorization effect was due to the label "group" *per se*, or to perceived similarity. Billig and Tajfel (1973) carried out an experiment to test the relative main effects of the two factors and found that the label "group" *per se* (unaccompanied by any similarity attribute) was sufficient to result in intergroup discrimination.

It looks as though the minimal social categorization procedure is sufficient in inducing the adoption of the intergroup mode of behaviour as indicated by the occurrence of intergroup discrimination. Turner (1975a, 1978), however, has cautioned us that two conditions must first be met. The intergroup division imposed by the experimenter must to some extent be internalized by the subject. In other words, there must be some correspondence between the external intergroup division and the internal identification by the subjects with the minimal ingroup. It is not clear from Turner's (*ibid.*) discussion whether the fulfilment of this condition is a function of the exact operation of the minimal social categorization procedure (one variant of the procedure being more effective than another), or of the personal characteristics of the subjects (some subjects find the external intergroup division and the task of allotting monetary points more silly than others). What seems to be important is that the experimenter must provide an interesting, realistic and relevant pretext to the introduction of social categorization; as well as to make the task of allotting monetary points meaningful to the overall purpose of the experiment.

The second prerequisite is that the self mode of behaviour should be prevented from moving to the fore. This was normally fulfilled in the traditional social categorization experiments because the subjects were never asked to allot monetary points to themselves. As reported by Turner (*ibid.*), once the subject's attention was focused on self, the intergroup mode of behaviour which would otherwise result from social categorization was superseded by the self mode of behaviour. This happened when the subject was asked to allot monetary points first to himself and another member (who was either an ingroup or outgroup member), and following this, to allot points to an ingroup and an outgroup member. When the subject's attention was focused on self in this way, he showed self-favouritism but not ingroup favouritism. On the other hand, when the subject was asked to allot points first to an ingroup and an outgroup member, and then to allot points to himself and another member, he showed the same intergroup discrimination as found in the traditional social categorization experiments.

The above review leads to the following expectation. Provided the two conditions named by Turner are met, the minimal social categorization procedure would be sufficient in inducing the intergroup mode of behaviour. The next – and most crucial – question for us is the prospect of using this procedure for the enhancement of the power distance reduction tendency of the Bottom member in a power hierarchy. Will minimal social categorization affect "power" behaviour in an analogous manner as it affects "economic" behaviour? In the absence of any known empirical study on the relationship between minimal social categorization and power change, the question can only be approached by examining the theoretical explanation of the social categorization effect, and then by assessing the applicability of the explanation to the problem of power change.

The effect of social categorization, which is characterized by the preponderance of the maximum difference choice, would rule out any explanation which is based solely on the subjects' rational pursuit of utilitarian gains. Furthermore, the minimal conditions under which the social categorization effect occurs would mean that the effect cannot be attributed to previous hostility among the subjects, or to an "objective" current conflict of interests between the groups, or to a simple version of the subjects' self-interest. The initial explanation offered was a normative explanation in terms of a learned generic norm of intergroup behaviour (Tajfel, 1970). This explanation has since been replaced by a theory which relates social categorization to intergroup social comparison and social identity. The first systematic and major exposition of social categorization, intergroup social comparison, and social identity in relation to intergroup behaviour was given by Tajfel (1974) in his Katz-Newcomb Lectures. A more recent and extended version can be found in Tajfel (1978b, c). The exposition was developed in relation to a theoretical and schematic formulation of the *general* problem of intergroup behaviour. Building on Tajfel's work, Turner (1975a) developed a theory specifically for the explanation of the social categorization effect. His more recent statement (Turner, 1978) will form the basis of the following discussion.

Turner (1978) sees the social categorization effect as an example of groups competing with one another for positive social identity or psychological distinctiveness. A person's social identity is that part of his self-image which derives from his knowledge of his membership of a social group (or groups). His group memberships contribute either positively or negatively to his social identity. The contribution is dependent on, and assessed by means of, social comparisons between ingroups and other groups in terms of some valued dimension. Hence, an ingroup will be able to maintain or enhance its contribution to its members' positive social identity only if it achieves a positively valued distinctiveness from other groups. The above reasoning leads to the hypothesis that

> in any situation where a group is able to compare itself with another group on some valued dimension, the group must attempt to differentiate itself from the other towards the positively valued pole of that dimension . . . . [And] where any two groups can compare themselves with each other on a dimension which they value similarly, both must attempt to differentiate themselves from each other towards the same positively valued pole. (*ibid.*, p. 105)

In the latter case where two groups strive for the same positively valued difference relative to one another, the reciprocal attempts at intergroup differentiation constitute a competition for positive social identity.

The above hypothesis would be applicable to the minimal social categorization situation provided the following two conditions are met. Firstly, if the subjects accept the intergroup division imposed by the experimenter and regard their assigned group membership as a potential source of contribution to their social identity. Secondly, if the monetary points function as a valued dimension of intergroup comparison betweeen the groups. It would then follow from the stated hypothesis that the subjects would act in terms of the ingroup – outgroup categorization and allot the monetary points in such a way as to enable their ingroup to achieve a relative superiority over the outgroup. That is to say, they would adopt the maximum difference strategy in the distribution of points to ingroup and outgroup members. Through such a strategy, a discriminative subject would enhance his social identity or psychological distinctiveness by virtue of his membership in the relatively superior group.

Two comments can be made about this mode of explanation. It contains an embryonic version of a kind of voluntaristic theory of action which we have discussed in Chapter 4 in relation to Parsons' (1973) work. As such, the theoretical framework which it provides has a much greater potential than that provided by either a positivistic or idealistic theory. The second comment can be expressed in the language of social stratification which we discussed in Chapter 4.

As noted above, positive social identity or psychological distinctiveness is the outcome of favourable intergroup comparison on some valued dimension. What would constitute or not constitute a valued dimension is left unspecified. Presumably, anything which can be evaluated in terms of superiority/inferiority would constitute such a valued dimension. The resemblance between the valued dimension and the status or social-evaluative dimension of social stratification is immediately apparent. For most practical and theoretical purposes, the two can be regarded as identical. From this point of view, an attempt to achieve positive social identity or psychological distinctiveness can be regarded as an attempt to change the intergroup positions on a social-evaluative dimension such that the ingroup occupies a position superior to the outgroup; or if such a dimension does not exist, to create one which will reflect the ingroup's superiority.

The above exercise in translation is intended solely for the purpose of bringing into focus the prominent role of the social evaluative dimension in the social identity theory of intergroup behaviour. The kind of intergroup behaviour which can be encompassed by the theory is of course not restricted to discriminatory behaviour of an *economic* nature. But it is noteworthy that the single most commonly used index of intergroup discrimination has been an economic index (monetary points). The economic notion of "profit" actually forms an integral part of the language describing the behaviour. It looks as though the stage is already set for the social identity theory to make inroads into economic behaviour. An article by Tajfel (1976), for instance, actually bears the intriguing title of "From the Economics of Expendable Objects to the Social Psychology of Intergroup Relations". Turner and Tajfel, of course, are not alone in assigning a high degree of prominence and autonomy to the social-evaluative dimension. We have seen in Chapter 4 how Dahrendorf (1968) and Wesolowski (1962) had attached a greater theoretical significance to the social-evaluative dimension than the economic dimension. Weber's (1948) position showed a similar emphasis, although to a lesser degree. Brown (1965) and Berkowitz (1975), two of the few social psychologists who have written on social stratification at any great length, have similarly put emphasis on the status or social-evaluative dimension. The social psychological studies of interpersonal and intergroup "conflict" also manifest a preference for the social-evaluative dimension both in the conceptualization and explanation of "conflict". A review of the literature by Turner (1975b) shows that most of the so-called conflict studies are in fact studies of social competition which centres round the status variable.

Would social categorization heighten the power distance reduction tendency of the Bottom member? The social identity theory suggests that the answer would depend on the social-evaluative connotation of the formal power dimension in the hierarchical system. If the formal power dimension were a valued dimension such that the top position enables its incumbents compare favourably with the other more lowly placed subgroups, the onset of social categorization would produce an enhanced effect on power change. The reasoning will run as follows. Under the condition of social categorization, the Bottom member acts in terms of his subgroup instead of self. In doing so he is under strong pressure to maximize the superiority of his subgroup *vis-à-vis* the other subgroups. This pressure is presumably stronger than the corresponding pressure of maximizing self superiority when social categorization is not introduced. If by occupying the top position it would contribute positively to the superiority of the member's subgroup, then he would be expected to show a higher power distance reduction tendency than when he is acting in terms of self.

However, there are indications which cast doubt on the assumption that the formal power hierarchy is positively correlated with social-evaluative or status superiority. As noted in Chapter 6, the image that power corrupts seems to be widespread. People may dislike to be in a position which carries with it the explicit responsibility and right of controlling or influencing the activities of others, even though after they actually have had a taste of that power they may, according to Russell (1938) and Mulder (1974), come to enjoy it so much that they would honestly feel disgraced when they have to resign from it.*

The opposite assumption seems more realistic though it may sound ridiculous on the surface, namely, that people would pride themselves with being faithful to a lowly but respectable position which they currently occupy. From their point of view, to stay put may not be glorious, but it is at least innocent; and innocence, to them, would seem virtuous. It is relevant to recall here the view put forward by Duverger (1966) concerning depoliticization, which we have come across in Chapter 4. It is always advantageous to those who are in power to persuade others that for them (the latter) to be actively involved in political action would be dishonest, unhealthy, sordid and selfish. The effect of this aspect of political socialization on the

* Two later studies carried out amongst university students at a New Zealand university strongly indicate that power is perceived as something bad or undesirable. While the respondents in these two studies were not strictly comparable to the subjects in the following experiment (who were secondary school boys in England), the results are at least consistent with the argument that power may be incompatible with a positive social identity. See Appendix.

people's general attitude towards participating in power change remains to be established, but at least a plausible conjecture can be put forth that far from being perceived as an opportunity for the enhancement of social identity, the opening up of the top position puts the political "virtue" of the people to a test. In this test, the normative demand on the people varies according to their structural positions in the power hierarchy. Thus the Bottom is expected to stay put to pay deference to the Neck, and through this, expresses his loyalty to the system. The Neck, on the other hand, would hesitate; for by hesitating, or putting on a public image of hesitation, he would still seem virtuous if and when he ascends to the throne. All these are socially proper and politically appropriate manners, which lends support to the maintenance of a certain degree of predictability and stability in times of change.

In order to complete the analysis of the possible effect of social categorization on power change, it is important to compare the nature and extent of social stratification in the minimal social categorization setting and the work group setting. Prior to and immediately after the induction of minimal social categorization, there was no hierarchical or stratified relation between the two contrived groups at all. Apart from the group boundary introduced by social categorization, the general background was homogeneous and the groups were presumably equal. Presentation of the experimental task, namely, the distribution of monetary points, rendered such an equality very vulnerable to change. The possibility was therefore created such that one side might be forced into an inferior position on the emergent economic dimension if no preemptive or counter action were undertaken. It was in the absence of any stratification that discriminatory behaviour occurred, leading to the establishment of a stratificational dimension which apparently was economic in nature but according to the social identity theory was basically social-evaluative. It was while still in the Garden of Eden that, to quote Dahrendorf (1968, p. 159), that "the undefinable yet effective force of prestige continues to create a noticeable rank order". The manifestation of the social categorization effect would seem to require an unstratified setting. In one of Turner's (1975b) experiments, for instance, the effect of social categorization on groups which were already hierarchically ranked along the social-evaluative dimension was much reduced. When social categorization is brought to bear on power change in the work group, it now has to operate in a context where stratification is already present, that is, stratification on the experimentally created formal power dimension. Hence, as far as the Bottom is concerned, there exists a structural constraint which would counteract the realization of the social categorization effect.

An experiment was carried out to provide a preliminary test of the effect of social categorization on power change. While the primary focus was on the Bottom, it was necessary to include the Neck in order to give a fuller picture. The role-play method described in the preceding chapter was used to set up the Neck and the Bottom conditions. To introduce social categorization into the work group situation, the Neck and Bottom positions were each filled by a three-member work team instead of by an individual member. There were one Neck team and four Bottom teams, labelled respectively as "Centre", "North", "South", "East" and "West". Team membership and the rank of the teams were determined by chance. There were nine subjects in each of the two conditions.

The main results of this experiment as well as the political categorization experiment (to be discussed later) were reported in Ng (1978). Like the findings of the previous experiment (Ng, 1977a) discussed in Chapter 8, the Neck in the present experiment showed a greater power distance reduction tendency than the Bottom. The mean strength of the Neck's tendency was 76·4, which was significantly greater ($P < 0{\cdot}05$) than that of the Bottom (57·4). These figures closely resemble the corresponding figures in the previous experiment (Ng, 1977a) in which social categorization was not introduced and the subjects acted purely in terms of self (72·7 and 51·0 respectively). The figure of 57·4 in the Bottom condition of the present experiment was only slightly higher than the corresponding figure in the previous experiment (51·0). In terms of the numbers of subjects who would definitely like their teams to take over, six (66%) did so in the Neck condition, compared with three (33%) in the Bottom condition. Fisher's exact probability test showed no significant difference between the two numbers. The figure of 33% in the Bottom condition was again only marginally greater than the corresponding figure in the previous experiment (25%). Thus the introduction of social categorization had altered only very slightly the power distance reduction tendencies of both the Bottom and the Neck.

It would appear that social categorization that relies only on the social-evaluative force of positive social identity cannot enhance the power distance reduction tendency of the Bottom. This may be due to a certain incompatibility between a position of power and positive social identity. It also may be due to a structural constraint arising from the already stratified setting into which social categorization was superimposed. This does not mean, however, that social categorization must always be applied in its pure form as represented by the minimal social categorization paradigm. Nor should we overlook the possibility that social categorization may, in combination with certain other factors, possess great potential for activating power change in a hierarchical system. This brings us to the study of power change through political categorization.

Power change through political categorization

In place of the minimal type of social categorization, a more complex form of social categorization called political categorization will be examined. The latter refers to the situation where categorization acquires political implications. In minimal social categorization, as we have noted, the categories are artificial and without any social-evaluative, economic, or political implication. The categorization of people into high-IQ and low-IQ scorers would be no longer minimal but is social-evaluative, because the resulting IQ ranking of the two categories is social-evaluative in nature. The social categories "white" and "black" are social-evaluative to the extent that they elicit differential evaluation of superiority/inferiority; they will also acquire political meaning to the extent that they reflect an existing superordination-subordination relation between them, as for example in South Africa.

In general, political categorization can result in three ways. The first and most obvious way has just been cited, that is, when the categories X, Y, . . . articulate differential positions on an existing relationship or dimension of superordination-subordination. Secondly, when no such dimension exists at present but the categories are later turned into an emergent dimension of superordination-subordination. A third mode of political categorization can be regarded as a mixture of the first two. This refers to the situation where the power relation between the categories has become dormant or submerged, but still retains the potentiality of being activated anew from time to time. To the Welsh people, for instance, the categories "Welsh" and "English" may represent such a relation, particularly amongst those who strongly identify with their Welsh origin (Branthwaite and Jones, 1976). Many instances of nationalist and racial movements are of this kind.

The focus of our present discussion will be on the second mode of political categorization. In the absence of political categorization, the hierarchical ranking of the positions in the work group forms the sole power dimension. The essence of the onset of political categorization is the *creation* of another power dimension to confront the initial power dimension. (It should be noted that this refers specifically to the second mode of political categorization. The function of the first mode of political categorization is the *activation* of a current power dimension to confront the initial power dimension. In the third mode of political categorization, the function becomes one of *reactivation*.) An individual's or group's ranks on the two dimensions may be either congruent (high on both, or low on both) or incongruent (high on the first and low on the second, or vice versa). The more the number of ranks that can be distinguished on each dimension other than the high and low ranks (e.g. a middle rank), the more complex will be the combinations. For the purpose of illustrating the theoretical analysis of the effects of the interaction between two dimensions, the above crude distinction between rank congruence and rank incongruence will be sufficient.

A large number of studies, known variously as status equilibration (Benoit-Smullyan, 1944; Kimberly, 1966, 1972), status crystallization or inconsistency (Lenski, 1954, 1967; Goffman, 1957; Jackson, 1962), status congruence (Adams, 1953; Homans, 1961; Sampson, 1963, 1969), or rank equivalence (Galtung, 1966), all deal with the consequences of rank incongruence. The theoretical reasoning which is most relevant to our present search for means of activating the Bottom stems from Benoit-Smullyan's (1944) status equilibration postulate. Benoit-Smullyan, in line with Weber's (1948) multi-dimensional model of social stratification, distinguishes between three chief hierarchies, namely, the economic , prestige and political hierarchies. The position or rank on a hierarchy is called status. Benoit-Smullyan (op. cit.) advances the status equilibration postulate, which states that there is a tendency for the three different types of statuses to reach a common level by matching one another. The mechanism through which status equilibration can be effected is the status conversion process, which refers to the transformation of one type of status into another. The cause of status equilibration is said to lie in the expectation of or preference for equilibrium. Benoit-Smullyan assumes implicitly that status equilibration is always in the upward direction, that is, a low status would be pulled up to match a high status rather than the other way round. Thus the revolutionary action brought about by the economically prospering French bourgeoisie against the *ancien régime* is interpreted as a manifestation of the status equilibration process which was set in motion when customary and legal barriers prevented the bourgeoisie from achieving political and prestige statuses which would be comparable to their rising economic status. The equilibrium desired by the bourgeoisie was one in which their low political and prestige statuses were pulled up rather than one in which their high economic status was crushed down.

The upward direction of equilibration is explicitly stated in Galtung's (1966) axiom of rank equilibration: "All individuals will try to equilibrate their status sets upwards, and only status sets with equal ranks are stationary" (p. 158). In this form, the axiom of rank equilibration is identical to Homan's (1961) view of the status consistency striving of the individual.

Status (or rank) equilibration, that is, the equilibration of a low status or rank upward to match a high rank, is by definition an instance of upward mobility in so far as it is referring to the case of an individual person. In the case of status equilibration by a group of people *en masse*, the result would be a kind of limited social change in the sense of Tajfel's (1975) definition of the term. Both Goffman (1957) and Geschwender (1967) believe that an individual will use rank equilibration to redress the discrepancy between his ranks before he will adopt other modes of responses, such as social change attempt, prejudice and/or discrimination, social isolation or withdrawal, or the development of psychosomatic symptoms. This belief assumes, of course, that the lower of the two ranks is equilibratable. Where the low rank is fixed or unchangeable (e.g. an ascribed rank), the person with incongruent ranks would turn to other modes of response such as attempting to effect a certain change in the social order. The reasoning behind the rank equilibration thesis would suggest that a high rank on a new power dimension introduced by political categorization would generate pressure on the Bottom to equilibrate his bottom rank upward, i.e. to take over the top position in the work group.

An experiment carried out by Ng (1978) provides some preliminary support of the above expectation. To set up a power dimension in the form of political categorization, the categories "Bristol" and "Newcastle" were used. A pilot study had established that pupils comparable to the experimental subjects (who were 15- to 16-year-old secondary school boys at Bristol, England) rated the categories of "Bristol" and "Newcastle" people very closely to one another on a number of attributes except in terms of their "similarity". The nature of these attributes made it possible to assume that prior to the experimental induction of political categorization, the Bristolian subjects would have regarded the Newcastle outgroup as equal to but dissimilar to themselves. This would minimize the extent to which the relative ranking to be established by political categorization would be confounded by any perceived inequality which might already exist.

The basic procedure in the experiment was generally similar to that reported in the social categorization experiment. To set up a *high* rank through political categorization, the subjects were told that the firm which sponsored the work group was a "Bristol" firm; that the group supervisor was a "Bristol" man; and that there were three "Bristol" teams and only two "Newcastle" teams. A "Bristol" team occupied the middle rank when the subject's team was assigned to the Bottom condition. Apart from setting up a high rank, a low rank was also created by replacing "Bristol" with "Newcastle" so that Newcastle now became the majority subgroup whose supremacy relative to the Bristolian subgroup was backed up by the facts that both the firm and the group supervisor belonged to "Newcastle". This resulted in a 2 (High, Low) × 2 (Neck, Bottom) factorial design. There were ten subjects each in the High/Neck and High/Bottom cells, and eight subjects in each of the remaining two cells.

The results are shown in Table 1, which includes also the baseline results from an earlier experiment (Ng, 1977a) in which the subjects acted in terms of self. Since the numbers of subjects in the four experimental cells were not identical, it was necessary to carry out some preliminary tests before the results were subjected to a 2 (High, Low) × 2 (Neck, Bottom) analysis of variance. All the preliminary tests (Bartlett's test, Kurtosis tests, and tests of the correlation of the absolute values of the residuals and the expected values) were nonsignificant. The subsequent 2-way analysis of variance yielded one significant main effect due to the High/Low factor introduced by political categorization ($F = 4{\cdot}73$, $df = 1, 32$: $P < 0{\cdot}05$). Comparison of means showed that the High/Bottom combination had a significantly greater strength of power distance reduction than the Low/Bottom combination ($F = 5{\cdot}44$, $df = 1, 32$; $P < 0{\cdot}05$). With regard to the numbers of subjects who would definitely take over, the difference between the above two combinations (7 out of 10 vs 4 out of 8) was not significant on the Fisher's exact test. Compared to the Bottom in the baseline condition, the High/Bottom combination showed a significantly greater strength of power distance reduction ($P < 0{\cdot}05$, two-tailed Mann-Whitney test) and a significantly larger number of subjects who would definitely take over the top position ($P < 0{\cdot}05$, Fisher's exact test).

TABLE 1
Power distance reduction tendencies

		Strengths of the tendencies		Number of subjects definitely taking over	
Conditions	*n*	Neck	Bottom	Neck	Bottom
High rank	10	75·9	77·9	7	7
Low rank	8	69·9	54·0	6	4
Baseline	40	72·7	51·0	30	10

As can be seen in Table 1, the power distance reduction tendency of the High/Bottom combination shown on both indices was as high as that of the Neck in the baseline condition. This result when considered alone may also be interpreted in terms of Mulder's Minimum Representation Theory, since a high rank introduced by political categorization would mean a smaller power distance from the top position. However, this interpretation can no longer hold when the result pertaining to the High/Neck combination is also considered. Compared to either the High/Bottom combination or the Neck in the baseline condition, the High/Neck combination showed no increase in the power distance reduction tendency, even though its power distance from the top position would be even less than that of the other two.

Our effort in extending the study of power change beyond Mulder's multiindividual paradigm was intended as no more than restating certain questions which were either answered prematurely or otherwise had been neglected. What constitutes the power distance variable? How is this variable related to the structural power parameters, and how do both of them mediate the bureaucratic rules which regulate power change? Does the Bottom always stay put? Under what condition would he *not* stay put? These questions should and could be raised in a meaningful way, and while the answers which we have tried to provide to these questions are only preliminary, at least they show how the questions can be approached with the aid of a broad perspective on power.

Concluding Remarks

In the foregoing pages, I have outlined a broad range of the problem of power and examined in some detail several major approaches to the problem. By way of conclusion, three of the main themes to emerge from the preceding discussions will be noted.

The first main theme concerns the complexity of the problem of power. Power is a multi-faceted phenomenon which finds its expression in a variety of situations. It can be seen in the action and behaviour of an individual as he relates to the physical and social environment. General psychology provides ample evidence of this, as indicated by such notions as competence, efficacy, helplessness, perceived locus of control, stimulus, and can. In most cases of this kind, the focus is on the individual's power (or the lack of it) in the "asocial" sense, i.e. without reference to an active social relation between two or more individuals. This does not mean that the social psychology of power will have nothing to do with asocial power. The reason for this is that an individual's asocial power, or the lack of it, is not only due to his maturation or interaction with the purely physical environment, but is also due to his socialization and the social condition he has been in. In view of this, the study of asocial power will be incomplete without a social psychological analysis. The study of asocial power, in turn, can contribute to the understanding of social power in at least two ways. The power relation and interaction between two individuals will be affected at least partly by their relative asocial power. The situation involving two individuals who are both high in asocial power would be quite different from the situation in which one individual is higher in asocial power than the other (e.g. the Machiavellianism studies reported in Christie and Geis, 1970a). Secondly, the parameters known to govern asocial power can be readily translated into the bases of social power. A prime example of this is the work of B. F. Skinner.

In contrast to the first, asocial, facet of power, the other facets are all social. The study of social power has been the professed aim of the contemporary social psychology of power in the past three or four decades. The two most important formulations are derived from field-theory and reinforcement/social exchange theory. Both of them, and the former in particular, have attended to a too narrow range of the problem.

The field-theoretical formulation of power was developed in conjunction with the study of social influence. The basic postulate is that an individual induces a change in the psychological state of another individual only by virtue of the power he has over the latter. This postulate, together with its more refined elaboration, has led to two unsatisfactory developments. Every instance of social influence is reduced to a power relation, resulting in a narrow view of social influence and its underlying process. Secondly, the locus of power is reduced to an act performed by the individual. This would define out of existence those instances of power which do not originate from the acts of individuals. In so far as one is concerned solely with isolated changes brought about by power at the dyadic level, the above criticism can perhaps be ignored. However, there is no convincing case to be made that such a narrow concern should continue to constitute the focus of the social psychology of power. There is certainly a definite place for this kind of concern; but at the same time, the social psychology of power must also attend to those instances of social power which are unrelated in any significant way to the acts performed by individuals. More specifically, it must take into account the three-dimensional view of power in the formulation of the problem and choice of research emphasis. Failure to do so would result in a discipline no less superficial than the one-dimensional view of political behaviourism.

The social exchange formulation of power equates power with outcome control, and analyses a power relation in terms of the configuration of outcomes and the presence or absence of alternatives. It usually relies on the principle of reinforcement for the analysis of outcomes and their subjective utilities. On the other hand, different authors writing from the social exchange perspective have assigned quite different emphases to the analysis of alternatives. Emerson (1962) deduced two behavioural mechanisms which would enable a person to improve his power position through altering the availability of alternatives (i.e. extension of the power network, and coalition formation). Thibaut and Kelley (1959), and Kelley and Thibaut (1969) were more interested in the cognitive process of comparing and seeking alternatives. Taken together, the behavioural and cognitive aspects of the analysis of alternatives would throw some light on the problem of power change. Unfortunately, they all contain an implicit assumption which restricts their applicability, namely, the assumption that a power relation is open-ended through which exit is always possible. Where exit from the power relation is impossible or is perceived to be impossible, power change has to be wrought from within. For an understanding of this type of power change, one has to look beyond social exchange theory.

The afore-mentioned limitation of the social exchange formulation of power is part of the consequences of a *laissez faire* type of liberal approach to the problem of power. The liberalism is implied by the very notion of exchange and the implicit (albeit unnecessary) assumption of voluntariness. Several major issues are thereby excluded from the analysis: coercion and force; the differential possession of exchangeable resources; and power relations which are unrelated to exchange. Furthermore, and in conjunction with the exclusion of the above issues, the social exchange formulation of power does not normally deal with the relationships between power on the one hand, and social conflict and stratification on the other. The import of pointing out these omissions and the over-emphasis on alternatives is twofold. It highlights the limited and partial scope of the social exchange analysis of power; and more importantly, it points out the ideological justification that such an analysis lends to the status quo. In the latter regard, social exchange theory shares the same platform with the Utopian's view of society.

What has been said above concerning field-theory and social exchange theory is not intended to deny the unique contributions which the two theories have made to the social psychology of power. It is to argue for a change of focus and the adoption of a perspective which is more in accord with the complexity of the problem. One cannot remain at the pre-Russellian stage, or align oneself with the Utopian's view of society, or be contented with the one- or two-dimensional view of power, and at the same time still hope to be able to develop a social psychology of power. Here again, we must note emphatically what we do *not* intend to mean by the preceding statement. We do not believe that the discipline we seek to develop here will be forthcoming automatically and solely by embracing Russell, the Rationalist, and the three-dimensional view. We have merely pointed out the direction in which the discipline should develop in the light of the many facets of power and their interrelatedness.

The second of the main themes to emerge from the present work has been the multitude of problems which are significant in themselves and with which power is closely related. First and among the most important is social control, a problem which is basic to every human group and is most clearly visible in formal organizations and the political state. Social control is only possible through a power or an authority structure for the application of sanctions of various kinds. It follows from this that no group can dispense with a power structure for long, although the formality and rigidity of the power structure would vary with time and the circumstances. Within this power structure, the interests of those in the superordinate and subordinate positions contain an element of irreducible contradiction, and hence potential conflict. Conflict of this kind can only be eliminated through the elimination of the power structure. The latter, however, is impossible for the reason of social control.

Power is therefore inextricably related to social control, and through the latter, is also related to an important and irreducible type of conflict. Power can also give rise to another type of conflict, i.e. conflict staged between parties which do not stand in any relationship of superordination and subordination to one another. The potential for conflict of this kind stems from power as a scarce and valued resource: when two parties desire to share or attain the same power which is not enough for both, they become enemies. There is still a third variant of conflict which is directly related to power. This is conflict which arises from unstable comparison of the relative power between the two parties. It is usually conducted through a contest of coercive force for the reason that a contest of this kind provides the most irrefutable evidence of relative strength and weakness.

The third major problem which is closely related to power is social inequality or stratification. Weber (1948) offered no more than a metaphorical description of the relation between power and inequality, while Dahrendorf (1968) has proposed that the unequal distribution of material rewards and status is a secondary, derivative phenomenon of power. We shall not concern ourselves here with the question of the origin of inequality, but with the question of discriminatory behaviour. The problem of intergroup discrimination is central to the study of social categorization, itself an important area of research in social psychology. It can be shown that as soon as we raise the question of what makes discrimination possible (in contradistinction to the question of what causes discrimination), the relevance of power will move to the fore. As has been discussed more fully elsewhere (Ng, in press), intergroup discrimination always occurs within a certain intergroup power relation, even though such a relation has rarely been explicitly stated. In the minimal social categorization paradigm, for instance, an implicity bilateral equal power relation between the contrived groups is created by the experimenter the very moment he asks — and therefore permits — the members of both groups to distribute monetary points to one another. This puts the groups in an equal power position *vis-à-vis* one another and makes it possible for discrimination to occur. It was within this particular kind of intergroup power relation that the observation of discriminatory behaviour was made. When this power relation was replaced by other kinds of power relation, the behaviour in question began to change accordingly (see Ng, *ibid.*). Thus, in the experimental situation where only one group (Group A) was allowed to allot the rewards, discrimination against the other, respondent group (Group B) was most marked when Group A had a secure power advantage over Group B. When the power advantage of Group A was insecure, discrimination gave way to equality.

To the extent that social psychology is concerned with the above three problems, it would be necessary to analyse more fully the roles played by power in these problems. The preceding discussions are only a small beginning in this direction, and serve no more than to illustrate the relevance of a social psychology of power which is grounded in both sociology and social psychology.

The fourth major problem is social influence, in which social psychology has a long and outstanding interest. The one-to-one correspondence between influence and power assumed (practically) by field-theory is no longer tenable. Neither is the opposite assertion made by Moscovici (1976) that influence should be studied apart from power. Both positions are based on a partial interpretation of power. The study of minority influence carried out by Moscovici will sooner or later have to reconsider the proper role of power and the problem which power poses for the active minority as they seek to amplify their influence into social change. The reason for this is that even though number and power may be unnecessary for the achievement of influence, the translation and amplification of specific instances of influence into a movement for social change have to confront the existent arrangement of power in society. Moreover, the process of conflict creation that underlies minority influence can be interpreted in terms of opposing claims to legitimation. In both regards, Weber's (1947) treatment of legitimacy would be useful. Then, one must also attend to the internal power relation amongst the minority* as well as the vested interests which the third party or parties may have in the status quo.

Power is a multi-faceted phenomenon and is closely related to a multitude of other significant problems. These are two of the three main themes emerging from the present work. The third theme has been power change.

There are several variants of power change of which only three have been noted. Where a power relation had not existed before, human beings can and have to create one. The reasons for the occurrence of power differentiation can be found in social control and whatever quanta of inequality that might exist. The forces of power differentiation must also imply that a situation of power equality is inherently unstable. Where a power relation has been established, it can undergo two kinds of changes depending on whether the existent power distance (inequality) gets bigger or smaller. An increase in the power distance is usually generated from the top, whereas a decrease in the power distance has often to be fought from below.

All three variants of power change should be given a prominent place in the social psychology of power. The present work has dealt with only the case of power distance reduction at some length. The discussion has been deliberately focused on the reduction of power distance from *within*, that is to say, not through exit from the existent power relation. Several parameters have been delineated to account for the low power distance reduction tendency of the members at the bottom of a power hierarchy. The inhibitory grip of these parameters on the more lowly placed members is however not unbreakable. From a consideration of the thinking behind social categorization and social stratification, the concept of political categorization was deduced. This concept, together with the rank equilibration thesis, holds some promise for raising the power distance reduction tendency of the lowly placed members in the experimental situation. The implication of this line of thinking for other types of situations, such as the colonial situation of Hong Kong, remains to be explored.

Social psychology must not shy away from either the general

* Sigmund Freud, for instance, was more than a Machiavellian in his relations with his colleagues and students.

problem of power or the more specific problem of power change. Social psychology cannot be a relevant discipline without at the same time being responsible to the object of its study, i.e. the people. The conditions under which human beings live are to a large extent shaped by the social arrangement of power which therefore should not be left out of social psychology. What is internal or subjective often bears an inalienable though complicated relation with the external or objective. Unless social psychology has no concern for the power or the lack of power of individual human beings, then it must endeavour to delineate the relationships between the subjective and the objective, as well as to translate private troubles into public issues. It must also seek to uncover those conditions which facilitate or inhibit power change. From then on, it will be up to the moral inclination and courage of the individual social psychologist to practise what he knows.

Appendix

The unfavourable connotation of power

(1) Sixty-five introductory psychology students at Otago University were asked to rate each of forty items on a 9-point scale in terms of how important (9) or unimportant (1) the item is to them personally. The items consisted of 36 human values taken from the Rokeach Value Survey (Rokeach, 1973), together with "power", "equity", "social justice" and "self-determination". The meaning of "Power" was amplified to read "Position of authority and importance, can influence other people". Of the 36 Rokeachean values, "national security" (mean rating of 5·4), "obedient" (5·0), and "salvation" (4·5) were rated as the least important. This finding is remarkably consistent with other cross-cultural results (Moore, 1976). Rated on the bottom of the whole list, however, was "power" (4·3).
(2) A second study with another class of introductory psychology students ($n = 265$) gives corroborative evidence of the unfavourable connotation of power. This study compared the power factor in impression formation with the well-known warm-cold factor (e.g. Kelley, 1950). The students read a short description about a stimulus person and then expressed their impression of that person by rating the latter on ten 7-point semantic differential scales (see Table 1 below). In the "warm" version, the stimulus person was described as follows.

> Miss Z is a third year student at the University. She has had a year's working experience in the Students' Union, is 20 years old, and unmarried. People who know her consider her to be a very warm person, industrious, critical, practical and determined.

In the "cold" version, the word "cold" replaced "warm" in the description. In the "power" version, there was no mentioning of warm or cold, and the last sentence in the description was altered to read "People who know her consider her to be a very industrious person, critical, practical, determined, and with a strong desire for power". Another set of descriptions had "Miss" replaced by "Mr", yielding a 3 (warm, cold, power) × 2 (male, female) design. The six versions of the description were randomly distributed to the students, with at least 43 students answering each version.

Analysis of variance showed a significant main effect ($P < 0 \cdot 05$) due to the sex of the stimulus person on three of the ten rating scales. "Miss Z', as compared to "Mr Z", was rated as significantly more *considerate*, more *good-natured*, and more *humane*. A highly significant main effect of the warm-cold-power factor was found on all the ten scales (all with $P < 0 \cdot 000001$). The means are shown in Table 1 and discussed in the next paragraph. One significant interaction effect ($P < 0 \cdot 05$) was observed regarding "not dangerous". When Mr Z was described as "cold", he was rated as more dangerous than a "warm" Mr Z; while a Mr Z "with a strong desire for power" was rated as more dangerous than a "cold" Mr Z. On the other hand, a power striving Miss Z was rated as equally dangerous as a cold Miss Z; while a warm Miss Z was rated as the least dangerous.

TABLE 1
Ratings of the warm, cold, and power striving persons

	Warm	Cold	Power striving
1. Dominant-submissive	5·6	5·8	6·5
2. Not dangerous-dangerous	5·2	4·2	3·8
3. Considerate-self-centred	5·0	3·1	2·8
4. Humane-ruthless	4·4	3·4	2·8
5. Trustworthy-untrustworthy	5·5	5·7	4·7
6. Informal-formal	4·4	2·8	3·8
7. Sociable-unsociable	5·8	3·1	4·9
8. Popular-unpopular	5·5	3·2	4·3
9. Humorous-humourless	4·3	2·6	3·6
10. Good natured-irritable	5·1	3·5[a]	3·6[a]

The responses were coded in such a way that the scale value decreased from 7 on the left end of the scale to 1 on the right end of the scale. A score between 3·5 to 4·4 may be regarded as neutral.
[a] Scores with the same superscript are not significantly different from one another at the 0·05 level based on Duncan's new multiple range test.

As shown in Table 1, a warm person was generally rated more positively than either a cold or a power striving person, although in the case of "dominant" there may be some doubt about this interpretation. There is nothing striking about this general finding. What is more interesting is the contrast between cold and power striving. Cold was already bad enough, but power striving was even worse in being extremely dominant, potentially dangerous, self-centred, ruthless and only slightly trustworthy (items 1 to 5). Where power striving was rated less negatively than cold (items 6 to 9), the ratings were more frequently neutral than positive. In any case, the four items in which this occurred appear to have less significant social consequences than those items in which the reverse had occurred (i.e. items 1 to 5).

References

Adams, J. S. and Romney, A. K. (1959). A functional analysis of authority. *Psychology Review* **66**, 234–251.

Adams, S. (1953). Status congruency as a variable in small group performance. *Social Forces* **32**, 16–22.

Adler, A. (1956). "The Individual Psychology of Alfred Adler" (Ed. and annotated by H. L. Ansbacher and R. R. Ansbacher). Harper and Row, New York.

Adler, A. (1966). The psychology of power. *Journal of Individual Psychology* **22**, 166–172.

Adorno, T. W., Frenckel-Brunswick, E., Levinson, D. J. and Sanford, R. N. (1950). "The Authoritarian Personality". Harper, New York.

Alinsky, S. (1971). "Rules for Radicals". Random House, New York.

Allport, G. W. (1968). The historical background of modern psychology. *In* "The Handbook of Social Psychology, Vol. 1" (G. Lindzey and E. Aronson, Eds), pp. 1–80. Addison-Wesley, Reading, Mass.

Apfelbaum, E. (1974). On conflict and bargaining. *In* "Advances in Experimental Social Psychology, Vol. 7" (L. Berkowitz, Ed.), pp. 103–156. Academic Press, New York.

Apfelbaum, E. (1979). Relations of domination and movements for liberation: an analysis of power between groups. *In* "The Social Psychology of Intergroup Relations" (W. G. Austin and S. Worchel, Eds), pp. 188–204. Wadsworth, Inc., Belmont, Calif.

Armistead, N. (1974). Introduction. *In* "Reconstructing Social Psychology" (N. Armistead, Ed.), pp. 7–27. Penguin, Middlesex.

Asch, S. E. (1951). Effects of group pressure on the modification and distortion of judgements. *In* "Groups, Leadership, and Men" (H. Guetzkow, Ed.), pp. 177–190. Carnegie Press, Pittsburgh.

Austin, W. G. (1979). Justice, freedom, and self-interest in intergroup conflict. *In* "The Social Psychology on Intergroup Relations" (W. G. Austin and S. Worchel, Eds), pp. 121–143. Wadworth, Inc., Belmont, Calif.

Austin, W. G. and Worchel, S. (1979). "The Social Psychology of Intergroup Relations". Wadsworth, Inc., Belmont, Calif.

Bachrach, P. and Baratz, M. S. (1962). Two faces of power. *American Political Science Review* **57**, 641–651.

Bachrach, P. and Baratz, M. S. (1963). Decisions and non-decisions: an analytical framework. *American Political Science Review* **57**, 641–651.

Bachrach, P. and Baratz, M. S. (1970). "Power and Poverty". Oxford University Press, New York.

Baldridge, J. V. (1971). "Power and Conflict in the University". John Wiley and Sons, New York.

Bales, R. F. (1950). "Interaction Process Analysis". Addison-Wesley, Cambridge.

Bales, R. F. (1968). Interaction process analysis. *In* "International Encyclopaedia of the Social Sciences, Vol. 7" (D. L. Sills, Ed.), pp. 465–470. Macmilland and Free Press.

Bandura, A. (1977). Self-efficacy: toward a unifying theory of behavioural change. *Psychological Review* **84**, 191–215.

Banton, M. (1972). Authority. *New Society* 12 Oct., 86-88.

Baritz, L. (1960). "The Servants of Power: A History of the Use of Social Science in American Industry". Wesleyan University Press, Conn.

Bauman, Z. (1974). Officialdom and class: bases of inequality in socialist society. *In* "The Social Analysis of Class Structure" (F. Parkin, Ed.), pp. 129-148. Tavistock, London.

Bendix, R. (1945). Bureaucracy and the problem of power. *Public Administration Review* V, 194-209.

Bendix, R. (1956). Indexes of bureaucratization. *Reprinted in* "Comparative Perspective in Industrial Society" (W. A. Faunce and W. H. Form, Eds), pp. 244-259. Little, Brown and Co., Boston.

Bendix, R. (1965). Max Weber and Jakob Burckhardt. *American Sociological Review* **30**, 176-184.

Bendix, R. and Lipset, S. M. (Eds) (1967). "Class, Status and Power". (Rev. Ed.). Routledge and Kegan Paul, London.

Benoit-Smullyan, E. (1944). Status, status types, and status interrelations. *American Sociological Review* **9**, 151-161.

Berger, P. L. and Luckmann, T. (1967). "The Social Construction of Reality: A Treatise in the Sociology of Knowledge". Penguin, Middlesex.

Berkowitz, L. (1975). "A Survey of Social Psychology". Dryden Press, Hinsdale, Ill.

Berkowitz, L. and Daniels, L. R. (1963). Responsibility and dependency. *Journal of Abnormal Social Psychology* **66**, 429-436.

Berkowitz, L. and Daniels, L. R. (1964). Affecting the salience of the social responsibility norm: effects of past help on the response to dependency relationships. *Journal of Abnormal and Social Psychology* **68**, 275-281.

Berkowitz, L. and Walster, E. (Eds) (1976). "Advances in Experimental Social Psychology, Vol. 9. Equity Theory: Toward a General Theory of Social Interaction". Academic Press, New York.

Billig, M. (1976). "Social Psychology and Intergroup Relations". Academic Press, London.

Billig, M. and Tajfel, H. (1973). Social categorization and similarity in intergroup behaviour. *European Journal of Social Psychology* **3**, 27-52.

Birnbaum, P. (1976). Power divorced from its sources: a critique of the exchange theory of power. *In* "Power and Political Theory: Some European Perspectives" (B. Barry, Ed.), pp. 15-31. John Wiley and Sons, London.

Blake, R. R. and Mouton, J. S. (1979). Intergroup problem solving in organizations: from theory to practice. *In* "The Social Psychology of Intergroup Relations" (W. G. Austin and S. Worchel, Eds), pp. 19-32. Wadsworth, Inc., Belmont, Calif.

Blau, P. M. (1964). "Exchange and Power in Social Life". John Wiley and Sons, New York.

Blau, P. M. (1970). A formal theory of differentiation in organizations. *American Sociological Review* **35**, 201-218.

Blau, P. M. (1972). Interdependence and hierarchy in organizations. *Social Science Research* **1**, 1-24.

Blau, P. M. (1974). "On the Nature of Organizations". John Wiley and Sons, New York.

Blood, R. O., Jr. and Wolfe, D. M. (1960). "Husbands and Wives: The Dynamics of Married Living". Free Press, Glencoe, Ill.

Bondurant, J. V. (1958). "Conquest of Violence". Princeton University Press, Princeton.

Bottomore, T. B. (1964). "Elites and Society". Penguin, Middlesex.

Branthwaite, A. and Jones, J. E. (1975). Fairness and discrimination: English versus Welsh. *European Journal of Social Psychology* 5, 323–338.

Brickman, P. (1974). "Social Conflict: Readings in Rules, Structures and Conflict Relationships". D. C. Heath and Co., Lexington.

Bridgwater, P. (1972). "Nietzsche in Anglosaxony: a Study of Nietzsche's Impact on English and American Literature". Leicester University Press.

Brown, L. D. (1977). Can "Haves" and "Have-nots" cooperate? Two efforts to bridge a social gap. *Journal of Applied Behavioural Science* 13, 211–224.

Brown, L. D. (1978). Toward a theory of power and intergroup relations. *In* "Advances in Experiential Social Processes, Vol. 1" (C. L. Cooper and C. P. Alderfer, Eds), pp. 161–180. John Wiley and Sons, Chichester.

Brown, R. (1965). "Social Psychology". Free Press, New York.

Cartwright, D. (1959a). Power: a neglected variable in social psychology. *In* "Studies in Social Power" (D. Cartwright, Ed.), pp. 1–14. Institute of Social Research, Ann Arbor, Mich.

Cartwright, D. (1959b). A field theoretical conception of power. *In* "Studies in Social Power" (D. Cartwright, Ed.), pp. 183–220. Institute of Social Research, Ann Arbor, Mich.

Cartwright, D. (1965). Influence, leadership, control. *In* "Handbook of Organizations" (J. G. March, Ed.), pp. 1–47. Rand McNally, Chicago.

Cartwright, D. and Zander, A. (1968a). Power and influence in groups: introduction. *In* "Group Dynamics: Research and Theory" (D. Cartwright and A. Zander, Eds), pp. 215–235. Harper and Row, New York.

Cartwright, D. and Zander, A. (1968b). Group and group membership: *In* "Group Dynamics: Research and Theory" (D. Cartwright and A. Zander, Eds), pp. 45–62. Harper and Row, New York.

Cartwright, D. and Zander, A. (1968c). The structural properties of groups: introduction. *In* "Group Dynamics: Research and Theory" (D. Cartwright and A. Zander, Eds), pp. 485–502. Harper and Row, New York.

Chadwick-Jones, J. K. (1976). "Social Exchange Theory: Its Structure and Influence in Social Psychology". Academic Press, London.

Chertkoff, J. M. (1970). Sociopsychological theories and research on coalition formation. *In* "The Study of Coalition Behaviour" (S. Groennings, E. W. Kelley and M. Leiserson, Eds), Chapter 15. Holt, Rinehart and Winston, New York.

"Chinese Chronicle" (1976). Compiled and published by the People's Press, Shanghai.

Christie, R. and Geis, F. L. (Eds) (1970a). "Studies in Machiavellianism". Academic Press, New York.

Christie, R. and Geis, F. (1970b). Implications and speculations. *In* "Studies in Machiavellianism" (R. Christie and F. Geis, Eds), pp. 339–358. Academic Press, New York.

Clark, K. B. (1971). The pathos of power. *American Psychologist* 26, 1047–1057.

Coleman, J. S. (1971). "Resources for Social Change: Race in the United States". John Wiley and Sons, New York.

Coleman, J. S. (1973). Loss of power. *American Sociological Review* 38, 1–17.

Collins, B. E. and Raven, B. H. (1969). Group structure: attraction, coalitions, communication, and power. *In* "The Handbook of Social Psychology, 2nd Ed., Vol. 4" (G. Lindzey and E. Aronson, Eds), pp. 102–204. Addison-Wesley, Reading, Mass.

Coser, L. (1956). "The Functions of Social Conflict". Free Press, New York.

Creel, H. G. (1960). "Confucius and the Chinese Way". Harper and Row, New York.

Crozier, M. (1964). "The Bureaucratic Phenomenon". Tavistock, London.

Dahl, R. A. (1957). The concept of power. *Behavioural Science* **2**, 201–215.
Dahl, R. A. (1961). "Who Governs? Democracy and Power in an American City". Yale University Press, New Haven.
Dahl, R. A. (1968). Power. *In* "International Encyclopaedia of the Social Sciences, V. 12" (D. L. Sills, Eds), pp. 405–415. Macmillan and Free Press.
Dahl, R. A., March, J. and Nasatir, D. (1956). Influence ranking in the United States senate. Cited in R. A. Dahl (1957).
Dahrendorf, R. (1959). "Class and Class Conflict in Industrial Society". Routledge and Kegan Paul, London.
Dahrendorf, R. (1968). On the origin of inequality among men. *In* "Essays in the Theory of Society" (R. Dahrendorf, Ed.), pp. 151–178. Routledge and Kegan Paul, London.
Danet, B. (1973). Giving the underdog a break: latent particularism among customs officials. *In* "Bureaucracy and the Public: A Reader in Official-Client Relations" (E. Katz and B. Danet, Eds), pp. 329–337. Basic Books, New York.
Davis, K. and Moore, W. E. (1945). Some principles of stratification. *American Sociological Review* **10**, 242–249.
Davis, J. H., Laughlin, P. R. and Komorita, S. S. (1976). The social psychology of small groups: cooperative and mixed-motive interaction. *Annual Review of Psychology* **27**, 501–541.
Davis, W. N. (1972). Drinking: a search for power or nurturance? *In* "The Drinking Man" (D. C. McClelland, W. N. Davis, R. Kalin and E. Wanner, Eds), pp. 198–213. Free Press, New York.
Deaux, K. and Emswiller, T. (1974). Explanation of successful performance on sex-linked tasks: what is skill for the male is luck for the female. *Journal of Personality and Social Psychology* **29**, 80–85.
de Charms, R. (1968). "Personal Causation: The Internal Affective Determinants of Behaviour". Academic Press, New York.
D'Entreves, A. P. (1967). "The Notion of the State: An Introduction to Political Theory". Oxford University Press, London.
Deutsch, M. and Gerard, H. B. (1955). A study of normative and informational social influence upon individual judgement. *Journal of Abnormal and Social Psychology* **51**, 629–636.
Djilas, M. (1957). "The New Class: An Analysis of the Communist System". George Allen and Unwin, London.
Doise, W. and Sinclair, A. (1973). The categorization process in intergroup relations. *European Journal of Social Psychology* **3**, 145–153.
Duverger, M. (1966). "The Idea of Politics: The Uses of Power in Society" (translated by R. North and R. Murphy). Methuen, London.
Ellenburger, H. (1970). "The Discovery of the Unconscious: The History and Evolution of Dynamic Psychiatry". Basic Books, Inc., New York.
Emerson, R. H. (1962). Power-dependence relations. *American Sociological Review* **27**, 31–41.
Emerson, R. H. (1972). Exchange theory, part 1: a psychological basis for social exchange and exchange theory, part 2: exchange relations and network structures. *In* "Sociological Theories in Progress, Vol. 2" (J. Berger, M. Zelditch, Jr. and B. Anderson, Eds), pp. 38–87. Houghton-Mifflin, Boston.
Etzioni, A. (1964). "Modern Organizations". Prentice-Hall, Englewood Cliffs, New Jersey.
Fanon, F. (1967). "The Wretched of the Earth". Penguin, Middlesex.
Feather, N. T. and Simon, J. G. (1971). Attribution of responsibility and valence

of outcome in relation to initial confidence and success and failure of self and other. *Journal of Personality and Social Psychology* **18**, 173–188.

Festinger, L. (1954). A theory of social comparison processes. *Human Relations* **7**, 117–140.

Festinger, L. (1957). "A Theory of Cognitive Dissonance". Row Peterson, Evanston, Ill.

Festinger, L. Schachter, S. and Back, K. (1950). "Social Pressures in Informal Groups: A Study of Human Factors in Housing". Harper, New York.

French, J. R. P. and Raven, B. H. (1959). The bases of social power. In "Studies in Social Power" (D. Cartwright, Ed.), pp. 118–149. Institute of Social Research, Ann Arbor, Mich.

Frenckel-Brunswick, E. (1948). Dynamic and cognitive categorization of qualitative materials: II. Application to interviews with the ethnically prejudiced. *Journal of Psychology* **25**, 261–277.

Fried, M. H. (1960). On the evolution of social stratification and the state. *In* "Culture in History" (S. Diamond, Ed.), Columbia University Press. *Reprinted in* "The Logic of Social Hierarchies" (E. O. Laumann, P. M. Siegel and R. W. Hodge, Eds), pp. 684-695. Markham Publishing Co., Chicago, 1970.

Friedrich, C. J. (1963). "Man and His Government". McGraw-Hill, New York.

Friedrich, C. J. (1967). "An Introduction to Political Theory: Twelve Lectures at Harvard". Harper and Row, New York.

Friedrich, C. J. (1972). "Tradition and Authority". Pall Mall Press, London.

Frisbie, P. (1975). Measuring the degree of bureaucratization at the societal level. *Social Forces* **53**, 563–573.

Galtung, J. (1966). Rank and social integration: a multi-dimensional approach. *In* "Sociological Theories in Progress, Vol. 1" (J. Berger, M. Zelditch, Jr. and B. Anderson, Eds), pp. 145–198. Houghton Mifflin, Boston.

Gamson, W. A. (1968). "Power and Discontent". Dorsey Press, Homewood, Ill.

Gerth, H. H and Mills, C. W. (1948). Introduction: the man and his work. *In* "From Max Weber: Essays in Sociology" (Translated, edited and with an introduction by H. H. Gerth and C. W. Mills), pp. 3–74. Routledge and Kegan Paul, London.

Geschwender, J. A. (1967). Continuities in theories of status consistency and cognitive dissonance. *Social Forces* **46**, 160–171.

Gibb, C. A. (1969). Leadership. *In* "The Handbook of Social Psychology, Vol. 4" (G. Lindzey and E. Aronson, Eds), pp. 205-282. Addison-Wesley, Reading, Mass.

Giddens, A. (1968). "Power" in the recent writings of Talcott Parsons. *Sociology* **2**, 257–272.

Giddens, A. (1974). Elites in the British class structure. *In* "Elites and Power in British Society" (P. Stanworth and A. Giddens, Eds), pp. 1–21. Cambridge University Press, London.

Gilbert, A. (1965). Commentary on the discourses. *In* "Machiavelli: The Chief Works and Others, Vol. 1" (Translated by A. Gilbert), pp. 186–187. Duke University Press, Durham, North Carolina.

Giles, H. (1978). Linguistic differentiation in ethnic groups. *In* "Differentiation Between Social Groups: Studies in the Social Psychology of Intergroup Relations" (H. Tajfel, Ed.), pp. 361–394. Academic Press, London.

Ginsburg, M. (1973). Nietzschean psychiatry. *In* "Nietzsche: a Collection of Critical Essays" (R. C. Solomon, Ed.), pp. 293–315. Anchor Books, New York.

Glass, D. C. and Singer, J. E. (1972). "Urban Stress: Experiments on Noise and Social Stressors". Academic Press, New York.

Goffman, I. W. (1957). Status consistency and preference for change in power distribution. *American Sociological Review* **22**, 275–281.

Gold, M. (1958). Power in the classroom. *Sociometry* **21**, 50–60.
Goldhamer, H. and Shils, E. A. (1939). Types of power and status. *American Journal of Sociology* **45**, 171–182.
Goode, W. J. (1963). "World Revolution and Family Patterns". Free Press, New York.
Goode, J. (1972). Presidential address: The place of force in human society. *American Sociological Review* **37**, 507–519.
Gouldner, A. W. (1954). "Patterns of Industrial Bureaucracy". Free Press, New York.
Gouldner, A. W. (1970). "The Coming Crisis of Western Sociology". Basic Books, New York.
Gurr, T. R. (1970). "Why Men Rebel". Princeton University Press, New Jersey.
Hamilton, M. (1976). An analysis and typology of social power (Part I). *Philosophy of Social Sciences* **6**, 289–313.
Hamilton, M. (1977). An analysis and typology of social power (Part II). *Philosophy of Social Sciences* **7**, 51–65.
Harsanyi, J. C. (1962). Measurement of social power, opportunity costs, and the theory of two-person bargaining games. *Behavioural Science* **7**, 67–80.
Hartmann, R. and Husband, C. (1974). "Racism and the Mass Media". Davis-Poynter, London.
Haufmann, E. (1935). Social structure of a group of kindergarten children. *American Journal of Orthopsychiatry* **5**, 407–410.
Hawley, A. H. (1963). Community power and urban renewal success. *American Journal of Sociology* **68**, 422–431.
Heider, F. (1958). "The Psychology of Interpersonal Relations". Wiley, New York.
Heinicke, C. and Bales, R. F. (1953). Development trends in the structure of small groups. *Sociometry* **16**, 7–38.
Herbst, P. G. (1952). The measurement of family relationships. *Human Relations* **5**, 3-35.
Hirschman, A. O. (1970). "Exit, Voice and Loyalty: Responses to Decline in Firms, Organizations, and States". Harvard University Press, Cambridge, Mass.
Hobbes, T. (1651). "Leviathan". Edited with an introduction by C. B. Macpherson. Penguin, Middlesex, 1968.
Hollander, E. P. (1958). Conformity, status and idiosyncrasy credit. *Psychology Review* **65**, 117–127.
Hollander, E. P. (1960). Competence and conformity in the acceptance of influence. *Journal of Abnormal and Social Psychology* **61**, 360–365.
Homans, G. C. (1961). "Social Behaviour: Its Elementary Forms". Routledge and Kegan Paul, London.
Homans, G. C. (1969). Prologue: The sociological relevance of behaviourism. *In* "Behavioural Sociology: The Experimental Analysis of Social Process" (R. L. Burgess and D. Bushell, Jr., Eds), pp. 1-24. Columbia University Press, New York.
Homans, G. C. (1976). Commentary. *In* "Advances in Experimental Social Psychology. Vol. 9. Equity Theory: Toward a General Theory of Social Interaction" (L. Berkowitz and E. Walster, Eds), pp. 231-244. Academic Press, New York.
Horowitz, I. L. (1963). An introduction to C. Wright Mills. *In* "Power, Politics and People, the Collected Essays of C. Wright Mills" (I. L. Horowitz, Ed.), pp. 1–20. Oxford University Press, New York.
Horwitz, M. (1958). The veridicality of liking and disliking. *In* "Person Perception and Interpersonal Behaviour" (R. Tagiuri and L. Petrullo, Eds), pp. 191–209. Stanford University Press, Stanford.
Hunter, F. (1953). "Community Power Structure: A Study of Decision-Makers". University of North Carolina Press, Chapel Hill.

Jackson, E. F. (1962). Status consistency and symptoms of stress. *American Sociological Review* **27**, 469–480.

Jones, E. (1954). "Sigmund Freud: Life and Work, Vol. 1". Hogarth Press, London.

Jones, E. E. and Gerard, H. B. (1967). "Foundations of Social Psychology". John Wiley and Sons, New York.

Katz, E. and Danet, B. (1966). Petitions and persuasive appeals: a study of official-client relations. *American Sociological Review* **31**, 811–822.

Katz, D. and Kahn, R. L. (1966). "The Social Psychology of Organizations". John Wiley and Sons, New York.

Kaufmann, W. (1950). "Nietzsche: Philosopher, Psychologist, Antichrist". Princeton University Press, New Jersey.

Kavanau, J. L. (1967). Behaviour of captive white-footed mice. *Science* **155**, 1623–1639.

Kelly, H. H. (1950). The warm-cold variables in first impressions of persons. *Journal of Personality* **18**, 431–439.

Kelly, H. H. and Thibaut, J. W. (1969). Group problem solving. *In* "The Handbook of Social Psychology, Vol. 4" (G. Lindzey and E. Aronson, Eds), pp. 1–101. Addison-Wesley Publishing Company, Reading, Mass.

Kelman, H. C. (1961). Processes of opinion change. *Public Opinion Quarterly* **35**, 57–78.

Kelman, H. (1972). Power: the cultural approach of Karen Horney. *In* "The Dynamics of Power" (J. H. Masserman, Ed.), pp. 71–82. Grune and Stratton, New York.

Kimberly, J. C. (1972). Relations among status, power, and economic rewards in simple and complex social structures. *In* "Sociological Theories in Progress, Vol. 2" (J. Berger, M. Zelditch, Jr. and B. Anderson, Eds), pp. 291–307, Houghton Mifflin, Boston.

Kimberly, J. C. (1966). A theory of status equilibration. *In* "Sociological Theories in Progress, Vol. 1" (J. Berger, M. Zelditch, Jr. and B. Anderson, Eds), pp. 213–226. Houghton Mifflin, Boston.

Kipnis, D. (1972). Does power corrupt? *Journal of Personality and Social Psychology* **24**, 33–41.

Kleinke, C. L. (1978). "Self Perception: The Psychology of Personal Awareness". W. H. Freeman and Co., San Francisco.

Koestler, A. (1967). "The Ghost in the Machine". Pan Books, London.

Krech, D., Crutchfield, R. S. and Ballachey, E. L. (1962). "Individual in Society". McGraw-Hill, New York.

Kuhn, T. S. (1962). "The Structure of Scientific Revolutions". University of Chicago Press, Chicago.

Lasswell, H. D. (1948). "Power and Personality". Greenwood Press, Conn.

Lasswell, H. D. and Kaplan, A. (1948). Appendix: on power and influence. *In* "Power and Personality" (H. D. Lasswell, Ed.), pp. 223–236. Greenwood Press, Conn.

Lasswell, H. D. and Kaplan, A. (1952). "Power and Society: A Framework for Political Inquiry". Routledge and Kegan Paul, London.

Lenski, G. E. (1954). Status crystallization: a non-vertical dimension of social status. *American Sociological Review* **19**, 405–413.

Lenski, G. E. (1966). "Power and Privelege: A Theory of Social Stratification". McGraw-Hill, New York.

Lenski, G. E. (1967). Status inconsistency and the vote: a four nation test. *American Sociological Review* **32**, 298–301.

Lewin, K. (1941). Analysis of the concepts whole, differentiation, and unity. *University of Iowa Studies in Child Welfare* **18**, 226–261. *Reprinted in* "Field Theory in Social Science" (D. Cartwright, Ed.), pp. 305–338. Tavistock, London.

Lewin, K. (1944). Constructs in psychology and psychological ecology. *University of Iowa Studies in Child Welfare* **20**, 1-29. *Reprinted* under the title of Constructs in Field Theory. *In* "Field Theory in Social Science" (D. Cartwright, Ed.), pp. 30-42. Tavistock, London.

Lief, H. I. (1972). Power in the family: a preface. *In* "The Dynamics of Power" (J. H. Masserman, Ed.), pp. 116-119. Grune and Stratton, New York.

Lind, E. A. and O'Barr, W. M. (1979). The social significance of speech in the courtroom. *In* "Language and Social Psychology" (H. Giles and R. St. Clair, Eds), pp. 66-87. Basil Blackwell, Oxford.

Lippett, R., Polansky, N., Redi, F. and Rosen, S. (1952). The dynamics of power. *Human Relations* **5**, 37-64.

Lively, J. (1976). The limits of exchange theory. *In* "Power and Political Theory: Some European Perspectives" (B. Barry, Ed.), pp. 1-13. John Wiley and Sons, London.

Lockwood, D. (1956). Some remarks on "The social system". *British Journal of Sociology* **7**, 134-166.

London, P. (1969). "Behavioural Control". Harper and Row, New York.

Lowry, R. J. (Ed.) (1973). "Dominance, Self-esteem, Self-Actualization: Germinal Papers of A. H. Maslow". Brooks/Cole Publishing Co., California.

Lukes, S. (1973). "Individualism". Blackwell, Oxford.

Lukes, S. (1974). "Power: A Radical View". Macmillan, London.

Machiavelli, N. (1965a). The Prince. *In* "Machiavelli: The Chief Works and Others, Vol. 1" (Translated by A. Gilbert), pp. 10-96. Duke University Press, Durham, North Carolina, 1965.

Machiavelli, N. (1965b). Discourses on the first decade of Titus Livius. *In* "Machiavelli: The Chief Works and Others, Vol. 1" (Translated by A. Gilbert), pp. 188-529. Duke University Press, Durham, North Carolina, 1965.

Macpherson, C. B. (1968). Introduction. *In* "Hobbes: Leviathan" (C. B. Macpherson, Ed.), pp. 9-63. Penguin, Middlesex.

Mahoney, M. J. and Thoresen, C. E. (Eds) (1974). "Self-control: Power to the Person". Brooks/Cole, Belmont, California.

Marcuse, H. (1964). "One Dimensional Man". Beacon Press, Boston.

Maritain, J. (1942). The End of Machiavellianism. "The Review of Politics **4**, 9-32. *Reprinted in part in* "Machiavelli: Cynic, Patriot, or Political Scientist?" (De L. Jansen, Ed.), pp. 91-97. D. C. Heath, Boston, 1960.

Maslow, A. H. (1937). Dominance-feeling, behaviour, and status. *Psychological Review* **44**, 404-429. *Reprinted in* R. J. Lowry (Ed.) (1973), pp. 49-70.

Maslow, A. H. (1941). Deprivation, threat and frustration. Psychological Review **48**, 364-366.

Maslow, A. H. (1942). Self-esteem (dominance-feeling) and sexuality in women. *Journal of Social Pyschology* **16**, 259-294. *Reprinted in* R. J. Lowry (Ed.) (1973), pp. 106-136.

Maslow, A. H. (1943a). The authoritarian character structure. *Journal of Social Psychology* **18**, 401-411. *Reprinted in* R. J. Lowry (Ed.) (1973), pp. 139-149.

Maslow, A. H. (1943b). A theory of human motivation. *Psychological Review* **50**, 370-386. *Reprinted in* R. J. Lowry (Ed.) (1973), pp. 153-173.

Maslow, A. H. (1968). "Toward a Psychology of Being". D. Van Nostrand Co., New York, second edition.

Masserman, J. H. (Ed.) (1972). "The Dynamics of Power. (Scientific Proceedings of the American Academy of Psychoanalysis, Vol. XX)". Grune and Stratton, New York.

Mattingly, A. (1958). Machiavelli's *Prince*: political science or political satire? *The American Scholar* **27**, 482-491.

May, R. (1972). "Power and Innocence: A Search for the Sources of Violence". Dell, New York.

McClelland, D. C. (1961). "The Achieving Society". Van Nostrand, New Jersey.

McClelland, D. C. (1970). The two faces of power. *Journal of International Affairs* **24**, 29–47.

McClelland, D. C. (1975). "Power: The Inner Experience". Irvington, New York.

McClelland, D. C. and Wilsnack, S. C. (1972). The effects of drinking on thoughts about power and restraint. *In* "The Drinking Man" (D. C. McClelland, W. N. Davis, R. Kahn and E. Wanner, Eds), pp. 123–141. Free Press, New York.

McDougall, W. (1948). "An Introduction to Social Psychology", 29th ed. Methuen, London.

McGuire, W. J. (1969). The nature of attitudes and attitude change. *In* "The Handbook of Social Psychology, Vol. 3" (G. Lindzey and E. Aronson, Eds), pp. 136–314. Addison-Wesley, Mass.

McKellar, P. (1977). The origins of violence. *In* "Violence: The Community and the Administrator. Studies in Public Administration, No. 22" (M. G. Kerr, Ed), pp, 14–27. New Zealand Institute of Public Administration, Wellington.

Merei, F. (1949). Group leadership and institutionalization. *Human Relations* **2**, 23–39.

Merton, R. K. (1957). "Social Theory and Social Structure". Rev. Ed. Free Press, New York.

Michels, R. (1962). "Political Parties" (Translated by E. Paul and C. Paul). Free Press, New York.

Milgram, S. (1974). "Obedience to Authority: An Experimental View". Harper and Row, New York.

Mills, C. W. (1948). "The New Man of Power". Harcourt and Brace, New York.

Mills, C. W. (1951). "White Collar: The American Middle Classes". Oxford University Press, London.

Mills, C. W. (1956). "The Power Elite". Oxford University Press, New York.

Mills, C. W. (1958). The structure of power in American society. *British Journal of Sociology* **9**, 2941.

Mills, C. W. (1959). "The Sociological Imagination". Penguin Books, Harmondsworth, Middlesex.

Minton, H. L. (1967). Power as a personality construct. *In* "Progress in Experimental Personality Research, Vol. 4" (B. A. Maher, Ed.), pp. 229–267. Academic Press, New York.

Mischel, W. (1968). "Personality and Assessment". Wiley, New York.

Mitchell, W. (1967). "Sociological Analysis and Politics: The Theories of Talcott Parsons". Prentice-Hall Inc., Englewood Cliffs, New Jersey.

Moore, M. (1976). A cross-cultural comparison of value systems. *European Journal of Social Psychology* **6**, 249–254.

Mosca, G. (1938). "The Ruling Class'. Translated by H. D. Kahn, edited and revised by A. Livingston, McGraw-Hill, New York.

Moscovici, S. (1974). Social influence I: conformity and social control. *In* "Social Psychology: Classical and Contemporary Integrations" (C. Nemeth, Ed.), pp. 179–216. Rand McNally, Chicago.

Moscovici, S. (1975). Reply to a critical note on two studies of minority influence. *European Journal of Social Psychology* **5**, 261–263.

Moscovici, S. (1976). "Social Influence and Social Change". Academic Press, London.

Moscovici, S. and Lage, E. (1976). Studies in social influence III: majority versus minority influence in a group. *European Journal of Social Psychology* **6**, 149–174.

Mueller, C. (1973). "The Politics of Communication: A Study in the Political Sociology of Language, Socialization, and Legitimation". Oxford University Press, New York.
Mugny, G. (1975). Negotiations, image of the other, and the process of minority influence. *European Journal of Social Psychology* 5, 209-228.
Mulder, M. (1959). Power and satisfaction in task oriented groups. *Acta Psychology* **16,** 178-225.
Mulder, M. (1965). Power motivation in behaviour on a level of reality. Paper read at the meeting of A.P.A., September, Chicago.
Mulder, M. (1971). Power equalization through participation? *Administrative Science Quarterly* **16**,
Mulder, M. (1972). The learning of participation. Paper presented at the First International Sociological Conference on Participation and Self-government. Dubrovnick, Yugoslavia.
Mulder, M. (1974). Power distance reduction tendencies: problems of power and power relations. Paper read at the conference "Research Paradigms and Priorities in Social Psychology". Otawa, Canada.
Mulder, M. (1975). Reduction of power differences in practice: the power distance reduction theory and its implications. Paper read at the seminar: European contributions to Organization Theory. Fontainbleau, France.
Mulder, M. and Wilke, H. (1970). Participation and power equalization. *Organizational Behaviour and Human Performance* 5, 430-448.
Mulder, M., van Kiijk, R., Stelwagen, T., Verhagen, J., Soutendijk, S. and Zwezerijnen, J. (1966). Illegitimacy of power and positiveness of attitude towards the power person. *Human Relations* **19**, 21-37.
Mulder, M., van Eck, J. R. R. and van Gils, M. R. (1967). Structuur en dynamiek van een grote organisatie. Institute for Social Psychology, Utrecht University and Dutch Institute for Preventive Medicine. T.N.O., Leiden. Cited in M. Mulder (1974).
Mulder, M., Van Eck, J. R. R. and de Jong, R. D. (1970). Het systeem van functioneren onder verschillende omstandigheden in een grote organisatie. In "Bedrijfpsychologie" (P. J. D. Drenth, P. J. Willems and Ch. J. de Wolff, Eds), pp. 431-434. van Loghum Slaterus, Kluner, cited in M. Mulder (1974).
Mulder, M. and Veen, P. *et al.* (1970). "Inadequate Power Exertion by the Powerful and Power-Distance-Reduction by the Less Powerful on a Level of Reality". Manuscript, Institute of Social Psychology, University of Utrecht.
Mulder, M., Veen, P., Hartsuiker, D. and Westerduin, T. (1971). Cognitive processes in power equalization. *European Journal of Social Psychology* **1**, 107-130.
Mulder, M., Veen, P., Hijzen, T. and Jansen, P. (1973a). On power equalization: a behavioural example of power distance reduction. *Journal of Personality and Social Psychology* **9**, 87-96.
Mulder, M., Veen, P., Rodenburg, C., Frenken, J. and Tielens, H. (1973b). The power distance reduction hypothesis on a level of reality. *Journal of Experimental Social Psychology* **9**, 87-96.
Murdock, G. P. (1949). "Social Structure". Macmillan Publishing Co., New York.
Murdoch, P. (1967). Development of contractual norms in a dyad. *Journal of Personality and Social Psychology* **6**, 206-211.
Nemeth, C. (1975). Understanding minority influence: a reply and a digression. *European Journal of Social Psychology* **5**, 265-267.
Ng, S. H. (1977a). Structural and non-structural aspects of power distance reduction tendencies. *European Journal of Social Psychology* **7**, 317-345.
Ng, S. H. (1977b). Power: the dimension of ranking in interpersonal and intergroup behaviour. Unpublished Ph.D. thesis, University of Bristol.

Ng, S. H. (1978). Minimal social categorization, political categorization, and power change. *Human Relations* **31**, 765–779.

Ng, S. H. (in press). Power and intergroup discrimination. *In* "Social Identity and Intergroup Relations" (H. Tajfel, Ed.). Cambridge University Press and Éditions de la Maison des Sciences de l'Homme.

Nietzsche, F. (1872). "The Birth of Tragedy". Translated by W. Kaufmann. Random House, New York, 1967.

Nietzsche, F. (1883–1888). "The Will to Power". Translated by W. Kaufmann and R. J. Hollingdale, and edited, with commentary, by W. Kaufmann. Vintage Books, New York. 1968.

Nietzsche, F. (1886). "Beyond Good and Evil". Translated by W. Kaufmann. Vintage Books, New York. 1966.

Olsen, M. E. (1970). Elitist theory as a response to Marx. *In* "Power in Societies" (M. E. Olsen, Ed.), pp. 106–113. Macmillan, New York.

Olson, D. H. and Cromwell, R. E. (1975). Methodological issues in family power. *In* "Power in Families" (by R. E. Cromwell and D. H. Olson, Eds), pp. 131–150. John Wiley and Sons (Sage Publications), New York.

Pareto, V. (1935). "The Mind and Society". Translated by A. Bongiorno and A. Livingston, and edited by A. Livingston. Jonathan Cape, London.

Parkin, F. (1971). "Class Inequality and Political Order: Social Stratification in Capitalist and Communist Societies". Paladin, Herts.

Parsons, T. (1937). "The Structure of Social Action". McGraw-Hill, New York.

Parsons, T. (1942). Max Weber and the contemporary political crisis. *Review of Politics* **8**, 66–71 (Part I), 155–172). (Part II) *Reprinted in* "Politics and Social Structure" (T. Parsons), pp. 98–124. Free Press, New York. 1969.

Parsons, T. (1951). "The Social System". Free Press, New York.

Parsons, T. (1957). The distribution of power in American society. *World Politics* **X**, 123–143.

Parsons, T. (1963a). On the concept of influence. *Public Opinion Quarterly* **27**, 37–62.

Parsons, T. (1963b). On the concept of political power. *Proceedings of the American Philosophical Society* **107**, 1963. *Reprinted in* "Sociological Theory and Modern Society" (T. Parsons), pp. 297–354. Free Press, New York. 1967.

Parsons, T. (1964). Some reflections on the place of force in social process. *In* "Internal War: Basic Problems and Approaches" (H. Eckstein, Ed.). Free Press, New York. *Reprinted in* "Sociological Theory and Modern Society" (T. Parsons), pp. 264–296. Free Press, New York. 1967.

Parsons, T. (1967). "Sociological Theory and Modern Society". Free Press, New York.

Parsons, T. (1976). Social structure and the symbolic media interchange. *In* "Approaches to the study of social structure" (P. M. Blau, Ed.), pp. 94–120. Open Books, London.

Pavlov, I. P. (1927). "Conditional Reflexes". (Translated by G. V. Anrep) Oxford University Press, London.

Peters, R. S. and Tajfel, H. (1957). Hobbes and Hull — metaphysicians of behaviour. *British Journal for the Philosophy of Science* **8**, 3044.

Phares, E. J. (1976). "Locus of Control in Personality". General Learning Press, New Jersey.

Plon, M. (1974). On the meaning of the notion of conflict and its study in social psychology. *European Journal of Social Psychology* **4**, 389–436.

Pollard, W. E. and Mitchell, T. R. (1972). Decision theory analysis of social power. *Psychological Bulletin* **78**, 433–446.

Polsby, N. W. (1963). "Community Power and Political Theory". Yale University Press, New Haven.

Presthus, R. (1962). "The Organizational Society". Knopf, New York.

Rabbie, J. H. and Horwitz, M. (1969). Arousal of ingroup-outgroup bias by a chance win or loss. *Journal of Personality and Social Psychology* **13**, 269–277.

Raven, B. H. (1965). Social influence and power. *In* "Current Studies in Social Psychology" (I. D. Steiner and M. Fishbein, Eds), pp. 371–382. Holt, Rinehart and Winston, New York.

Raven, B. H. (1974). The comparative analysis of power and power preference. *In* "Perspectives on Social power" (J. T. Tedeschi, Ed), pp. 172–198. Aldine Publishers, Chicago.

Raven, B. H. and French, J. R. P. Jr. (1958). Group support, legitimate power and social influence. *Journal of Personality* **26**, 400–409.

Raven, B. H. and Kruglanski, A. W. (1970). Conflict and power. *In* "The Structure of Conflict" (P. Swingle, Ed.), pp. 69–109. Academic Press, New York.

Raven, B. H., Manson, H. H. and Anthony, E. (1962). The effects of attributed ability upon expert and referent influence. University of California at Los Angeles (Technical Report No. 10, Nonr 233 [54]). Cited in B. H. Raven (1974).

Rex, J. (1961). "Key Problems of Sociological Theory". Routledge and Kegan Paul, London.

Robinson, D. N. (1976). "An Intellectual History of Psychology". Macmillan, New York.

Rokeach, M. (1973). "The Nature of Human Values". Free Press, New York.

Rogow, A. A. and Lasswell, H. D. (1963). "Power, Corruption, and Rectitude". Prentice-Hall, Englewood Cliffs, N.J.

Rollins, B. C. and Thomas, D. L. (1974). A theory of parental power and child compliance. *In* "Power in Families" (R. E. Cromwell and D. H. Olsen, Eds), pp. 38–60. Halstead Press, New York.

Rosen, S. (1959). Effects of adjustment on the perception and exertion of social power. *In* "Studies in Social Power" (D. Cartwright, Ed.), pp. 69–82. Institute of Social Research, Ann Arbor, Mich.

Rotter, J. B. (1966). Generalised expectancies for internal versus external control of reinforcement. *Psychological Monography* **80**, whole no. 609.

Rotter, J. B., Seeman, M. and Liberant, S. (1962). Internal versus external control of reinforcement: a major variable in behaviour therapy. *In* "Decisions, Values and Groups, Vol. 2" (N. F. Washburne, Ed.), pp. 473–516. Pergamon Press, New York.

Runciman, W. G. (1966). "Relative Deprivation and Social Justice". Routledge and Kegan Paul, London.

Russell, B. (1938). "Power: A New Social Analysis". George Allen and Unwin, London.

Ryder, R. G. (1970). Dimensions of early marriage. *Family Process* **9**, 51–68.

Salter, W. M. (1968). "Nietzsche the Thinker". Frederick Ungar, New York.

Salzinger, K. (1973). Inside the black box, with apologies to Pandora. A review of Ulric Neisser's Cognitive Psychology. *Journal of the Experimental Analysis of Behaviour* **19**, 369–378.

Sampson, E. E. (1963). Status congruence and cognitive consistency. *Sociometry* **26**, 146–162.

Sampson, E. E. (1969). Studies in status congruence. *In* "Advances in Experimental Social Psychology, Vol. 4" (L. Berkowitz, Ed.), pp. 225–270. Academic Press, New York.

Schattschneider, E. E. (1960). "The Semi-Sovereign People: A Realist's View of Democracy in America". Holt, Rinehart and Winston, New York.

Schopler, J. (1965). Social power. *In* "Advances in Experimental Social Psychology, Vol. 2" (L. Berkowitz, Ed.), pp. 177–218. Academic Press, New York.

Schopler, J. and Bateson, N. (1965). The power of dependence. *Journal of Personality and Social Psychology* **2**, 247–254.

Schopler, J. and Laytan, B. D. (1974). Attributions of interpersonal power. *In* "Perspectives on Social Power" (J. T. Tedeschi, Ed.), pp. 34–60.

Seeman, M. (1959). On the meaning of alienation. *American Sociological Review* **24**, 783–791.

Seeman, M. (1975). Alienation Studies. *Annual Review of Sociology* **1**, 91–123.

Seligman, M. E. P. (1975). "Helplessness: On Depression Development and Death". W. H. Freeman, San Francisco.

Sherif, M. (1936). "The Psychology of Social Norms". Harper and Row, New York.

Sherif, M. (1962). Intergroup relations and leadership: introductory statement. *In* "Intergroup Relations and Leadership" (M. Sherif, Ed.), pp. 3–21. John Wiley and Sons, New York.

Sherif, M. (1966). "Group Conflict and Co-operation: Their Social Psychology". Routledge and Kegan Paul, London.

Simmel, G. (1950). "The Sociology of Georg Simmel". Free Press, Glencoe, Ill.

Simon, H. A. (1947). "Administrative Behaviour". Macmillan, New York.

Skinner, B. F. (1938). "The Behaviour of Organisms: An Experimental Analysis". Appleton-Century-Crofts, Inc., New York.

Skinner, B. F. (1948). "Walden Two". Macmillan, New York.

Skinner, B. F. (1953). "Science and Human Behaviour". Macmillan, New York.

Skinner, B. F. (1969). "Contingencies of Reinforcement: A Theoretical Analysis". Appleton-Century-Crofts, New York.

Skinner, B. F. (1971). "Beyond Freedom and Dignity". Knopf, New York.

Skinner, B. F. (1972). "Cumulative Record: A Selection of Papers". Appleton-Century-Crofts, New York. Third edition.

Skinner, B. F. (1973). Are we free to have a future? *Impact* **3**, 5–12.

Skinner, B. F. (1977a). The experimental analysis of operant behaviour. *In* "The Roots of American Psychology: Historical Influences and Implications for the Future. (Annals of the New York Academy of Sciences, Vol. 291)" (R. W. Rieber and K. Salzinger, Eds), pp. 374–385. New York Academy of Sciences, New York.

Skinner, B. F. (1977b). Human behaviour and democracy. *Psychology Today*, September.

Skinner, B. F. (1978). "Reflections on Behaviourism and Society". Prentice-Hall, Englewood Cliffs, New Jersey.

Smith, A. (1975). "Powers of Mind". Ballantine Books, New York.

Sorokin, P. A. and Lunden, W. A. (1959). "Power and Morality: Who Shall Guard the Guardians?" Porter Sargent Publishers, Boston.

Steiner, I. (1972). "Group Process and Productivity". Academic Press, New York.

Stryker, S. (1977). Developments in "Two social psychologies": toward an appreciation of mutual relevance. *Sociometry* **40**, 145–160.

Swingle, P. G. (1976). "Management of Power". John Wiley and Sons, New York.

Tajfel, H. (1970). Experiments in intergroup discrimination. *Scientific American* **223**, 96–102.

Tajfel, H. (1972). Experiments in a vacuum. *In* "The Context of Social Psychology: A Critical Assessment" (J. Israel and H. Tajfel, Eds), pp. 69–119. Academic Press, London.

Tajfel, H. (1974). "Intergroup Behaviour, Social Comparison and Social Change". Katz-Newcomb Lectures, University of Michigan, Ann Arbor.

Tajfel, H. (1975). The exit of social mobility and the voice of social change: notes on the social psychology of intergroup relations. *Social Science Information* **14**, 101–118.

Tajfel, H. (1976). From the economics of expendable objects to the social psychology of intergroup relations. Manuscript, Department of Psychology, University of Bristol.

Tajfel, H. (1978a). Interindividual behaviour and intergroup behaviour. *In* "Differentiation Between Social Groups: Studies in the Social Psychology of Intergroup Relations" (H. Tajfel, Ed.), pp. 27–60. Academic Press, London.

Tajfel, H. (1978b). Social categorization, social identity and social comparison. *In* "Differentiation Between Social Groups: Studies in the Social Psychology of Intergroup Relations" (H. Tajfel, Ed.), pp. 61–76. Academic Press, London.

Tajfel, H. (1978c). The achievement of group differentiation. *In* "Differentiation Between Social Groups: Studies in the Social Psychology of Intergroup Relations" (H. Tajfel, Ed.), pp. 77–98. Academic Press, London.

Tajfel, H. and Billig, M. (1974). Familiarity and categorization in intergroup behaviour. *Journal of Experimental Social Psychology* **10**, 159–170.

Tajfel, H. and Turner, J. (1979). An integrative theory of intergroup conflict. *In* "The Social Psychology of Intergroup Relations" (W. G. Austin and S. Worchel, Eds), pp. 33–47. Wadsworth, Inc., Belmont, Calif.

Tajfel, H., Flament, C., Billig, M. and Bundy, R. (1971). Social categorization and intergroup behaviour. *European Journal of Social Psychology* **1**, 149–175.

Tedeschi, J. T. (Ed.), (1974). "Perspectives on Social Power". Aldine Publishers, Chicago.

Tedeschi, J. T. and Bonoma, T. V. (1972). Power and influence: an introduction. *In* "The Social Influence Processes" (J. T. Tedeschi, Ed.), pp. 1–49. Aldine-Atherton, Chicago.

Tedeschi, J. T., Bonoma, T. V. and Schlenker, B. R. (1972a). Influence, decision and compliance. *In* "The Social Influence Processes" (J. T. Tedeschi, Ed.), pp. 346–418. Aldine-Atherton, Chicago.

Tedeschi, J. T., Schlenker, B. R. and Lindskold, S. (1972b). The exercise of power and influence: the source of influence. *In* "The Social Influence Processes" (J. T. Tedeschi, Ed.), pp. 287–345. Aldine-Atherton, Chicago.

Tedeschi, J. T., Schlenker, B. R. and Bonoma, T. V. (1973). "Conflict, Power and Games". Aldine Publishers, Chicago.

Tedeschi, J. T., Smith, R. B. III and Brown, R. C., Jr. (1974). A reinterpretation of research on aggression. *Psychological Bulletin* **81**, 540–562.

Thibaut, J. (1968). The development of contractual norms in bargaining: replication and variation. *Journal of Conflict Resolution* **12**, 102–112.

Thibaut, J. and Faucheux, C. (1965). The development of contractual norms in a bargaining situation under two types of stress. *Journal of Experimental Social Psychology* **1**, 89–102.

Thibaut, J. and Gruder, C. L. (1969). Formation of contractual agreements between parties of unequal power. *Journal of Personality and Social Psychology* **11**, 59–65.

Thibaut, J. W. and Kelley, H. H. (1959). "The Social Psychology of Groups". Wiley, New York.

Thibaut, J. W. and Riecken, H. W. (1955). Some determinants and consequences of the perception of social causality. *Journal of Personality* **24**, 113–134.

Thomas, W. I. and Thomas, D. S. (1928). "The Child in America". Alfred A. Knopf, New York.

Thoresen, C. E. and Mahoney, M. J. (1974). "Behavioural Self-control". Holt, Rinehart and Winston, New York.

Triandis, H. C. (1977). Subjective culture and interpersonal relations across cultures. *In* "Issues in Cross-Cultural Research. Annals of the New York Academy of Sciences, Vol. 285" (L. L. Adler, Ed.), pp. 418–434. The New York Academy of Sciences, New York.

Triandis, H. C. (1979). Commentary. *In* "The Social Psychology of Intergroup Relations" (W. G. Austin and S. Worchel, Eds), pp. 321–334. Wadsworth, Inc., Belmont, Calif.

Tumin, M. M. (1953a). Some principles of stratification; a critical analysis. *American Sociological Review* **18**, 387–397.

Tumin, M. M. (1953b). Reply to Kingsley Davis. *American Sociological Review* **18**, 672–673.

Tumin, M. M. (1967). "Social Stratification: the Forms and Functions of Inequality". Prentice-Hall, Englewood Cliffs, New Jersey.

Turner, J. C. (1975a). Social comparison and social identity: some prospects for intergroup behaviour. *European Journal of Social Psychology* **5**, 5–34.

Turner, J. C. (1975b). Social categorization and social comparison in intergroup relations. Unpublished Ph.D. thesis, University of Bristol.

Turner, J. (1978). Social categorization and social discrimination in the minimal group paradigm. *In* "Differentiation Between Social Groups: Studies in the Social Psychology of Intergroup Relations" (H. Tajfel, Ed.), pp. 101–140. Academic Press, London.

Uleman, J. (1966). A new TAT measure of the need for power. Unpublished Ph.D. thesis, Harvard University. Quoted in "The Power Motive" (D. G. Winter). Free Press, New York, 1973).

Uleman, J. S. (1972). The need for influence: development and validation of a measure, and comparison with the need for power. *Genetic Psychological Monograph* **85**, 157–214.

Veen, P. (1972). Effects of participative decision-making in field hockey training: a field experiment. *Organizational Behaviour and Human Performance* **7**, 288–307.

Verof, J. (1957). Development and validation of a projective measure of power motivation. *Journal of Abnormal and Social Psychology* **54**, 1–8.

Wahrman, R. and Pugh, M. D. (1972). Competence and conformity: another look at Hollander's study. *Sociometry* **35**, 376–386.

Walton, J. (1966). Substance and artifact: the current status of research on community power structure. *American Journal of Sociology* **71**, 430–438.

Weber, M. (1930). "The Protestant Ethic and the Spirit of Capitalism". (Translated by Talcott Parsons). Allen and Unwin, London.

Weber, M. (1947). "The Theory of Social and Economic Organization". (Translated by A. M. Henderson and T. Parsons). Oxford University Press, New York.

Weber, M. (1948). "From Max Weber: Essays in Sociology". (Translated and edited by H. H. Gerth and C. W. Mills). Routledge and Kegan Paul, London.

Weber, M. (1968). "Economy and Society: An Outline of Interpretive Sociology". (G. Roth and C. Wittich, Eds). Bedminster Press, New York.

Wesolowski, W. (1962). Some notes on the functional theory of stratification. *Polish Sociological Bulletin* **3–4**, 28–38. *Reprinted in* "Class, Status, and Power: Social Stratification in Comparative Perspective" (R. Bendix and S. M. Lipset, Eds), pp. 64–69. Routledge and Kegan Paul, London. 1966. Second edition.

Westergaard, J. and Resler, H. (1975). "Class in a Capitalist Society". Heinemann, London.

White, R. W. (1959). Motivation reconsidered: the concepts of competence. *Psychological Review* **66**, 297–333.

White, R. W. (1960). Competence and the psycho-sexual stages of development. *In* "Symposium on Motivation" (M. R. Jones, Ed.), pp. 97-141. University of Nebraska Press, Lincoln, Nebraska.

White, R. W. (Ed.) (1963). "The Study of Lives". Atherton Press, New York.

White, R. W. (1964). "The Abnormal Personality". The Ronald Press Co., New York. Third edition.

Whyte, W. F. (1945). "Street Corner Society". University of Chicago Press, Chicago.

Whyte, W. H. (1956). "The Organization Man". Simon and Schuster, New York.

Wilke, H. and Mulder, M. (1971). Coalition formation of the gameboard. *European Journal of Social Psychology* **1**, 339–355.

Williams, R. M., Jr. (1947). "The Reduction of Intergroup Tensions: A Survey of Research on Problems of Ethnic, Racial, and Religious Group Relations". Social Science Research Council, Bulletin, 57, 1947, New York.

Winter, D. G. (1972). The need for power in college men: action correlates and relationships to drinking. *In* "The Drinking Men" (D. C. McClelland, W. N. Davis, R. Kalin and E. Wanner, Eds), pp. 99–119. Free Press, New York.

Winter, D. G. (1973). "The Power Motive". Free Press, New York.

Winter, P. G. (1975). "Power Motives and Power Behaviour in Women". Paper prepared for Symposium on Women: Studies of Power and Powerlessness. American Psychological Association Convention, August, 1975.

Worchel, S., Arnold, S. E. and Harrison, W. (1978). Aggression and power restoration: the effects of identifiability and timing on aggressive behaviour. *Journal Experimental and Social Psychology* **14**, 43–52.

Wrong, D. H. (1959). The functional theory of stratification: some neglected considerations. *American Sociological Review* **24**, 772–782.

Wrong, D. H. (1976). Force and the threat of force as distinct forms of power. *In* "Skeptical Sociology" (D. H. Wrong, Ed.), pp. 183–195. Heinemann, London.

Zimbardo, P. G. (1975). Transforming experimental research into advocacy for social change. *In* "Applying social psychology" (M. Deutsch and H. A. Hornstein, Eds), pp. 33–66. Halsted Press, New York.

Zimbardo, P. G., Ebbesen, E. B. and Maslach, C. (1977a). "Influencing Attitudes and Changing Behaviour: An Introduction to Method, Theory, and Applications of Social Control and Personal Power". Addison-Wesley, Mass. Second edition.

Zimbardo, P. G., Haney, C., Banks, W. C. and Jaffe, D. (1977b). The psychology of imprisonment: privation, power and pathology. *In* "Contemporary Issues in Social Psychology, 3rd Ed.". (J. C. Brigham and L. S. Wrightsman, Eds), pp. 202–216. Brooks/Cole, Monterey, Calif.

Subject Index

R

S

European Monographs in Social Psychology

Series Editor: HENRI TAJFEL

E. A. CARSWELL and R. ROMMETVEIT
Social Contexts of Messages, 1971

J. ISRAEL and H. TAJFEL
The Context of Social Psychology: A Critical Assessment, 1972

J. R. EISER and W. STROEBE
Categorization and Social Judgement, 1972

M. VON CRANACH and I. VINE
Social Communication and Movement, 1973

CLAUDINE HERZLICH
Health and Illness: A Social Psychological Analysis, 1973

J. M. NUTTIN, JR (and Annie Beckers)
The Illusion of Attitude Change: Towards a Response Contagion Theory of Persuasion, 1975

H. GILES and P. F. POWESLAND
Speech Style and Social Evaluation, 1975

J. CHADWICK-JONES
Social Exchange Theory: Its Structure and Influence in Social Psychology, 1976

M. BILLIG
Social Psychology and Intergroup Relations, 1976

S. MOSCOVICI
Social Influence and Social Change, 1976

R. SANDELL
Linguistic Style and Persuasion, 1977

H. GILES
Language, Ethnicity and Intergroup Relations, 1977

A. HEEN WOLD
Decoding Oral Language, 1978

H. TAJFEL
Differentiation between Social Groups: Studies in the Social Psychology of Intergroup Relations, 1978

M. BILLIG
Fascists: A Social Psychological View of the National Front, 1978

C. P. WILSON
Jokes: Form, Content, Use and Function, 1979

J. P. FORGAS
Social Episodes: The Study of Interaction Routines, 1979

R. A. HINDE
Towards Understanding Relationships, 1979

A-N. PERRET-CLERMONT
Social Interaction and Cognitive Development in Children, 1980

In preparation

P. SCHÖNBACH
Education and Intergroup Attitudes